C000299901

MIKE SANCHEZ

Thanking you

MIKE SANCHEZ
BIG TOWN PLAYBOY

Michael Madden

MUSIC MENTOR BOOKS

York, England

© 2014 Michael Madden. First edition. All rights reserved.

The right of Michael Madden to be identified as Author of this Work has been asserted in accordance with the UK *Copyright, Designs and Patents Act 1988.*

Every effort has been made to trace the copyright holders of material used in this volume. Should there be any omissions in this respect, we apologise and shall be pleased to make the appropriate acknowledgments in future printings.

A full list of photo and illustration credits appears on page 307.

All rights reserved. No part of this publication may be reproduced, stored in a retrieval system or transmitted in any form by any means, electronic, mechanical, reprographic, recording or otherwise without prior written permission from the publisher.

This book is sold subject to the conditions that it shall not, by way of trade or otherwise, be lent, resold, hired out or otherwise circulated without the publisher's prior consent in any form of binding or cover other than that in which it is published and without a similar condition including this condition being imposed on the subsequent purchaser.

Whilst every effort has been made to ensure the correctness of information included in this book, the publisher makes no representation – either express or implied – as to its accuracy and cannot accept any legal responsibility for any errors or omissions or consequences arising therefrom.

British Library Cataloguing-in-Publication Data
A catalogue record for this book is available from the British Library.

ISBN-13: 978-0-9562679-7-9

Published worldwide by Music Mentor Books *(Proprietor: G.R. Groom-White)*
69 Station Rd, Upper Poppleton, York YO26 6PZ, North Yorks, England.
Telephone: +44 (0)1904 330308 *Email:* music.mentor@lineone.net

Cover design by Tony 'Diavolo' Coni.

Printed and bound in Great Britain by Bonacia Ltd, Peterborough.

For my dear Mum and Dad.

Mike Sanchez

Acknowledgements

Growing up in the late sixties and early seventies, I was heavily influenced by the musical choices of my older sisters. I was exposed to the glam rock of Slade and T. Rex, the youthful Michael Jackson, and heartthrobs such as David Cassidy and Donny Osmond. I became a fan of T. Rex, but the rest of them were not really for me. I will always, therefore, be grateful to my dad and particularly my mum for sharing their own record collection. Johnny Cash, Buddy Holly, and an intriguing cassette tape, *Kings of Rockabilly,* featuring Sleepy LaBeef amongst others, introduced me to sounds from long ago. It was a musical collection that I embraced and supplemented with Jerry Lee Lewis, Chuck Berry, Fats Domino and Little Richard. Throughout the years, my car has changed from cassette, to CD, to MP3 player, but the music has largely remained the same. The passengers, mainly my children Gabriella, Ole and Zachary, have all listened to and been influenced by these classic artists, and it is a source of amusement to see a record collection that contains Britney Spears, Miley Cyrus and Johnny Cash.

It was a trip to see Sleepy LaBeef at the *Rockers' Reunion* in Reading in 2009 that first brought Mike Sanchez to my attention, and I was accompanied by my wife Sally to this and several subsequent shows to see Mike in action. Indeed, it was Sally who first suggested the idea of this book to Mike at Greystones in Sheffield, and so she probably deserves the biggest thanks of all for this and the endless support that she has provided during the writing process. Throughout the research, planning, interviewing and cross-checking, everyone concerned has – without exception – been keen to contribute, which is a great testament to Mike. There are too many to mention individually, but I must acknowledge Robert Plant for providing the *Foreword*, and particularly Jo Hill for being instrumental in this, and for being a fantastic point of contact for any questions, email addresses, telephone numbers and other important details. There are many sources of reference available to the biographer, but I must give special mention to

Acknowledgements

John Combe's book, *Get Your Kicks On The A456 (Volume 2)*, which provided confirmation of many of the events and timelines that Mike's notes and memories proposed.

As the book neared completion, I must acknowledge the contribution of Janet Fisher, my copy editor, who ensured that the manuscript was in a condition that could be shared with a wider audience, and Tony Coni who provided the wonderful artwork for the cover. I must also thank the publisher, George Groom-White, with whom it has been a pleasure and an education to work. Finally, I must thank Mike and his wife Sarah for providing endless material, for taking calls at all hours of the day, and for welcoming me into their lives. It has been a pleasure in the making, and I hope that you enjoy reading it as much as I enjoyed writing it.

Michael Madden
March 2014

Foreword by Robert Plant

Mike first came into my near vision
more than 30 years ago..
I was drawn to him..
bright eager + crazed..
His references, a musical paradise fume..
As his gift developed he grabbed the
genre by the throat and shook new life
into it .. preaching sweat + grind + from
his Church of the 88 keys..
He is admired + respected by all who come
before him.

R.P.

Contents

Introduction 13

1   From Madrid to Bewdley 15

2   Sounds and Styles 29

3   High School Confidential 33

4   Starting Out 47

5   Mr. Electricity 81

6   Fame! 91

7   Train Keeps A-Rollin' 113

8   Going Solo 163

9   Rhythm King 177

10 You Better Dig It! 199

11 Almost Grown 237

12 Mike on Music 267

Discography 277

Index of People's Names 291

Index of Songs & Album Titles 301

Index of Films & Shows 305

Photo & Illustration Credits 307

Introduction

Mike Sanchez has seen it all. He has shared a stage with many rock'n'roll greats, including Eric Clapton, Robert Plant, Jeff Beck and Bill Wyman, and he is considered their equal in many musical circles. 'Mike's the Man' is a common accolade when opinions are sought as to his musical appeal, and he remains one of the foremost names in rock'n'roll and boogie-woogie piano playing in the world today.

However, he is so much more than that. Whilst many artists are measured in terms of album sales, Mike's appeal goes far beyond his recordings. He is known for striving to make every performance the best that it can possibly be, delivering shows with his all-action style and undoubted charisma onstage. When the music is pumping, the keys are jumping, the sweat is pouring and the rhythm really does satisfy your soul: that is Mike Sanchez.

Offstage Mike devotes a huge amount of time to his fans, staying behind until the last one has gone, signing CDs and other merchandise. Every one of them means something to him, and he means so much to them all. They all want to be a part of Mike Sanchez, sharing stories as to where they first saw him, how many times they have seen him, and where they will see him next. It is probably true that there are not many people who have only seen Mike Sanchez once, as after the first experience he simply must be tasted again to see if he can recapture the energy and exhilaration of the previous show – and he usually can.

Mike Sanchez: Big Town Playboy charts his roots in Spain, his early years in London and his move to Bewdley where he formed his first band, the Rockets. It tells of his time with Ricky Cool & The Big Town Playboys, the band that he eventually made his own, his time with Bill Wyman's Rhythm Kings, his solo career, and so much more besides. He is now a family man, living with his wife Sarah and their son Louie on a hillside in El Tiemblo, just outside Madrid, considering the next significant step in his colourful career.

CHAPTER 1

From Madrid to Bewdley

Mike's formative years include his Spanish roots and the twist of fate that saw him move from London to Bewdley.

When Jesús Miguel 'Mike' Sánchez Bastida was born at the Salvation Army Mothers' Hospital in Hackney in the East End of London on 17 February 1964, the sound of the Bow bells could clearly be heard proclaiming their message from the church of St Mary-le-Bow. Though a cockney by any definition of the term, his roots are deeply entrenched in Spain, as his name suggests. His maternal grandparents, José Bastida Montoya and Josefa Gil Martínez, were typical of many Spaniards at the end of the nineteenth century, with a large family of seven children to support. These were Mike's mother, Manuela Bastida Gil, who was born on 3 December 1923; her sisters Vicenta, Josefa ('Fifi'), Tomasa ('Tomi'), María and Isabel; and her brother Miguel, who died in 1950 from typhus which was prevalent in Spain at the time. José worked as a labourer on dam construction and as a miner to bring in much-needed income, but the family learnt to survive on very little. They lived in the small town of Montejaque, 87 miles inland from the bustling port of Malaga, but in 1927 they moved to the municipality of El Tiemblo, between Avila and Madrid, where José found a job as a labourer working on a huge dam at El Burguillo in the Valle de Iruelas. After three years the work at El Burguillo was complete, so the family moved to Puentes Viejas in the province of Madrid where more construction work was available.

In 1933, José passed away at a young age due to ill health induced by poor working conditions in mines, as well as chain-smoking the crude cigarettes that were the only ones labourers could afford. This left Mike's grandmother, Josefa, to bring up a large family on her own, against the backdrop of a troubled Spain that was soon to be torn apart by civil war. Shortly after José died, the family moved to Calle Canillas in central Madrid, where they shared a house. In the city, it was easier for Josefa's children to find work. Miguel became skilled in ironmongery, whilst Tomi became a servant at the home of Spanish nobleman and politician José Antonio Primo de Rivera.

After the Spanish Civil War broke out in July 1936, parts of Spain became increasingly dangerous for families to live in, and after around a year most of the Bastida family became refugees to escape the bombings in Madrid and the rest of central Spain. However, Manuela's brother, Miguel, joined the republican army, and had already experienced war on the front line before it was discovered that he was still only 16 years old, whereas soldiers had to be aged at least 18 to enlist. Josefa intervened, and Miguel then travelled to La Carolina in the province of Jaén, where he became an ironmonger for the remainder of the war. Manuela's two older sisters, Vicenta and Fifi, went to Murcia and Malaga respectively, but Josefa and the rest of her children fled to the Catalonian port of Villanueva y Geltrú in the province of Barcelona. Manuela lived with and worked for a family who ran the restaurant at the town's main railway station, whilst her mother and siblings found similar work in the area.

After a while, word spread that their new hometown would be subject to a bombing raid. The whole community hid in the hills, and Josefa and her children spent the night watching from their vantage point overlooking the town. Wave after wave of German bombers which had been loaned to Franco's cause lit up the sky with their deadly cargo. The citizens were helpless and returned to the town the following morning to witness the destruction. Manuela's room was completely destroyed, with charred bedsprings and piles of rubble marking the place where she would have slept had it not been for the early warning.

After the bombings, the refugees were taken even further away from home towards Girona and southern France, where many Spaniards remained until after the war ended in April 1939. It was a confusing time as they left Villanueva y Geltrú and the family were split up. Manuela's younger sisters, María and Isabel, were still just children. They stayed at Girona for a few days before they were given the all-clear to be returned on a long bus drive back to Madrid. Fortunately, the two girls found their previous home at Calle Canillas, and were taken in by the family who had previously shared the house with Josefa and her children.

Josefa and her daughters Manuela and Tomi stayed in France for over a month until the civil war finally came to an end. They then returned to Madrid, where they were reunited with María and Isabel. Vicenta, Fifi and Miguel returned to Calle Canillas, and the family were all together once again.

After the war, the area around Madrid returned to normality, and Manuela and her siblings remained close under the caring eye of Josefa. This changed in May 1946, when Manuela gave birth to a son, Juan José – later known as 'Juanjo', as it is common in Spain to abbreviate the first and middle names and make them into one.

Towards the end of the 1940s, Manuela took a job as a nanny, maid and cleaner for the family of a diplomat whose work had brought him from Peru to Spain. The diplomat was Javier Pérez de Cuéllar, who later became Secretary General of the United Nations, and the family took Manuela and young Juanjo with them when they moved to the Netherlands. Manuela's life improved enormously as a result of her new role, being able to keep her young son with her all of the time and not having to struggle to make ends meet.

After remaining in the Netherlands for over four years, the family moved to London, again taking Manuela and Juanjo with them. Eventually, the de Cuéllars bade farewell to their Spanish help when they returned to Peru, and as a parting gift they enrolled Juanjo into the exclusive Blackfriars boarding school in Llanarth. This allowed Manuela to settle down on her own, working first as a house cleaner and then in a variety of hotels and restaurants – workplaces that were shared by many other Hispanics who had arrived in the UK for precisely that reason.

In the 1950s, Britain was a popular destination for immigrants from across the globe who were seeking work. They came from as far afield as Asia and the Caribbean, as well as the Mediterranean, and the catering industry was a willing employer. The finest hotels and restaurants in London, such as Claridge's, the Dorchester, the May Fair, the Cumberland and many others featured a host of Italian, Spanish and Portuguese waiters and other front-of-house staff. Manuela held a string of positions until she found herself working in the Cumberland Tea Rooms in 1960.

Mike's father, Jesús Sánchez Díaz, was born in Madrid on 17 May 1932 to Manuel Sánchez Garcia and Remedios Díaz Noriega. Manuel's family came from the small town of Salmoral, close to

Salamanca, whilst Remedios originally came from Noriega in the northern province of Asturias.

In his youth, Manuel owned a horse and went from village to village selling animal skins. By the time his children were born, he owned a dairy with a herd of cows, but when the civil war broke out he was forced to sell the cows by the Franco government. He then found work as a baggage handler at the Estación del Norte train station in Madrid, where he stayed for forty years until his retirement. The station, today known as Principe Pio, is close to Madrid's Royal Palace, and Manuel's home was a flat on Paseo del Rey overlooking the busy terminal.

Remedios was a dressmaker and had a number of wealthy clients. She used the money she made to send Jesús and his three sisters, Angelita ('Angela'), Teresa and Victoria, to the private Jaime Balmes school, as she wanted the children to have a good education rather than suffer Franco's public education, which she considered disastrous. Jesús was a keen scholar. He would frequently immerse himself in a variety of books on history, drama, poetry and romance. The past was a particular passion, and he loved to demonstrate his encyclopaedic knowledge of Spanish and world history. Jesús was also a talented artist, depicting still lifes as well as people and portraits in a host of oil paintings.

Madrid has always been a vibrant city, and Jesús particularly liked the variety of cinemas along La Gran Via, just a short walk from his home. He became a big fan of movie stars such as Esther Williams (his particular favourite), Clark Gable and Rita Hayworth, and would spend all of his spare money watching the latest releases. His sister Teresa believes he saw the movie *Escuela de Sirenas (Bathing Beauty)* thirty times, whilst Angelita remembers him telling her all about *The Third Man* and other great films. He also loved police movies, and every night he would tell his sisters the story of the film he had just seen as they drifted off to sleep. He would often take his sister Teresa to the 'Palace of the Pipas', which was a cinema where everyone ate pipas (sunflower seeds) until the floor became a carpet of pipas, and they would sit for four hours eating the seeds and watching back-to-back movies.

In 1948, at the age of 15, he started work in Pontejos, a textile and clothing store next to the Puerta del Sol. He stayed there for ten years, and by the time he reached his mid-twenties he had received letters from friends who had emigrated from Spain to England. They told of the abundance of jobs and the better pay that could be had in London. One day, Jesús had completed an overtime shift at work and walked past the office. Inside, the owners were counting their money, and when he saw the piles of cash and thought about the meagre wage that he earned, his mind was made up. He would seek his fortune elsewhere. And so, in 1957, at the age of 25, he decided to make the trip to England.

However, he first had to do three months' National Service. It would have been twelve, but he won a lottery to reduce the term. He enlisted in the cavalry and became an expert horse handler.

When he eventually reached England, things did not start well. For the first two nights he was forced to sleep in a doorway, then found work in a hospital that provided him with a bed. The glamour of a life in the English capital seemed a long way off, as his duties extended to moving corpses from one department to another – often with unpredictable results, as his route took him along uneven pathways which caused the bodies to jolt and shift beneath their white death shrouds. He soon decided that he needed a different occupation, and in 1960 found employment as a waiter in the main restaurant at the Cumberland Hotel.

His sister Angelita explains just how much he meant to the family: 'Jesús was the best brother that anyone could have had, even in their dreams. When he established himself in England, he brought me to London to learn the language. I was 16 years old and I had studied English in Madrid for two years. He paid for me to go to a school in Regent Street, and he arranged a room for me just two buildings away from where he lived. It was there that I met his future bride, Manuela, in 1960.'

The handsome Jesús often caught the eye of Manuela, though she assumed that he must be dating one of the many pretty waitresses around at the time. For his part, Jesús was really quite shy and finally plucked up the courage to ask Manuela if she was from Italy, due to her Italian appearance. They soon started dating, with the Gaumont State cinema in Kilburn being a favourite haunt. The two Spaniards working in service were made for each other, and as soon as Jesús discovered that Manuela had the luxuries of a refrigerator and a black and white television, he realised that he was in heaven! They were married at St Mary of the Angels, Bayswater, in 1962. Two years later, on 17 February 1964, Manuela gave birth to a son, Jesús Miguel, who soon became known as Mike Sanchez.

In 1968, the family moved from Paddington to Claremont Avenue off Kenton Road in the suburban North London town of Kingsbury, Middlesex. Jesús had started work at the prestigious Grosvenor House Hotel, Park Lane, where he remained for several years, undertaking a variety of waiting jobs before concentrating his efforts on wine. His studies in this area certainly paid off, as he progressed to the role of head sommelier. The Grosvenor was very popular with the leading artists, actors and musicians of the day, and Jesús struck up a friendship with many of the guests, including Omar Sharif, who would always ask for him whenever he stayed at the hotel. It is probably no coincidence that, when Sharif retired from acting, he opened up a gentleman's clothing store in Madrid, close to where Jesús used to work. Jesús often spoke of the times he used to deliver breakfast to songwriter Henry Mancini in his suite at the top of the hotel, who would already be sitting at a piano, composing music so early in the day.

At the age of four, Mike started school at Uxendon Manor Primary & Junior School in Kingsbury. This was a confusing time for a young cockney boy with Spanish parents. At home, Spanish was the native language, with only the television providing spoken English. The teachers at Uxendon Manor assumed that Mike was simply a slow learner and placed him in remedial classes. He would be taken in a van to other schools or hospitals to undergo various tests, including eyesight and hearing, when really they should have recognised him as an advanced Spanish student!

Although the Swinging Sixties were seen as a time of liberation, freedom and 'anything goes', 1960s Britain was still a very insular place, with racial prejudices very much to the fore. Mike's darker skin and thick black hair set him apart from the other children. He was also overweight, giving him a podgy appearance and inevitably contributing to him coming last in almost every race on school sports day. Despite this, he participated in all of the school's activities and events, regularly attending its fetes and fairs. However, his opinion of school and his general melancholy were made worse by a number of occasions when he proudly won a goldfish at the fete, only to typically find it dead a few hours later. The highlight of his early school years was definitely the glass marbles that the children played with during break and lunch times. He was an excellent shot with a small glass ball in his hand and often went home with many more marbles than he had started out with.

Mike followed his father's inclination towards art, and he spent many long hours scribbling sketches of motorbikes, soldiers, flowers and other diverse subjects. Other friends followed his artistic leaning and influenced his subject matter. George Sagoe, a Jamaican boy, had exceptional skill as an artist. He would draw images from the Stan Lee Marvel comics, each with his own interpretation, and Mike would sit next to him in class, trying to copy the caricatures. At school, at home and anywhere that he could find some space and spare time, Mike would draw enthusiastically, trying in his own way to be as great an artist as his father.

His parents both held down full-time jobs, but the family were far from affluent. Toys were few and far between, and although the young Mike enjoyed his Action Man, he accepted the realisation that he would never be able to get the huge tank and other accessories, as his mum and dad would never spend that kind of money on such things.

In common with many Spaniards, particularly those who settled in the UK, religion played an important part in the busy lives of Jesús and Manuela, and they took Mike to the Roman Catholic Church of All Saints, Kenton Road every Sunday. He owned a children's Bible, and though the spectacular images of Moses parting the sea, the Last Supper and the cross being dragged to its destination brought the otherwise dreary stories to life, he knew from bitter experience not to make any adverse comments regarding his parents' faith. The church was filled with Irish, Italians and Hispanics, and Mike would sit impatiently listening to the monotone voice of the priest delivering his sermon. The ritual of the body and blood of Christ did little to ease his discomfort, and it was a welcome relief when the ceremony ended and he could return home.

The previous residents of the house at 14 Claremont Avenue had left behind an ancient, almost unplayable upright piano, and Mike's parents decided to keep it as a unique piece of furniture rather than a musical instrument. Jesús had a Spanish friend, Emma Langdon, who was a part-time piano teacher. Emma taught Mike piano every week for three years, enabling him to reach Grade 5 in his piano exams, with a good level of aural awareness making up for his lack of ability at sight-reading.

School was an increasingly fraught affair, and it became even more unbearable when Mike started to become the victim of bullies. The English and the Irish boys ganged together and picked on the Hispanic boy, starting with verbal abuse directing him and his family to go home. 'Spaniard' was seen as almost as big an insult as 'foreign bastard', and the words were soon accompanied by physical assaults. These began in a small way, with the child that he sat next to prodding him constantly whilst the teacher looked away. Fights broke out, and although Mike tried to turn the other cheek and avoid the violence, inevitably he would sometimes have to fight back. At the end of the school year in 1973, his headmaster added a note to his report saying simply, 'Michael's violent behaviour must change.'

The piano should have been an escape, but Mike was so preoccupied with the misery at school that he would not practise from week to week, and when Emma came around he could demonstrate that he had learnt absolutely nothing in the previous seven days. Perhaps exasperated, or perhaps because she recognised some genuine talent, Emma entered Mike in the *Southall Festival of Music, Speech and Dance*. Her faith was justified, as he finished ninth out of a total of around 60 young pianists.

At school and elsewhere, the bullying and racism continued – so much so that, when Mike was given a brand new bicycle, he kept it inside for three years, fearing what might happen if he went out on it. The bullying was particularly bad outside the confines of the school yard, with many of the bullies having older brothers who would be even more forceful in their language and violence. The aura of hate made the young Spanish boy long to be elsewhere. He began to fear the impending move to high school, and his mind was filled with dark thoughts of how to deal with the terror and intimidation.

None of Mike's school friends were of British origin. They were West Indian, Jewish or Italian, and they suffered the same abuse. Howard Parker, a Jewish boy, was picked on for being Jewish and also for being overweight. Mike found some common ground, as he also had a weight problem, and they stuck together as much as possible. Every day was a struggle, and they knew that the bullying could happen anywhere: at school, in the street, or even in front of their houses.

At home, the young Mike was doted on by his parents, and whilst the sounds of the Beatles and the Rolling Stones filled the charts in the sixties, Mike's early musical influences came from his father's love of more traditional music. He would have the radio on whenever he was at home, particularly in the morning whilst preparing for a day at work, treating Mike to the sounds of Louis Armstrong, the big band jazz of Duke Ellington and Count Basie, and the mature voice of Frank Sinatra. Even at such a young age Mike developed a preference, and that was for the silky-smooth vocals of Nat 'King' Cole.

In contrast to these seasoned performers, Mike also discovered a taste for the raw sounds of traditional rock'n'roll. Elvis Presley's 'Heartbreak Hotel' and 'She's Not You', the rockin'-bass sound of Bill Haley & His Comets and, particularly, Chuck Berry's 'Johnny B. Goode' were interspersed with quirky numbers such as Bobby 'Boris' Pickett's 'Monster Mash', and they were all played repeatedly in Mike's formative years, when the early morning radio became a great source of inspiration and affection.

In the sanctity of his own home Mike found comfort and solace in this music. His brother, Juanjo, saw the interest at an early age: 'There was an old Dansette record player at home, and I was a substantial collector of records from the '50s: Buddy Holly, Eddie Cochran, Elvis and anyone else from that era. I used to go into record shops in London, and back then you could go into a booth and listen to what you were thinking of buying. I often took a girl with me if I was trying to impress her, and, as the booths were quite small, we would have to squeeze in together. It was the closest you could get! I almost always bought what we had listened to, and when I got it home Mike would often ask about it. I would play music as a background to whatever else I was doing when I got home from work, but he had a real interest in it. When I got married and moved to the Midlands, I left my record collection behind, and he pounced on it. In fact, he never did return it!'

Mike played his new record collection constantly, one after another: Brenda Lee, Johnny Burnette, Cliff Richard, Adam Faith, Buddy Holly – the beats gripped him. The wild Little Richard, the smooth Pat Boone, whose career was founded on recording black rhythm & blues songs for the white American market, Chubby Checker, Johnny & The Hurricanes and, of course, Elvis Presley. For a few hours, Mike could disappear into another world – a world away from the miserable times at school and a world that was to lay the foundations for his whole career – but eventually he would have to put the records away for another day and face reality.

The racism started to extend to his parents, often emanating from the parents of the bullies. Jesús would travel the ten miles of Edgware Road to work on his Puch Maxi moped, dressed in suit and trilby – long before the days when crash helmets became compulsory. When he came home, one of the neighbours was always ready to hurl vile abuse at him. She would shout and scream about foreigners, foreign languages and even the smell of garlic whilst her husband cowered inside, no doubt fearful that he might find himself on the receiving end if he asked her to stop. Occasionally, Jesús would try to halt the tirade, pointing out that he had the right to be there and that he and his family were doing no harm, but with a backdrop of television shows such as *Till Death Us Do Part*, with the infamous Alf Garnett, and *Love Thy Neighbour* making a joke of racism, it was an impossible task.

The only escape for the family came in the form of the Austin J4 van which eventually replaced Jesús moped. They took every opportunity to travel around in the van, visiting Southend-on-Sea and South Coast towns such as Brighton. They also went further afield, to the never-ending beaches of Weston-super-Mare, then over the Severn Bridge into Wales. They travelled into the West Midlands to Bewdley, where Mike's half-brother Juanjo had settled with his wife, Rosemary.

Juanjo had left his privileged schooling in 1962 and found employment at a travel agent's near Piccadilly Circus. He had stayed there until 1964, when he had been called upon to do his Spanish military service, which lasted for eighteen months. He had then returned to London and the travel industry, as he became a rep for the early holiday resorts on the Spanish costas. At this time, Benidorm was a relatively modest coastal town with plans to build a number of large hotels to cater for British and other Northern European holidaymakers in the 1960s and 1970s. He had married Rosemary Bishop, and they had settled in Bewdley, a small town on the River Severn near Worcester. They had chosen Bewdley as it had the advantage of being close to his latest employer, the Horizon Group in Birmingham.

Mike and his parents loved their trips to Bewdley and the surrounding countryside of the Wyre Forest. It was such a world away from London and with none of the problems that they found when they returned to the capital.

Unfortunately, the bullying extended to crank calls, and the emergency services turned up on more than one occasion having been told of a fire at the Sanchez house. When the door opened, the firemen rushed in carrying their hose, as the bemused family looked on. Finally, Jesús cracked, and after one particularly abusive episode from his neighbour, he marched next door and punched her in the face. He was prosecuted in court and paid a fine for his actions. This was the last straw, and Jesús and Manuela decided they would have to move out of London.

They had a number of options: West Palm Beach in Florida, Melbourne in Australia, or Bewdley in Worcestershire. Jesús' sister, Angela, had fallen in love with an American soldier whilst working at a US military base near Madrid. They were eventually married and settled in West Palm Beach, where they had a child named Marcus. Angela frequently told her brother how beautiful it was in Florida and that they could become American citizens and settle there too if they really wanted to. Jesús also knew a former colleague who had moved to Melbourne. He too enthused over the beauty of his chosen land, as well as the quality of life and the ease of becoming an Australian citizen. Despite these obvious attractions, Manuela wanted to be near her son in Bewdley. There was never any doubt, and the decision was made. They had spent seven years on Claremont Avenue, but in 1975 were driven away from their home by racism and bullying. Ironically, they sold the house to a large African family and headed for Worcestershire.

The house was sold quickly, and they put all of their possessions into storage until they could find a suitable replacement. They were in no hurry; they were just pleased to be out of the poisonous atmosphere that had developed around them, and they decided to take a long holiday in Europe. The Austin van was their saviour as they drove through France to Monte Carlo and St-Tropez, then along the coast to Barcelona. They passed through the Spanish costas, meeting up with long-lost family members in Salou, Oliva, Benidorm, Alicante, Torrevieja and Benalmadena. They went on past Malaga and down to Gibraltar, finding a new camping area each night and roughing it in the back of the van. Eventually they headed inland, travelling to meet the rest of their family in Madrid and El Tiemblo. They were happy times, and for two months Jesús and Manuela could be carefree, albeit with Mike never far from their side, and they were feeling good about life as they headed to their new hometown of Bewdley. They stayed with Juanjo and Rosemary at Ironside Close for two months until they found a new home on Coniston Way, across the neighbouring estate. Manuela was particularly pleased, being just a five-minute walk away from her elder son.

After one of the most joyful summers of his eleven years, Mike started at Bewdley High School in 1975. He was nervous at first, as he knew no one there, but the surroundings were so naturally beautiful that he felt at ease. The school was small and modern, and there were trees everywhere. The Severn flowed by the school grounds, and there were ducks, swans and many other birds in abundance. Every breath was a joy, with fresh air unlike anything he had experienced in the city. The majority of his fellow pupils were from Bewdley and the surrounding farmlands, and although this made Mike a stranger in their midst, there was none of the racial tension that was so prevalent in London.

Jesús and Manuela noticed the difference too, with the locals bidding them a polite 'Hello' or 'Good morning', and they became used to offering a friendly greeting to everyone that they met, without expecting abuse in return.

The surroundings encouraged an interest in nature, and Mike started sketching wild birds and the landscape by the river. He began to read through books on the birds of Britain and Europe, and not surprisingly he studied ornithology. By 1977, he had dozens of his sketches on display across the main corridors and reception areas of Bewdley High School, and he was genuinely proud of his achievements. His skill as an artist and his interest in nature made up for his inability to grasp scientific principles in physics and chemistry, and whilst he was now confident with the English tongue, like so many for whom English is not their first language, he struggled with English literature.

Sport was another shortcoming – the exception being rugby, where his sheer size meant that he could outmuscle and trample on smaller rivals – but he came alive in the art and music classes, where he always felt that he was able to make a positive and valuable contribution.

When his mind drifted back to the dark days in Kingsbury and he recalled the happy memories of the Dansette record player and his brother's singles collection, he realised that his love of music did not follow the established order of the Top 40 and the choices of mainstream radio disc jockeys. He appreciated the early Beatles tracks such as 'She Loves You', but not the *Sgt. Pepper* era. The haunting sound of Procol Harum's 'A Whiter Shade Of Pale' was fine as far as it went, but the spooky echoes of bass and deep vocals on Elvis Presley's 'Heartbreak Hotel' were much more to his liking. The twangy guitar of Duane Eddy was surpassed by Brenda Lee's string section on 'I'm Sorry', stirring emotions that he never really understood until much later. 'Yellow Submarine' and 'Tie A Yellow Ribbon Round The Ole Oak Tree' did not just have the word 'yellow' in common. To Mike's discerning ear they were also both trivial rubbish, whilst the hippy music seemed so lame and shallow, and the glam rock crowd was just not what he wanted to follow. Rock'n'roll, traditional blues and soul classics were infinitely preferable, and he particularly loved the Motown groove featuring tambourines and crusty baritone solos.

When he went shopping with his parents back in London, his dad would often drive past the legendary 100 Club on Oxford Street, and he would see the queues of crazy-looking punk rockers waiting to go in. He felt much more of an affinity with these trendsetters who courted controversy than any of the middle-of-the-road pop singers that were so prevalent in the mid-1970s.

His piano lessons were long forgotten, but at least he remembered how to find middle C and how to run up and down the scales and octaves. When he heard Jerry Lee Lewis belting out 'Great Balls Of Fire' on the radio, it didn't take him long to work out the basics of the song. Mike felt like that was all he needed to know, and frequently asserts that he only knows three notes on the piano, but that he knows how to make all three of them rock!

His parents were unaware of his musical inclinations, and their record collection was very different to that of his brother. Edgy singles were replaced by easy listening box sets from artists such as James Last, Jim Reeves and Nat 'King' Cole. They also had a few old singles by vintage Spanish singers, but nothing that would expose Mike to musical subcultures and styles. Those influences were to come in abundance in high school.

CHAPTER 2

Sounds and Styles

Mike's encyclopaedic knowledge of roots music spans many decades. Discover his major influences and how he adopted his rock'n'roll style.

Mike devoured music throughout his youth and soon realised that it was not just his roots that were different from the other kids in school. Not content with the bland pop songs of his generation, his musical inspiration crossed several decades. He loved the loud and clear vocals so common in the rock'n'roll of the fifties, with simple lyrics and a strong beat. He loved those songs that had a clear message, as long as that message was right out there and not hidden away. He loved the simplicity of the double bass, acoustic guitars – particularly those with a rockabilly or Latin influence, real drums, and the raunchy tones of saxophones and other lively members of the horn section. It was the energy of the punk era, but without feeling the need to get political or preach to the masses. The messages in the songs were simple, and Mike loved them. The Eddie Cochran classics 'Summertime Blues' and 'Somethin' Else' bounced around his head, alongside Larry Williams' more frenetic 'Slow Down'. Buddy Holly, Johnny Burnette and the Everly Brothers were all on his playlist, whilst Gene Vincent & His Blue Caps provided such inspiration that Mike would later record an album of covers of their 1956-57 songs.

In Mike's world the characters were different, the styles were different, and the sounds were different, but they all came from a time when the music was classic, raw, rocking and so exciting to a young rock'n'roll musician. It was a powerful combination of talented but poor musicians and crude and still-developing recording techniques contrasted with the social atmosphere of a booming post-war America graced with the tallest buildings, the finest cars, the phenomenon of a brand new youth culture known as teenagers, and a number of record label bosses who knew talent when they heard it.

He loved the vocalist-pianists such as Little Richard, Fats Domino and Jerry Lee Lewis, and these legends later led him to other talented but lesser-known artists such as Clarence 'Frogman' Henry, Paul Gayten, Dave Bartholomew, Billy Wright, Esquerita, Roy Montrell, Amos Milburn and Billy 'The Kid' Emerson. The styles and sounds of New Orleans had a huge musical influence on Mike, though he could only wonder at the intricacies being laid down by the likes of Professor Longhair, Allen Toussaint and Dr John, whose playing had been honed by many years of mastering that unique Crescent City style. Add to these the Texan pianist Little Willie Littlefield, with whom Mike later shared a long friendship, and the influences become much clearer.

It is said that imitation is the sincerest form of flattery, and Mike loved the way that some singers imitated their heroes whilst developing a style all of their own. Billy Fury was heavily influenced by Elvis Presley, yet he was still uniquely Billy Fury; Adam Faith styled himself on Buddy Holly, but he was instantly recognisable as Adam Faith, and there were many more. This is a trait that Mike has taken into his own career, easily adopting the styles of Fats Domino, Little Richard and others as he loses himself in their songs.

Mike was 13 years old when Elvis Presley died, and the passing of the King was almost a blessing in disguise for a young rock'n'roller. The radio was filled with his songs, and the television broadcast his shows and movies endlessly. There were scenes of Teddy boys crying throughout Britain and thousands of fans gathering outside Graceland. It was almost back-to-back and wall-to-wall Elvis, and it was all the impetus that Mike needed. He saw the Teddy boy look, with slicked-back hair and thick-soled shoes, and he decided to try it out. The iconic Elvis was one of the greatest-looking people that he had ever seen, and if he could shape his own image to mimic the young King, then that would be just fine.

By 1977, Mike started to regularly check out which other artists were being played on the radio in addition to his beloved Elvis. Radio Luxembourg was a late-night thrill, but the reception was invariably poor and the selection of songs was usually loaded with modern-day pop music. Fortunately, the BBC had listened to a campaign in London the previous year, when over 6,000 rock'n'roll fans marched to the BBC Broadcasting House demanding to have more rock'n'roll played on BBC Radio. The march was organised by deejay, musician and record producer Stuart Colman with another deejay, Geoff Barker, and as a result the BBC agreed to play rock'n'roll in a weekly show hosted by Colman. *It's Rock'n'Roll* aired every Saturday at 5.30 p.m. on Radio 1 and became essential weekly listening for Mike. Many years later, it was Colman's production talents that helped to create the historic Jeff Beck and the Big Town Playboys album, *Crazy Legs*, which was released worldwide by Sony Music.

Most weekends, Mike would go shopping in Birmingham with his parents, and it was a time when rock'n'rollers were prevalent on the streets of the city. The boys wore drape suits of various colours, suede beetle-crushers or winkle-pickers, drainpipe trousers and fluorescent socks. Bootlace ties and huge belt buckles were also the vogue – the Teddy boys of the seventies were very different to their fifties counterparts. The girls played their part too, with big skirts and bouncy ponytails, and always accompanied their boyfriends in distinct gangs. Mike found a shop named Nelson House that could supply this attire in abundance, but with a jacket alone costing around £40, he had to content himself with bootlace ties, drainpipes and pink socks.

Although he longed to complete his outfit, the most important feature of the day was definitely the hairstyle. Everyone who was anyone had to have a DA (short for 'Duck's Arse', as that was exactly what it looked like from the back) and Mike was no exception. He experimented with Brylcreem, but found that it was not strong enough to hold his hair in place. This led to constant combing and smoothing, giving him the greasiest hands around. He then tried Tru-gel, which gave him a much better effect, until he finally discovered what some of the Teddy boys really used: vintage pomade. Pomade came in similar pots with names such as Dax, Black & White and Royal Crown, but Mike settled on the one that appealed by name as well as aroma: Sweet Georgia Brown. His image was complete – albeit without the expensive jacket at this stage – and he was ready for whatever the world had to offer.

CHAPTER 3

High School Confidential

Mike's high school years were a heady mixture of musical influence and education, friendship and fights.

Throughout his years at high school, Mike's parents worked as hard as any family could to make ends meet, but despite their apparent hardship they managed to put some money aside, always with their boy in mind. At the time, his mother was a dressmaker and would spend most hours of the day sat with her two vintage sewing machines buzzing away, making the most beautiful wedding dresses for a store in Bewdley. Mike knew that she was paid poorly for her craft and to see her dresses on display in the store, complete with a sizeable price tag, made him feel sick inside.

His mother seemed to sleep very little. She was frequently up before dawn, preparing food and washing clothes before disappearing into her sewing room for most of the rest of the day. The young Mike realised that it was extremely difficult for her to escape from her work, even for just a few hours, as it was all around her in their home.

His father also worked long hours, securing a position as head waiter at a hotel restaurant in nearby Stourport-on-Severn soon after their arrival in Bewdley. A short time later, he became wine sommelier at the prestigious Stone Manor Hotel just outside Kidderminster. In his spare time, Jesús attended evening classes to obtain a City & Guilds certificate for car body maintenance and spray-painting. Having received his qualification, he then took on two jobs simultaneously: the hotel work, as well as spray-painting cars. With his mother working endlessly in her sewing room and his father working two jobs, Mike did not get to spend much quality time with his parents except for the occasional weekend and holidays.

The ethic of hard work is something that Mike is justifiably proud of in his parents. However, he has a sense of frustration at their exploitation, which meant they had to spend their entire working lives living just to work, with very little hope of significantly raising their level of income. At one point, his father was offered the manager's job at the restaurant where he worked, but he turned it down as he did not want the grief and hassle that came with the new position in return for a pittance of a pay rise.

Eventually, Jesús decided to speculate on property, and he bought a house in Kidderminster. When he had enough money, he also acquired the house next door and then spent several years trying to rent out rooms with little success.

At Bewdley High School, Mike began to feel different. His clothing and hairstyle were a part of it, and he became aware of different teenage subcultures that affected life in and out of school. Once again he found himself in the minority, but this time he had a very close ally. He often found himself sitting next to a real comedian who had the ability to make everyone laugh – a great asset in situations when things threaten to get out of hand. His name was Ian Jennings, and Mike describes him as 'one of the funniest people I ever met'.

Ian remembers Mike joining his school: 'We were both aged 11 when Mike came to Bewdley High. We were in the same class in our first year at *big school*, but he was the new boy, as the year had already started. I remember Mike coming to school with his hair in a quiff: he wanted to look like the Fonz in *Happy Days*. I was already listening to Elvis, as there were lots of his songs on the radio just after he died. I was also discovering other Sun artists like Carl Perkins and Jerry Lee Lewis.'

At around the same time that Mike started to develop his quiff, Ian started brushing his own mass of greasy locks into the same style. Ian's older brother, Malcolm, was a punk rocker, which provided an interesting contrast to Ian's musical tastes. It was a great time for the rock'n'roll image, but 1978 also saw the release of the movie *Grease*. Occasionally, Mike would get shouts of 'Hey, Elvis!' which was quite a compliment; however, more often it was 'Hey, John Travolta!' which was not really what he wanted to hear. By now he had taken to wearing a black leather jacket over a white T-shirt – the drapes were still out of his price range – giving him even more of a resemblance to Travolta's character, Danny Zuko.

The friendship with Ian quickly blossomed into a wider circle.

Neil Wright was one such friend who shared Mike and Ian's love of Elvis, and had picked up a copy of his Sun collection. He wrote down the lyrics of all of the songs and shared them, so that they could memorise each and every one. By the time he was 14, Mike had temporarily discarded his piano lessons in favour of an acoustic guitar, and he started the significant task of learning all of Elvis's records from the Sun era. The acoustic strumming was a success, but he soon returned to the keyboard, where he started to learn and develop left-hand boogie-woogie riffs. He copied Vince Taylor's 'Brand New Cadillac' and Henry Mancini's 'Peter Gunn', and then discovered the Winifred Atwell single 'Rampart Street Rock' amongst his collection of old 45s. Atwell was best known for 'Black And White Rag', which became the theme tune to the BBC snooker programme, *Pot Black*, but in 'Rampart Street Rock' Mike found a crazy left-hand rhythm that he just had to learn.

Back on the guitar, he picked up Buddy Holly's 'Mailman, Bring Me No More Blues', and the frequent changing between guitar and piano brought him an obvious realisation: he came to understand that the simplest structures of songs were all based around the traditional twelve-bar blues, whether fast or slow. If it was fast, it was boogie-woogie or rock'n'roll, and if it was slow it was the blues.

Mark 'Beefy' Davies was not yet in Mike's circle, but he recalls how their friendship came about: 'On wet days at school Mike would go up to the art room and play "Great Balls Of Fire" on the piano. He also sang, and I realised that he was a big rock'n'roll fan just like myself. From then on, I really wanted to be his friend.'

Ian Jennings had a different motive for encouraging Mike's musical side: 'I first heard him play the piano during school break time. I remember him playing "Yesterday" by the Beatles in a classroom. We both loved it because the girls we liked actually spoke to us after that!'

Alongside Mike, Ian, Neil and Beefy, with their growing love for rock'n'roll music, came several other schoolmates including Wayne Dixon, Robert Milichip, Huw Benjamin, John Fearnal and Anthony Smalley, all of whom professed varying degrees of interest in rock'n'roll. At times it seemed that Mike had stumbled across his own gang, which gave him comfort, security and an outlet for his thirst for rock'n'roll. Most of them were in the same class and inevitably, over the next couple of years, the music became their centrepiece.

Later on, after leaving high school, they would eventually split into two bands. Mike would recruit Ian, Beefy, and another boy named

Tracy Witherspoon to form the Rockets, whilst Neil would enlist Robert, and later Beefy, to form the Rockin' Renegades. At this early point in his rock'n'roll career Mike played very little on the piano, his primary instrument being the guitar that was his constant companion until he joined the Big Town Playboys.

Mark Davies shared art and metalwork classes with Mike and was amazed at the quality of his artwork: 'He was particularly good at battle and fight scenes. One piece showed Teddy boys and punks fighting, with a graphic image of a Ted slashing a punk's throat. It was displayed on the wall in the school. I can't imagine anything like that being allowed today.'

As well as the fight scenes, Mike also created detailed pencil and biro drawings of Teddy boys in sexually explicit scenes. These were not put on display or shown to any of the teachers, and that was not the only secret art that he created. In technical drawing he sat next to Neil, whilst Ian sat next to Mark. Over the course of two lessons Mike drew a full-colour confederate flag on the drawing board using his collection of ballpoint pens, whilst their teacher, Mr Bant, was oblivious to it all.

Another pastime that Mike enjoyed at school was chess. His father had taught him the basics of the game, but at school there were a lot of pupils spending their lunchtimes playing. Their unofficial chess teacher, Mr Smith, was a daunting opponent. He had black hair, black clothes, black gloves, and looked very intense. He was a very good player, and once Mike started to play against him regularly, his own game improved for the experience.

Bewdley High School was a happy place for the boys and their music, but there was one man who made it even more special. As their interest in rock'n'roll blossomed, they realised that they had a ready-made role model amongst them. For four years they had a teacher named Richard Rogers. By day, Mr Rogers taught them woodwork in school, but by night and at the weekends he was on stages across the UK playing his version of good old rock'n'roll, blues and soul under the name of 'Ricky Cool'.

During lunch breaks at school he would often remain in the classroom by himself and practise on his tenor saxophone. Mike and Ian would hear him playing and wondered to themselves where he would be performing that coming weekend. A couple of times, they plucked up the courage to ask him questions about his musical persona, but it was always difficult for 'Sir' to relax and talk to his pupils on that level, particularly as there was always a class that he had to attend to.

One evening, Mike was at home watching television and caught a regional special titled *This Is Ricky Cool & The Icebergs*. He was amazed when, there before him, on television, was Ricky Cool. His teacher, still better known to him as Mr Rogers, was performing in his living room, and Mike was thrilled. Ricky sang Bo Diddley's 'You Can't Judge A Book By The Cover' whilst jumping around the stage with his band. He was full of energy, his hair was spiked up like a punk, and his performance was frenetic. All too soon it was over, and the following day Mike looked at the smartly dressed man walking calmly up the high school drive with flattened hair. He wore a suit and tie and carried his briefcase professionally. It was a surreal moment, and the first glimpse that Mike had into the Jekyll-and-Hyde world of people within rock'n'roll. However, the 'secret' was well and truly out, and Mike looked forward to how exciting things were going to be at school from that moment on.

Richard Rogers had been playing live since 1967. He started out performing solo gigs, playing country blues songs on guitar and harmonica, before creating the persona of Ricky Cool in 1976. The character was an American who had been present at every major development in popular music since the 1940s and who, having somehow missed out on fame and fortune, decided to try his luck in the UK. Ricky Cool & The Icebergs were formed in 1976, and the band accordingly played a set of three-minute rock'n'roll, rhythm & blues and western swing numbers. Rogers joined the teaching staff at Bewdley High School in 1977, a short time before the television special was aired.

After the show, Mr Rogers gained a kind of celebrity status among certain sections of the school. He also noticed that Mike and some of the other pupils were really starting to look like they were into his kind of music. This was particularly evident on non-uniform days, when the majority of the school adopted a variation of the punk style, whilst Mike, Ian and their friends stood out in their Teddy boy gear.

'I believe this used to get them into a few fights,' he recalls, although he saw that Mike had an advantage. 'He had previously been to school in London and was therefore a lot more streetwise than other pupils at Bewdley High. I'm sure that he felt like a bit of an outsider, but it also gave him the confidence to be different.'

Ricky Cool's relationship with Mike and Ian really began to grow, and he recalls the contrast between them in school: 'Mike was, generally speaking, a good pupil, whereas Ian liked to joke around a lot. I have to mention them together, as they were best friends and seemingly never apart.'

He even advised them of places in Birmingham where they could find white leather brothel-creepers and other quality items.

Mike had other friends in school, and one that had a special place in his heart was Stephen Draper. Stephen was blond-haired, tall and strong. He was not into rock'n'roll like the rest of Mike's circle of friends; instead, he had a passion for motorbikes and speed. Nevertheless, Mike and Stephen became good friends, riding around on their bicycles after school long before Stephen could get a real motorbike. They went on day-long hikes through the Wyre Forest outside Bewdley, returning Mike to his love of the forest, the River Severn and the beauty of nature that was all around them. Stephen encouraged him to take up fishing. They picked up all of the gear that they needed, as well as a district angling licence, and set off looking for quiet parts of the river in the hope that they could catch a few barbel fish along the way. The fishing trips were frequent, and it was a relaxing way to spend a sunny day, even if the fish refused to bite. This escape was just a mile from the town centre and throughout his early teens Mike considered the entire area to be a huge, wild, green playground, with rolling hills intersected by colourful pathways. It was an enchanting place for a youngster, but as his adolescence faded, so did his love for this natural fairground, and his awareness of the purer elements of earth, air and water were replaced by a more basic passion for music and girls.

Over the next few years, Mike's interest in music became more time-consuming, and he saw less and less of Stephen, who had started riding a little motorbike and mixing with a different crowd, but they still kept in touch. His friend lived a couple of miles from Bewdley along the A456, on a hill known as Long Bank. Local and national television cooking celebrity Rustie Lee also lived in a fine house on this hill, and she would often drop by to see Mike's mother, who would measure her up. Manuela made many of the clothes that she wore on her cookery programmes – another claim to fame for Mrs Sanchez!

In school, Mike's gang would often get together and run through ideas that they had come up with on their guitars. There were no drummers or bassists yet: everyone was just strumming acoustic or electric guitars. The question of vocals was also an interesting one, with only Mike and Neil being brave enough to sing in front of the rest of the boys. This is undoubtedly one of the reasons why they ultimately formed their own bands.

After school, if parents would allow it, they often met at the house of one of the gang members. These get-togethers consisted of Mike, Ian, Beefy, Tracy and Huw 'Bunny' Benjamin. Huw lived just a few hundred yards from Mike, and though he was never really a band member, his mother was fine with a group of boys coming over to sit in the living room and strum and practise newly discovered chords on their guitars. It was an interesting musical ensemble, and although Huw never really learnt enough to play guitar or sing, he often tapped out the rhythms on the back of an acoustic guitar and was generally helpful and full of encouragement. Huw had a younger brother, Julian, who was already a very talented musician. Their living room also contained an upright piano, and Julian would often give excellent renditions of Lennon & McCartney songs, demonstrating his passion for the music of the Beatles

Though the intricate nature of these compositions was a million miles away from the simplistic twelve-bar rock'n'roll rhythms favoured by Mike and the rest of the band, Julian also recognised the talent in Mike: 'I remember the first time he came round. He picked up a guitar and played the most incredible and haunting version of "Love Me Tender". I was totally in awe. To me, it was like Elvis was in the room, with his slick black hair and good looks. It's little moments like these that make us what we are.'

Bunny's living room became an important place, particularly when Mike met local musician Tony Goodwin. Tony was the partner of Bunny and Julian's mother, and he was an accomplished performer. He had started his musical life during the skiffle craze of the late fifties and became something of a local star. He fronted the Severn Valley Skiffle Kings, who went on to gain second place in the *Grand World Skiffle Group Contest* at the Mecca Ballroom, Birmingham, in 1957. Legendary skiffle pioneer Lonnie Donegan once sent Tony a congratulatory tape in praise of his musical talents, and in Mike's world this was his first encounter with a real star. It was also the first time that he had ever seen a professional singer-guitarist up close, singing the very songs that Mike himself wanted to perform. Tony was in his forties when they first met, but his looks and style created a lasting impression on the budding musician.

On that first day, the boys were all sitting around practising their instruments when Tony joined them. He realised that they were trying to play rock'n'roll and helped them out with a few pointers. Afterwards, he ran through a few Buddy Holly songs like 'Peggy Sue', and as he thumped out the chords and raised the volume of his vocals, Mike realised that this was exactly how it was supposed to be done. It remains a great memory for him and probably goes some way towards explaining his exuberant stage presence.

Regrettably, Tony Goodwin never really found the stardom that he perhaps deserved, but he was often seen with his acoustic by his side. With a wild and handsome gypsy look about him, he remained a much-loved and well-respected character in the Bewdley area, often going out of his way to help out in the neighbourhood. His family ran a building business, and Tony could claim that he had worked on every roof in the town. Mike still kept in touch with him whenever he played the Bewdley area, until Tony sadly passed away at the age of 77, having been diagnosed with cancer. His funeral was attended by hundreds of mourners, and Mike ensured that he was there to pay his last respects to a man who gave him inspiration in the early days of his musical experimentation.

Julian Benjamin to this day remains a professional musician. His older brother, Huw, was always proud of having been such a help in getting the boys together at his house and encouraging them to continue their rehearsals. Music was never a major factor in Huw's life, and as the group progressed they saw very little of him. He later became a publican and ran an assortment of pubs around the Midlands, eventually marrying a Scottish woman. Many years later, Mike discovered that he had passed away after an accidental painkiller overdose.

Although the musical side of school gave Mike so much pleasure, it became a dangerous place as the kids started to grow up. Hormones kicked in, and they became frustrated, bored, aggravated and aggressive. As with most classes at school, the boys grew at different rates. Mike sprouted into a six-foot teenager, whilst his peers remained of a smaller stature. He also had the biggest quiff, making him an even more imposing figure. This had its advantages, but in gang situations it meant that he was more likely to be seen as the leader. He never actually started a fight himself, but at school it seemed that the fights were always finding him.

His appearance set him up as a target for scooter-riding skinheads from neighbouring towns, who would connect with some of the known troublemakers from Bewdley and turn up outside the high school during disco evenings. Mike had already encountered many fights that started when a gang of boys would follow him as he walked home, offering insults and spitting on his back. Eventually, they would trip him up and start kicking him in the face. His heart beat faster as he anticipated the attacks from behind, but there was little that he could do. If he turned around, they would attack, and if he kept on going, so would his assailants. There was a slim hope that they might fade away, but more often than not a fight ensued. Mike got used to the beatings, realising that adrenaline would often numb the pain, even when numerous Doc Martens boots were kicking him in the face at the same time. In the end, he learnt to fight back, or at least to defend himself, and this he did to good effect.

One night, it turned particularly nasty. The boys had just left the school grounds, and there were several menacing figures on the streets who were unfamiliar to Mike and his friends. The situation got out of hand very quickly. One of his friends avoided being kicked by crawling under a parked car, whilst the rest of them fled. Mike remained to take a beating off one of the hardest kids in town, egged on by all of his mates. He fought back, grappling with his aggressor and pinning his body onto the bonnet of a car whilst wrapping his arm around the bully's head. Time stood still for a moment, as Mike looked at the metal ridge of the car's roof. He considered whether he should back off, or try to ram home his advantage by cracking his opponent's head open on the sharp edge.

Suddenly, time was moving again, and there was a large *bang* as the head came into contact with the metal. His victim fell to the floor, unconscious, and Mike struck his head twice more with his beetle-crusher shoe. Still full of adrenaline, he started to quietly walk away from his vanquished assailant and the surrounding crowd, who remained motionless. Moments later, his victim was up again, and this time he was like a wild animal with death written into his face. Before the fight had chance to start again, two of the high school teachers intervened and restrained the attacker. This quelled the crowd that had started to scent blood and the situation was temporarily diffused. Another teacher, the friendly Mr Norbury, gave Mike a lift home in his car. His parents' home on Blossom Hill was at least two miles away from the school on the other side of Bewdley, and as he sat in Mr Norbury's miniscule MG car he noticed several unknown young men on scooters waiting on different street corners for the entire journey, right up to the last little alley before his destination.

Mike was scared and confused, asking himself why this had happened. Was it simply because he looked different to the other kids? Was it because he had a different taste in music to the other kids? The gang in school was not a real gang. It was not organised in any way. It was just a bunch of lads who shared a love for rock'n'roll and who liked to dress in a certain style. They didn't steal other boys' girlfriends; they had no motorbikes or cars; they were still at school with no money and no ambition outside of their music. It was a confusing time all around.

The day after this historic fight, Mike made his way to school wearing a couple of bandages and sunglasses to hide the bruises around his eyes. They were seen as battle scars and he instantly gained huge respect from everyone in school. From that day onwards, not a single person dared to pick on him, and he could simply get on with his musical education.

Nevertheless, Mike, Neil and Beefy decided that it would be better if they learnt how to defend themselves properly, just in case the incident was ever repeated. Martial arts were very popular at the time, and they decided to learn judo. Every Wednesday, they walked three miles to a pick-up point in Stourport-on-Severn, from where they were taken by minibus to Hallow, near Worcester. Part of their lessons involved how to deal with an attacker who grabbed your hair from behind. Unfortunately, the three Teddy boys had well-groomed and very greasy locks, and any attempt to grab hold proved to be entirely useless. The experiment with judo did not last very long, as no one wanted to grab their hair, and anyone who did found that they could not hold onto it long enough for an attack.

A few months later, news spread throughout the school that Mr Rogers was soon to leave his teaching job at Bewdley High to pursue a professional career within the music scene. His involvement with the Icebergs had ended, and he now fronted Ricky Cool & The Rialtos, a band which contained other Midlands-based musicians. The announcement of his departure was tinged with sadness, but then it emerged that he was to give a farewell gesture to the pupils by performing a real live show for them with his new band.

Evening events in the school hall were already quite popular with a lot of the pupils, especially those who found their identity through the various teen cultures of the time. Bewdley High School was reasonably small, but its students had a wide variety of musical tastes. Mike and his friends were into traditional rock'n'roll, but there were also punk rockers, New Romantics, semi-hippies and long-haired, leather-clad youths who lived in the farming areas and tiny villages outside Bewdley town, around Cleobury Mortimer and the Clee Hills towards Shropshire. They were headbanging to the sounds of Status Quo, Led Zeppelin and Black Sabbath, no doubt encouraged by the fact that Black Sabbath bassist Geezer Butler lived nearby in the village of Far Forest.

School discos were held every few months, and for 50p the kids could escape for a few hours into their own musical worlds. Sometimes there would be live music onstage consisting of fifth- or sixth-form pupils who had put together a new band, usually playing very loud rock or punk in front of a willing audience filled mainly with their classmates. Teachers served soft drinks and there was absolutely no alcohol allowed, as it was on the school premises, but it was a good excuse to hang out with school friends in a very different atmosphere. Each of the musical cliques would take turns to get up and dance to their favourite songs. The deejay would play tunes by the Buzzcocks and the Sex Pistols, and Ian's brother Malcolm would join the rest of the punks as they pogoed around the hall. Next up, there would be the disco sounds of Donna Summer and Stevie Wonder. Then either Duran Duran or Spandau Ballet would entice the New Romantics into the centre of the hall. They revelled in their silk scarves and permed hair as they waved their arms around in an exaggerated and very camp manner. Finally, a couple of rock'n'roll songs would hit the turntable, and Mike and his friends would strut their stuff.

Each musical group would see the rest of the audience standing around watching the ridiculous show happening right in front of them – but with a good deal of trepidation, as it would soon be their turn. Occasionally, though, the subcultures mixed, and Mike freely admits to letting his greasy locks down on more than one occasion, headbanging and sweating it out to songs such as Status Quo's 'Down Down'.

When Ricky Cool & The Rialtos performed, it was a different evening altogether. This was the first time that Mike had ever seen a real group of seasoned musicians live on stage, playing tightly rehearsed arrangements of blues and rock'n'roll, with rasping saxophones and a powerful rhythm section. What made it even better was that it was fronted by Mike and his friends' very own favourite teacher, Mr Rogers.

The performance had a profound effect on Mike, as he realised that this was what he wanted to do with his life, if it was at all possible.

And why wouldn't it be possible? His examination results were never great, and in his mind he was never likely to excel in subjects such as maths, physics, chemistry or English literature. Art, technical drawing and music were his strengths, with history, religious education and physical education coming a very poor second. The school reception area had a variety of information leaflets on the tables, with titles such as *Choose a Career*, or *Get a Job*, but after that night watching Ricky Cool & The Rialtos the decision was made. A career in music seemed the obvious choice, and he was determined that nothing was going to stop him.

There were other pupils at the school with musical inclinations that Mike could only aspire to. Nick Allsop was a year below him, but he wrote a number of pop songs and put together a synthesizer-based band called Rouen. Rouen were already getting the attention of a major record company long before Mike's first band even took to the stage, and he saw them live a number of times. They cultivated a New Romantic image onstage, with bare feet, white tunics and bleached hair styled towards Duran Duran. They were consummate performers, and Mike will always remember waking up at a flat in London and hearing their single, 'Ordinary Life', on Radio 1.

Another pupil with a very different musical leaning was Bruce Hinton. Bruce was a stereotypical punk rocker who looked like a larger-than-life version of Sid Vicious. He was an imposing figure who sometimes dyed his hair in a leopard-skin style, and when he was with a gang of other punks, Mike and his friends often chose to cross to the other side of the street to avoid a confrontation. The truth of the matter was that, although they looked scary, the punks never gave Mike and his rock'n'roll friends any trouble.

Mike also had a classmate named Christian Metti who left school and created a hugely successful business selling slippers. Christian had a musical brother named Justin who later formed a successful band called Cantaloupe, with punk Bruce Hinton on bass guitar. Bewdley High School had a wealth of musical talent, and Mike was convinced that he was part of that movement.

After failing most of his O levels in the fifth form, Mike decided to remain in school for the following two years with very little idea as to what to do with his life, except for the burning desire to perform just like Ricky Cool. Many of his friends remained in school with him, but Ian Jennings headed for college. However, this did not keep him away from their music: 'I remember bunking off college and going back to the school to see everyone. They let me in through the window. They were messing with an electric guitar, and I was the only one who knew how to play bar chord blues like Chuck Berry, so I was in the band from then on – although at that point there was no band!'

Other than music, Mike struggled with his career options. He had occasionally helped his father in the car repair and respraying business but could not see his future in that line of employment. He also helped out washing wine glasses, followed by two months as a part-time silver service waiter in a restaurant in Bewdley. Although he did not enjoy the experience, it remains as the only employment that he has ever held down outside music. Despite his disinterest, he excelled at the job. He was polite with the customers and efficient in his duties. He would often carry two or three plates of soup on his left arm and another on his right, and this was what eventually brought about his downfall.

One evening the restaurant was full, and there was very little space for squeezing through the seated crowd. The chef poured the hot soup onto the soup plates but had a tendency to overfill them. Mike wisely decided to carry fewer of these brimming plates at the same time to avoid a spillage, but it was of no use. As he squeezed through a small gap between tables, ensuring that he could see where he was going at all times, he noticed that one of the plates had tilted. The angle was just enough to allow the steaming-hot green liquid to trickle onto the bare back of an elderly lady who happened to be sitting next to the owner of the restaurant. Mike instantly realised the pain and discomfort that the lady must have suffered as the scalding soup met her exposed flesh, but also realised at the same time that the restaurant business was not for him.

He finally left Bewdley High School after once again failing his O levels, and decided to do a three-month welding and craft practice course at Kidderminster College. Most of his time was spent wearing overalls and learning how to make roll-up cigarettes whilst admiring the female hairdressing students in the common room. He started to ride around on a smart-looking Yamaha 99 cc moped that had the appearance of a much more powerful motorbike, and he enjoyed the respectful glances and camaraderie that he received from the real bikers on the road. He always had a thing for motorbikes, but at the time he could not really afford to turn his interest into anything more serious, and when he finally did get enough money together, he was too busy travelling around and performing his music.

One of the more significant events at Kidderminster College happened when he performed to a class of students. He was playing his guitar and singing when one girl stood up and ran out of the room in tears, so moved was she by his performance. At that moment, Mike realised that whatever he was doing was working, and that it was what he wanted to do for a living.

CHAPTER 4

Starting Out

Follow Mike's fledgling rock'n'roll career in his own band, the Rockets, as well as his transition into Ricky Cool & The Big Town Playboys.

1981

After leaving school, Mike, Ian, Tracy and Beefy got together and decided to make something of their previous musical thrashing. They talked about calling themselves the Sputniks, but there was already a band with that word in its name, and then they considered Fireball XL5, but it didn't really fit with their idea. However, they definitely wanted a space theme, and after due consideration the Rockets were born.

They rehearsed in the back room at Mike's parents' house. Ricky Cool had made a bass guitar – a Fender copy with a short neck – which he had given to an ex-pupil. Beefy bought it for £10, securing his position. Tracy was the one with the guitar-playing ability, so he was on lead, whilst Ian and Mike beat out rhythms. Mike provided the musical direction, deciding which songs they should play and how the parts would be divided up, and after ten or eleven practice sessions they were almost ready to hit the road. They were still raw musicians from their early days at Bewdley High School, and they all played acoustic or electric guitars. The one essential ingredient that was missing was a drummer, and without that they would never be able to do a real show.

Stephen Draper lived with his mother and stepfather, Nigel. According to Stephen, Nigel was a semi-professional drummer, and he was happy to give the band some assistance to get them ready to perform a live gig. In the spring of 1981, they rehearsed at Stephen's house on Long Bank, and after a week or so they packed themselves off to the Market Tavern in Kidderminster, eager to perform. Sundays were a free and easy night, where local artists were backed by a drummer called Nigel Turrell and an organist named Cherry. This was to be their big chance to play their music in front of a genuine crowd, and although the audience were mainly elderly folk, they were noisy and enthusiastic.

Mike had finally acquired a black drape jacket with purple velvet trim, and the whole band wore their best rockabilly clothes: drainpipes, pink socks, black suede brothel-creepers, an eagle bootlace tie, the finest quiffs and huge sideburns. The Rockets were certainly not going to be let down by their looks on their first public appearance.

Mike sang 'That's All Right', 'Good Rockin' Tonight', 'I'm Left, You're Right, She's Gone', 'Twenty Flight Rock', 'Tear It Up' and 'The Train Kept A-Rollin''. Ian recalls their version of 'Johnny B. Goode' as having 'loads of mistakes, but loads of energy'. Tracy Witherspoon and Mark Davies played their parts, all plugged into an undoubtedly overloaded Sound City combo amp. The sound was distorted, but the band simply did not care. This was their debut, and although the crowd were not quite rocking in the aisles, they were more than happy with the Rockets' all too brief set.

After the gig they were approached by Geoff Belson, caretaker at the local All Saints Infants School, Wribbenhall. He was impressed by their performance and asked if they fancied getting some proper gigs. They were thrilled, and Geoff arranged for them to move their rehearsals from the cramped back room at Mike's house into the school.

The first practice session under Geoff's watchful eye was something of a disaster. They still had no drummer and no PA system either. However, the ever-resourceful Geoff was not discouraged, and he arranged for local boy Tim Bearne to come to the next rehearsal. Tim was very shy, but he was an accomplished drummer and just what the band needed.

At one rehearsal the band's main guitarist, Tracy Witherspoon, announced that he intended to buy a 1970s sunburst Antoria semi-acoustic that he had seen in Sean Dee's music store in Kidderminster. Something within Mike told him that he was destined to be the frontman, and so he went out and bought the guitar before Tracy ever got the chance. This was the beginning of the end for Tracy, but it was Geoff who delivered the final blow. Tracy played some great licks on his Les Paul copy, but Geoff considered that he did not really fit in with the band's style. He had to go, and after this momentous event the band started to progress more quickly. Another rather more esoteric change made by Geoff was to replace Beefy's old bass guitar with a new Commodore, completing the stylish look of the band.

The Rockets were now a four-piece, getting tighter with every rehearsal, and it was time to get them onstage. They decided that they should promote their own show at the nearby White Swan pub in Bewdley, so they put up posters and spread the word, creating quite a buzz amongst the youngsters throughout the town. When the evening came, the place was packed, and the boys were filled with nerves and adrenaline. They played two 45-minute sets and rocked the place. The audience responded to the show, and the band responded to the audience. There were a lot of familiar faces, notably ex-pupils from Bewdley High School, including a number of punk rockers. At school, Mike and his friends had always avoided the punks as they looked so scary, but now they were joining in and listening to the Rockets' particular brand of rock'n'roll. After the gig, the punks even admitted that they were just as scared of Mike and his friends, which probably explains why they never actually got into any fights with each other. Mike loved the respect that the punks had for his music and for the band, and that night at the White Swan gave him the confidence to take it further.

They went back to the Market Tavern and spoke to Don Phillips, who was the manager of the pub. He agreed to give the Rockets a six-week residency on Thursday evenings, just to try them out. Fame beckoned! After just one free and easy night and one real gig, the band had secured a regular slot, and they were thrilled.

The residency brought about its own pressures. They had to learn several new songs each week just to keep the shows fresh, and they had to come up with new ideas, as well as expanding on what they already had. Rehearsals engulfed them, and even when Mike was at home he would sit for hours in his bedroom, practising chords on his guitar. He started to create solos, as well as copying those that he had heard on his favourite tracks. Scotty Moore, Paul Burlison, Cliff Gallup and Eddie Cochran were all imitated, and Mike developed an obsession with trying to re-create the guitar-work of his heroes. As well as singing and playing, he was also trying to memorise the lyrics, striving for that perfect sound. The perfectionist in Mike could have been daunting for his fellow band members, but most of them were just as excited to have secured a regular gig.

Mike's brother, Juanjo, understood why Mike was so keen to perform: 'I deliberately distanced myself from his band at an early stage. I decided that I didn't want to turn up and be *Mike's big brother*, intruding on what they were doing or inhibiting him. He occasionally asked my opinion on things, but it was important that he could stand on his own two feet. I knew that he felt comfortable playing that kind of music: it gave him an avenue where he could be loud and extravagant. He was really rather shy and not very forthcoming. He was never the kind of person who could walk into a crowded room and introduce himself. Onstage he was able to show off. It was almost like an alter ego.'

When the Rockets were not performing, they were just like any other group of teenage boys. Ian and Beefy would chase girls, whilst Mike would concentrate more on the music. They would frequently get the bus to Birmingham and hang out at the Trees pub, which was popular with rock'n'roll fans. They would then walk around town, occasionally buying records or vintage clothes, but always ready to run away from the local skinheads, who were bigger and who outnumbered them.

Jesús, Mike's father, usually came home with around £20 from his job in a local restaurant. When he saw Mike earn £22 from a single gig, he decided that he should get involved, and so for a while he drove the van containing the band's equipment as well as most of the band.

Beefy introduced Mike to Will Wakefield, a friend of his from Kidderminster. Will was an all-round good guy, and he and Mike became close friends. They were around the same age, and they shared a love of rock'n'roll and particularly Elvis. Will was great with machinery, and he had a sense of discipline and a certain amount of reliability.

When they first met, Mike had not yet learnt to drive, and Will decided to teach him. Mike's first car was a Bedford HA van, tastefully painted in gold and dusty pink, and this was used for his early lessons with Will. Later on they progressed to a rusting old 1969 Renault 8, and although it was not much to look at, it had a good engine. They started to work on the body, painting it red and silver with a black line running across the whole bodywork. It was not exactly cool, but Mike and Will went out in it almost every night. Will was in the passenger seat, patiently giving instructions to Mike behind the wheel. He taught him what was right and what was wrong on the highways as they drove around the West Midlands, dropping into bars and pubs, drinking a

Coke and then moving on. After almost a year Mike decided that it was time to take his test. He had every confidence in Will's instruction, and with some justification. He took his first official lesson, quickly followed it up with a second, and later that afternoon he took his test and passed first time. It was a joyous occasion, with Will almost as proud as Mike to see his pupil throw away his L-plates. They continued their teacher-pupil relationship for several more months, with Will passing on his wealth of experience on what it *really* takes to be a good driver.

Will was also popular with the rest of the Sanchez household. Mike's father was looking for a new job in the car spraying industry, and Will found him just such a position in a Bewdley garage. The family really took to Will, who had had a tough start in life. He was raised by foster parents after his natural parents split up, and he'd never really had the attention he craved.

Mike's father still had an old J4 van, and this was essentially what got the band and their equipment to the gigs. 'Mike's dad thought that I was the sensible one,' Will recalls, 'and so I was the only one that he trusted to drive the van.' Very soon he had virtually been adopted by the band. As well as driving, he was responsible for helping them load and unload their equipment, ensuring they got home safely at night, and generally keeping them from harm. He also learnt how to operate the mixing desk and was therefore regarded as an essential part of the line-up. Eventually, he took on the unofficial role of publicist, as he had a great knack of letting people know where and when the next gig was to take place, always ensuring that there would be a decent crowd.

The residency at the Market Tavern was not the immediate success that they expected, and the only people who regularly showed up to support them were a group of Kidderminster's Teddy girls. Occasionally, others would drop by, strangers from the bar next door who just happened to hear the music, but they would often just pay the 50p admission, watch a set, and then wander off into the night never to be seen again.

At end of the six-week residency things felt a little flat. Their musical future had not really taken off, and although they still got together regularly to rehearse and learn new songs, they had to make do with occasional gigs in the Bewdley and Kidderminster areas. They still hoped and believed that they were just one good show away from fame and fortune; it was just a matter of time and of finding the right audience.

Most of their Teddy girl fans were Polish and generally attractive. Mark and Tim didn't have girlfriends at the time, and Tim was still quite introverted, so Mark set him up with Anna, the first girl that the band had ever seen him with. Mike was rarely seen with a girlfriend, spending most of his time wrapped up in the music. When he did have a girl on his arm she was invariably good-looking – like Krysia, one of the Polish girls. Their relationship lasted around eight weeks, after which she became Mark's girlfriend and they even went as far as getting engaged. This could have caused a conflict within the band, but Mike was not really bothered about it, and he managed to get his own back later.

Mike then met Donna Edgar from Kidderminster, and they saw each other frequently. She became the first girlfriend that he ever took on holiday to Spain when his parents went on their annual summer trip. On that particular occasion they stayed at the flat of his Auntie Teresa and her husband Nicholas in Alicante. Mike and Donna were the same age and the relationship blossomed, despite his involvement with the Rockets.

The image of the band was definitely enhanced by the presence of a series of girlfriends, but it caused something of a logistical problem, as they needed enough transport for all of the equipment as well as the girls. They just about managed to cram everything into Mark's minivan and the van Will drove.

Mike arranged for the band to practise in the small upstairs ballroom at the George Hotel in Bewdley. They were delighted to have such a spacious area in which to rehearse, except for the need to carry all of their equipment up the narrow staircase. In return for the use of the practice room, they agreed to perform a few shows at the George.

It was to one of these gigs that Mark brought statuesque brunette Melanie Foster on their first date. Mark describes Melanie as 'a player' and quite a catch, even for a budding rock'n'roll star. Unfortunately, Melanie seemed to take more of a liking to Mike, and the pair disappeared for a couple of hours. Although Melanie claimed that they were just chatting, Mark felt obliged to dump her on the spot. This suited Mike, who continued to see her for some time afterwards, perhaps sensing some karmic retribution for the time that Mark got engaged to his ex-girlfriend Krysia.

With occasional shows at the George, the word started to spread about the new rock'n'roll band in town. Sometimes this came quite literally from beneath their feet. At one of the rehearsals at the George, their sounds were heard by Led Zeppelin frontman Robert Plant, who was enjoying Sunday lunch and a pint with his family and friends in the bar below. He decided to check out the band and jokingly suggested that they should keep the noise down. They did not immediately recognise the international superstar, but it became the start of a long friendship between Mike and Robert that still endures to this day.

Robert made a number of impromptu visits upstairs at the George, and on more than one occasion grabbed the microphone and joined in. He also recommended that his daughter, Carmen, and her friend Carrie, two 15-year-old peroxide blondes who were big fans of the Stray Cats, should check out the band. Mike decided that, if Robert was going to continue to pop in, he had better learn more about him, and so he went out and bought his first Led Zeppelin records. Unbelievably, he had to do the same thing after meeting Bill Wyman, Mick Fleetwood and Eric Clapton, and Mike maintains that this is part of his appeal to these music gods.

Behind the scenes, Mike decided that Geoff Belson was having too much of an influence on the direction and style of the band, and told him that he was no longer required. After six months of having someone to organise their gigs, the Rockets were once again on their own, with Mike at the helm.

They were slowly getting noticed, even though the majority of their shows were performed in social clubs in neighbouring towns such as Droitwich or Stourbridge. Rehearsals continued in the ballroom at the George, and they constantly expanded their repertoire with a regular influx of new songs. Local businessman Micky Blunt, of Blunts Shoes fame, was sufficiently impressed with the band to want to get them into a studio. He invited them to do a session at Rook Studios in Stourport, where they laid down 'Tear It Up', 'The Train Kept A-Rollin'' and 'Brand New Cadillac'. The recordings were never taken any further, but this remains the first studio experience that Mike and the Rockets ever had.

More shows followed locally, in venues such as Murdoch's Wine Bar and the Sutton Arms in Kidderminster, the Severn's Club in Stourport, and Droitwich Working Men's Club. Some were rather sad social club affairs where the music had to be kept at a reasonable level, whilst others were in somewhat insalubrious pubs. At times, the only thing that kept them going was the few real rock'n'roll fans who would turn up and make it all worthwhile. After Geoff Belson's departure, the strain of organising and promoting their own gigs proved to be a burden for the band, and, as Mike later admitted, a mistake.

After a typical social club gig in Birmingham, they saw a different side to drummer Tim Bearne. He had started to come out of his shell by actually finding himself a girlfriend as a result of being in the band, and suddenly he wanted to live life on the edge. On this occasion, the equipment was spread between Beefy's minivan and Tim's Ford Fiesta, and they had decided to have a race back to Mike's. The minivan was leading as they hit the top of the hill in Hagley, but then Tim appeared alongside doing around 100 m.p.h., with manic eyes that saw nothing but victory. Mike sat in the passenger seat, hanging on for dear life as the Fiesta flew past the minivan, and they were all very relieved to reach the Sanchez household in one piece that night.

Mrs Sanchez would never go to bed until her boy was safely back home, and this was one of the things that she entrusted to Will Wakefield. She also ensured that they were well looked after, and always had an assortment of cakes and drinks ready for their arrival. 'It was always good to know that there would be a nice Spanish cup of coffee waiting when we got back, no matter what time it was,' Will remembers.

The difficulties involved in promoting and arranging their own gigs were all too apparent, and the Rockets were happy to return to the Market Tavern for another residency. This time, they were on familiar ground and their audience was starting to grow. There were their old school friends and new fans from the neighbouring towns of Stourport, Stourbridge and beyond. Word had spread further afield, and rock'n'roll enthusiasts appeared from as far away as Cleobury Mortimer, Leominster and Worcester.

Things were looking up for the band until one night old school friend Ian Moone brought Mike some tragic news. Stephen Draper, Mike's close friend from their days at school, had been killed in a head-on collision with a car in Bewdley. He had only recently bought himself a brand new 250 cc Yamaha, and had been bragging about how quickly he could get from one pub to another about a mile away. His love of speed and motorbikes had combined to bring about this tragedy, and Mike felt sour and empty in his soul.

Ian Jennings had known Stephen since their days at primary school in Far Forest: 'When Stephen was killed in the motorbike accident in Bewdley, it was probably our first experience with mortality. On the night it happened, I was walking home from Bewdley and could see the flashing blue lights in the distance behind me. If I had been half an hour later, I would have been there when it happened. We didn't find out until we were at a gig a couple of days later.'

Mike was one of the pall-bearers at the funeral, and they laid Stephen's body in his grave at an old church graveyard in Far Forest. Mike was deeply touched by the loss of his 17-year-old friend and still visits his grave whenever he is in the area.

In December 1981, they played a gig to celebrate Beefy's 18th birthday. Although they did not know it at the time, the band was about to undergo a seismic change.

1982

In January 1982, Mike and Ian went to the Odeon in Birmingham to see the Stray Cats, and it had a profound effect on both of them, influencing their style, their musical direction and ultimately the make-up of the band.

The Stray Cats were an American rockabilly band who reached the height of their popularity in the early 1980s. The Odeon was packed for the visit of the Americans and they gave a devastating performance. Mike could feel their inspiration from the first note to the last encore, as they ripped through some wild rock'n'roll in a frenzy. They had inherited some of the anger and energy of the punk era, but musically they were much tighter and more stylish. Their show was frenetic as they jumped around the stage, abusing their instruments and thrilling the audience as the adrenaline of performing live coursed through them. It was dangerous; it was high octane; it had attitude; and it projected into the crowd the desire to have sex, get drunk, drive too fast and above all, *rock!*

Meanwhile, Ian Jennings had picked up on another American band called the Cramps. With albums such as *Songs The Lord Taught Us*, the Cramps fitted right in with the psychobilly style, with dark, intense, echo-twanging renditions of long-forgotten songs about death and lost love that had been so popular during the 1950s. The Cramps did it their way and became a huge hit for so many teenagers who were searching for angry, but more stylish alternatives to punk.

Mike wanted to change the direction of the band overnight and told Mark that he needed to switch his Commodore bass guitar for an upright model: 'I told Mike that I couldn't afford a double bass, but he was determined to make it happen. Ian turned up with a Boosey & Hawkes upright that he got from Crotchet & Quaver music store in Kidderminster, so I asked what I was going to do. Mike was quite clear that it would be guitar or nothing, and so I started to learn a few chords on the acoustic. Ian actually hired the double bass with the option to buy it after six months. This he did, and it was a fortuitous purchase, as he still plays it to this day.'

The next change to occur was a more personal one: both Mike and Ian had their heads shaved around the sides to create a 'flat-top'. Tim Bearne would never agree to this, but as he was the drummer, it did not matter as much. As a guitarist, however, Mark was expected to follow suit: 'I told them point-blank that I was not shaving my head, and that was always kind of resented.' Musically, Mark quickly learnt what he needed to as the new rhythm guitarist, and the Rockets moved on with Ian playing the double bass.

The Rockets had developed a sizeable and loyal following in the local area and beyond, with two gigs at the Waterside Club in Worcester being particularly popular. Lovers of their music and fans of all ages came out to see the band play, as well as Mr and Mrs Sanchez, who were now starting to feel proud of their son and his growing reputation. Manuela Sanchez would do anything to preserve their energetic performances, including taking photographs and making cassette recordings and occasionally video recordings. She had also started to make stage clothes for her son, such as shirts and the occasional jacket, whilst still being there at the end of the night to rustle up some food and drink for the hungry band and their adopted roadie. Mike remains proud of what his parents did for him, particularly the efforts of his mother, whose energy and determination knew no bounds where Mike was concerned.

Although they now had a large sound system and a Bedford CF van of their own, the band realised that the whole ensemble was held together with string. The vehicle was in a dreadful state, whilst the PA had been bought from an old roadie who must have had the microphones and cabinets for many years before finally offloading them to the Rockets. Despite their apparent green shoots of success, they knew that things still had to change. The PA stayed around for a while, whilst the van was replaced by a similar model from a cheap Midlands dealership, but there was a major upheaval within the band's ranks.

Mark Davies takes up the story: 'One Saturday afternoon, Ian and Mike came round to my house and told me that they didn't want me in the band any more. My mum gave them a few expletives, but I told them it was OK. Although it was the two of them that delivered the message, it was clear to me that it was Mike's decision.'

Meanwhile, Mike's old school friend Neil Wright had seen the Rockets at the Market Tavern and decided 'I can sing better than Mike Sanchez.' He formed his own band, and the day after Mark had parted company with the Rockets, Neil called round and asked him to join the Rockin' Renegades as their bass player. Old school friend Robert Milichip was already a band member, as was Stephen Draper's brother Ian on saxophone, and so it was an easy decision to make. That made two rockabilly bands playing out of the Kidderminster area, and for a while there was some hostile rivalry, but in general they got along just fine.

The reduction to a three-piece gave the Rockets more space and more freedom onstage. Their shows became wilder and edgier, with more of a resemblance to the Stray Cats, who had so influenced Mike several months earlier. However, they still had to accept the consequences of managing all of their bookings themselves.

One particular gig was in the back room of a run-down pub called the Bird In Hand in the Horse Fair, a notorious area of Kidderminster. The only person who actually came to see the show was a drunk who managed to collapse into the large bass cabinet, which fell and almost crushed the drum kit. On another occasion, in Dudley town centre, they had arranged to play at the Smiling Man that was infamous for hosting a large population of local black pimps. They spent the night before the show driving around the town, sticking home-made posters onto anything that was visible. The glue proved to be rather strong, and the posters remained for many months. The gig itself was unremarkable, with just a handful of rockabilly fans turning out to support them, but one of the fans put them in touch with a promoter of Teddy boy events at the Old Vic in Wolverhampton, and this resulted in a few more appropriate bookings.

Not everyone was an instant fan. Guitarist Antonio 'Tony' Coni thought they were 'plastic' and recalls: 'I first saw Mike at the Old Vic when I was with Colbert Hamilton. The band had just started, when in walked this guy with a big quiff. He was very friendly, and I saw him in the Rockets about a month later at the same place. I didn't really like them, although I did steal some of Mike's licks. He always put 110 per cent into his shows, and he did a great version of "Lonesome Tears In My Eyes". After that, we always went to see each other play, and we spoke about music frequently. We would advertise them when we played, and they would advertise us.'

As time went on, the number of gigs increased, and the Rockets' audiences continued to grow. The Market Tavern shows had a regular and enthusiastic audience, and after one of these they were asked by local promoter Norman Dickens if they would like more regular work at bigger venues. The answer, of course, was an emphatic 'Yes', and they were given an address to visit the following day.

A block of flats next to Kidderminster viaduct was hardly what they expected as their next step on the road to stardom, but it was there that they once again met Norman, along with his sidekick, Howard Jones. Together they comprised local booking agency Dual Management.

Norman had been a promoter for many years, including hosting gigs at Kidderminster Town Hall in the days when the Who and the Rolling Stones were on the club circuit, before they were really famous. Jones recalls: 'We could see the potential in the band, so we took the trouble to speak to their parents and then arranged for them to sign contracts which ran for a year with an option to renew annually.'

Dual Management booked the Rockets to perform at various showcase events at social clubs across the West Midlands. The band had already had their fill of social clubs, but it was guaranteed work and maybe, just maybe, a stepping stone to bigger and better things. They accepted the engagements, but they made it clear that they were an ambitious young band and that they were really aiming to create a much wider fan base throughout the country. They wanted to impress upon Norman and Howard that they were not just a cheap, dull cabaret act. Dual Management could sign them, but they needed to know that they were real musicians with rock'n'roll running through their veins!

Howard Jones spent a lot of time with the band, trying to get to know them and to understand what they were about. He was genuinely interested in them, and drove them to gigs as well as arranging flyers and publicity, including promotional shots with local photographer John Pitt. He achieved good exposure for them around the UK, but much of the work that they got through Dual Management became staid and predictable.

Shows at places such as Bartley Green Social Club, Oldhill Labour Club, Amblecote Royal British Legion and Evesham Working Men's Club served only to get the band valuable stage time, but very little else. Their fee was rarely more than £50 per show, and with fuel for their van and the agency fee to be deducted, there was not much left to share between the three band members. Sometimes they played three consecutive nights, which made it a more financially viable proposition, but the actual gigs were soul-destroying, with the band having to play as quietly as possible in front of an audience of elderly club members who did not really care who was onstage, as long as they were not too loud. Some venues even had a traffic light system, so that when a certain decibel level was reached the power to the stage was cut for thirty seconds, making the whole set-up a most surreal experience.

Mike describes their life on the road as 'glittery and cheap cabaret stages, dusty and smelly dressing rooms, fat old men drinking beer and fat old women in fluorescent petticoat skirts'.

The night would often end with the boys trying to fix something inside the ageing van and eating vinegar-soaked chips with oil-stained fingers. It was not the rock'n'roll dream that they all hoped it would be, but the reality was they were still good friends and actually had a lot of fun throughout.

They had started to use a recording studio in the converted garage of music store owner Sean Dee in Kidderminster, funded by Dual Management, and recorded a number of original pieces which were never released. A couple of the tracks required a saxophone, and it seemed perfectly natural to ask their old schoolteacher Ricky Cool to help out. From that point on they kept in touch with Ricky more frequently and occasionally invited him as a special guest to their appearances at local venues such as Ye Olde Crown Inn in Stourport. It was still considered a special event when Ricky agreed, and in return he started to use the Rockets as his opening band when they decided they would like to try out to a wider audience in London.

Their first London shows were at traditional and well-known music venues: the King's Head in Fulham and the Dublin Castle in Camden. With Ricky Cool heading the bill, they were guaranteed to have a favourable audience, and his influence provided them with a much-needed foot in the door to the London music scene.

At one such gig, at the Grey Horse in Kingston upon Thames, a young Nick Lunt was in the audience. Nick now plays saxophone with Jools Holland, as well as performing with Mike whenever he can, but back then he played drums with the Rockettes. He decided to check out the Midlands-based rock'n'rollers, and he was suitably impressed. 'It was obvious from the start that Mike and Ian were already stars in the making,' he says. 'Mike was unbelievably charismatic, mixed with a lot of natural talent.'

Mike and Ian quickly became aware of the neo-rockabilly scene developing around the capital. Many of the bands released albums on the London-based Nervous Records label, with throwback names such as the Deltas, the Ricochets, Restless and Dave Phillips & The Hot Rod Gang. Prior to that, their knowledge of the UK rockabilly scene was restricted to outfits such as Matchbox and Crazy Cavan & The Rhythm Rockers, and this was a whole new world. It was also such a refreshing change from the stereotypical Shakin' Stevens and Showaddywaddy, who flooded the charts and gained regular appearances on *Top Of The Pops* with their sanitised popabilly.

They went to see many bands around that time, constantly picking up new ideas, rather than seeing them as rivals. In Northampton they checked out the Jets, a very tight trio produced by Stuart Colman, who were already making an impact on the UK charts. Other new bands, such as the Polecats, the Shakin' Pyramids and the Stargazers, were all signing deals with major record labels and having varying degrees of success with their debut albums. The Stargazers signed with Epic, a subsidiary of CBS. Their bass guitarist, Anders Janes, was later a member of the Big Six and worked extensively with Mike.

The Rockets' brand of music was gaining popularity throughout the land, and there were a lot more people greasing back their hair and wearing Eddie Cochran patches on their denim jackets. However, the Rockets preferred the authentic American 1950s hepcat look. This was already the fashion in London, and the band realised that, in this respect, Bewdley and even Birmingham were very much behind the times.

London was a whole new world to Mike and the band. He renewed his acquaintance with Elizabeth Conde, the daughter of a family friend from when they used to live there, and Eli developed a love for the same music that Mike was already into. Pubs such as the Charlie Chaplin in Elephant & Castle, the Pink Elephant Club at the Southgate Royalty and Bumbles in Wood Green all hosted fantastic nights. There were no seventies-style Teddy boys to be found; instead, it was as though the whole scene had been transformed into one big fifties' party. The girls looked like Natalie Wood or Mamie Van Doren, whilst the boys modelled themselves on James Dean or Ersel Hickey. The sounds were strange and new to Mike, but they were not from the current charts. There was the white fifties' rockabilly sound of Carl Perkins, Charlie Feathers and Sonny Fisher, as well as the thumping blues of Doctor Ross and Slim Harpo. It was as though the whole room were moving to the powerful beat, and in the early 1980s it felt like a

Mike's maternal grandparents, José Bastida Montoya and Josefa Gil Martínez.

Left to right: Manuela (Mike's mother), Isabel, Josefa, Maria and Tomi.

Mike's paternal grandparents, Manuel Sánchez Garcia and Remedios Díaz Noriega, on their wedding day.

Mike's father with sister Angela in 1959, not long after his arrival in London.

Mike's mum and dad on their wedding day, 1962.

Mike and mum, summer 1964.

Mike's 1st birthday, with brother Juanjo and the old Dansette record player in the background.

Mike with the kids from next door, 1966.

Mike and his dad in 1969, shortly after moving to Claremont Avenue, Kingsbury.

Juanjo, age 17.

Mike, age 12.

Jesús and Teddy boy son stretch their legs next to the family's Austin J4 van.
Mike's mum can just be glimpsed through the window.

Rockets promo taken on fire escape at the George Hotel, Bewdley ca. 1981.
Top to bottom: Tim Bearne, Mark Davies, Mike, and Ian Jennings.

Rockets publicity, 1983, with Robert Plant's car.
Left to right: Ian Jennings, Mike and Tim Bearne.

The Rockets at Murdoch's, Kidderminster, 1983.
Left to right: Mike, Ian Jennings, Tim Bearne and Will Wakefield.

The Rockets performing at a social club, 1983.
Left to right: Tim Bearne (hidden), Mike and Ian Jennings.

The Big Town Playboys recording at Radio London for Stuart Colman's show, March 1985.
Left to right: Andy Silvester, Ricky Cool, John Spinetto, Ian Jennings and Mike.

Promo shot for *Playboy Boogie!* (1985).
Left to right: Ian Jennings, Mike, John Spinetto, Andy Silvester and Ricky Cool

On tour: August 1985.

70

Leeds University Union
presents

THE BIG TOWN PLAYBOYS

featuring

**Robert Plant plus
The Rent Party**

Tonight
Wed. 12th March
Tickets £5.00

Warm-up gig for the *Heart Beat '86* concert
at Birmingham NEC with Robert Plant.

Band On The Wall, Manchester, November 1986.
Left to right: Andy Silvester, John Wallace, John Spinetto, Ian Jennings and Mike.

Publicity shot taken at Covent Garden, 1988.
Left to right: Al Nicholls, Andy Silvester, Mike, Ian Jennings, Dai Powell and Paul Clarke.

The Talbot, Wrexham, May 1988.
Left to right: Ian Jennings, Dai Powell and Mike.

statement for the real rock'n'roll subculture. It also gave Mike a transition from the popular music of his beloved fifties era to the lesser-known artists and music from the same period. He loved the new sounds and delved deeper into their musical origins, eagerly consuming the album sleeve notes to enhance his knowledge of the artists, their backgrounds and even where the tracks were recorded.

The stream of regular shows meant that they needed a whole wardrobe of stage gear. Fortunately, there was an abundance of vintage American clothes available on King's Road in Chelsea, as well as on Camden Market. A trip to the market always ended up with a visit to Ted Carroll's nearby record store, Rock On. Ted was one of the founders of the Chiswick Records label, which was so significant throughout the punk era. He also founded Ace Records, a subsidiary of Chiswick, which released numerous collections of rockabilly and rock'n'roll. Charly Records also had an impressive catalogue of releases, whilst other city markets often had stalls selling newly pressed singles of obscure rockabilly, hillbilly, boogie-woogie and blues recordings. Mike and Ian lapped up these precious pieces of vinyl and, to top it off, they found a hairdresser in Brixton who was well known for his iconic cuts, and it was there that they maintained their trademark flat-tops. Visits to the capital were rarely made just for the stage performances and, indeed, often led to the band exploring their roots even further than before.

1983

With exciting times to be had in London, the Midlands social club circuit became even more of a drag. However, the Rockets' fame was spreading, and rock'n'roll promoters from North and South were beginning to take an interest. The group entered a talent contest in Worcestershire which involved recording a few tracks at ADR Studio on London Road in Worcester at the end of January 1983. A single track would be chosen to compete against tracks from over sixty other entrants, most of them following the more contemporary styles of current UK chart bands, and Mike did not really think that they had much chance of success against this barrage of modern pop songs.

He had always been quite lazy when it came to songwriting, particularly as there are so many great rhythm & blues songs out there already. However, his original 'Without You' triumphed in the contest, and suddenly the regional newspapers became interested.

In February they went to Jennings Farm, where photographer John Pitt took some promotional photographs, including one of them sitting on Robert Plant's 1957 Chrysler Imperial – although Robert insisted that they removed their shoes to avoid marking the white leather seats.

It was now the spring of 1983, and the Rockets played their most prestigious gig yet as headliners on a six-band bill at the Malvern Winter Gardens. In April, they played a total of ten shows around the Midlands, and were finally starting to see breaks from the dreaded social clubs. They appeared at the legendary JB's club in Dudley, a venue that has hosted such varied performers as Elvis Costello, U2 and the Stone Roses. At the Mitre in Stourbridge they did a rockabilly night and were able to perform with the raw energy that was so prevalent in their rehearsals, but which was more or less forbidden on the social club scene.

The following month, the Rockets played an even bigger show, supporting the Alarm at Kidderminster Town Hall. The Alarm had shot to fame on the back of the punk and new wave movements with their recent hit single, '68 Guns', and the town hall was packed, with the crowd pushed up to the front of the stage. They were a seething mass, jumping and spitting, which was the thing to do at the time. Mike could feel their electricity, and he knew that he simply had to get onto that stage and perform like never before. They had to be as powerful as that Stray Cats show from just over a year earlier, and they had to rock. They needed to thrill the crowd, and yes, they even had to scare the crowd. That's what the punks expected, just like the punks scared Mike at school.

Onstage the Rockets were sensational. Mike imagined that this adrenaline rush was how it felt to be on drugs. He was hooked on it, and he wanted more.

The Rockets' increasing fame found them regularly appearing in local newspapers such as the *Kidderminster Shuttle* and the *Worcester Evening Post*. This drew the unwanted attention of the Department of Health & Social Security, as at the time the band were all claiming unemployment benefit. The DHSS wanted to investigate the potential undeclared income that these musicians were earning, and it was left to Dual Management to diffuse the situation. Howard Jones explained that the boys would love to be earning enough to pay tax, but at that time their fees barely covered their outlay in terms of travelling, equipment and other expenses. He persuaded them that the boys actually needed more money than they were making at that time to progress within the music industry, and he secured them a grant of around £40 per week which contributed to better PA equipment and van repairs. Fortunately, this halted any investigation, and another media appearance almost certainly worked in their favour. BBC Radio 1 contrasted a Barry Manilow show at Blenheim Palace with the Rockets' appearance at the King's Head in Fulham on the same evening. Whilst Mr Manilow would obviously have earned a tidy sum that night, Howard Jones announced to the world that the Rockets would probably clear enough to be able to afford a bag of chips between them.

Robert Plant continued to climb the stairs and check out the Rockets' rehearsals at the George, and at the end of September 1983 he finally got to see their entire show. They were booked to play at Brinton's Social Club in Kidderminster, opening for Birmingham soul singer Ruby Turner and her band. It was no ordinary social club. Brinton's was one of the largest and most successful factories in the carpet-making industry, and its social club was considerably larger and more extravagant than the band's usual Midlands venues. Plant and his wife, Maureen, were in the audience, together with daughter Carmen and her friend, Carrie. The girls, in particular, wanted more, and Mike soon arranged a regular invite for them to future Midlands shows.

After a while, Robert accepted that the 15-year-old girls had taken a liking to the 18- or 19-year-old musicians, and it was with his blessing that he allowed Mike and Will to drive over to his house and pick them up to take them to the shows. An image that will always live long in Mike's memory is one of Robert in dressing gown and slippers, wagging a fatherly finger at him and insisting that his daughter be back home safely by midnight, or one o'clock at the latest.

Cars played a significant part in the budding relationship between Robert and Mike. On one occasion, Mike and Will were at the Sutton Arms in Kidderminster, where they met Carmen and Carrie. They took the girls back to the Plant house and stayed for a while. When it came time to leave, Will's white Mk3 Ford Cortina refused to start, so Robert had to come out and help them push it up the drive.

On another evening, Mike and Will brought the girls home late, but there was no one at home. They were teenagers and did what most teenagers would do, with some kissing and cuddling in the car in the dark shadows of the Plant household. They saw a light coming up the drive and stopped what they were doing, but the light went away, so they naturally resumed. Unfortunately, Robert had decided to sneak up on them in his own car, and after turning off the lights and the engine, he allowed it to roll up to Will's vehicle, giving it a sturdy bump as it came to rest. The jolt shocked the boys into stopping their amorous activities, and they hastily bade the girls goodnight.

It was New Year's Eve 1983 when the Rockets played a gig in West Bromwich. As usual, Mike and Will picked up Carmen and Carrie to see the show, and Mike and the band were a little late getting the girls back to Robert Plant's house. Robert's New Year's Eve party was in full swing, and he hardly noticed the lateness of the hour, inviting the Rockets inside to join in the fun. He introduced Mike to Andy Silvester, former Chicken Shack and Savoy Brown bass player, who was also a member of Robert's original Honeydrippers. In fact, it was Robert who persuaded Andy to switch from bass to lead guitar.

They also bumped into Ricky Cool, and the transition from ex-teacher to friend was quickly completed as they started to use his nickname, 'Trix'. The Rockets staged an impromptu acoustic gig which left a big impression on the party-goers, and afterwards Ricky and Andy told them to stay in touch.

1984

Ricky Cool continues the story: 'Ricky Cool & The Rialtos finished in 1981. By that time Andy Silvester was a member of the band, most of whom had been involved with Robert Plant in his first Honeydrippers line-up. Andy and I remained close friends, with a shared passion for rhythm & blues, and the desire to put together an authentic Chicago-style blues band, including piano and double bass. I was living in Bewdley at the time and Andy lived in Stourport, so it was easy for us to get together. We worked on this for a couple of years without success.

'In early 1984, a month or so after Robert's party, I heard that the Rockets were playing a gig in Stourport, and I went along with Andy to see the band. We were both taken with Mike and Ian's enthusiasm and passion for their music. Mike was playing guitar, and at this point we did not know that he also played piano and had taken lessons. We met up with them on a few occasions and told them about our idea to form a Chicago-style band, and they were very enthusiastic.'

Meanwhile, in the spring of 1984 it seemed as though things might start to take off for the Rockets, when Dual Management secured them the offer of a recording contract with Nervous Records. This had always been a goal for the band, but it happened at exactly the wrong time. Mike and Ian were already considering the more exciting prospect of working with Ricky Cool and Andy Silvester, and there was the desire to get away from Dual Management, who would inevitably have been involved, so the contract remained unsigned.

The year progressed with a mixture of social clubs and some better venues. They started to appear in Fulham and Camden as the headline act rather than the support, and they also started to venture further afield. They performed in Newcastle upon Tyne for the Prudhoe rock'n'roll crowd, Middlesbrough, Bristol, Great Dunmow in Essex, and many other cities and towns. They played an all-dayer in Brighton, where Mike got a kicking for kissing the wrong girl, and many London venues such as the Mitre at Greenwich and a classic Teddy boy pub called the Tower, south of the Thames. Rock'n'roll booking agent Paul Barrett began to find them gigs, which made a welcome change from the sad social clubs favoured by Dual Management.

There were also nights at some less salubrious joints that were quite simply wrong for the style of the Rockets. One such was the Tin Can Club in Digbeth, Birmingham, normally reserved for extreme punks. The band were booked in, and a month before the gig Mike and Ian decided to do a bit of research. They went to see London psychobilly band the Meteors, and were a little taken aback by the make-up of the audience. There were a few rockabilly types, but the majority were hardcore punks looking every inch like the 'wrecking crew', as Meteors' fans were known. There were also a few alternative punks, and the atmosphere was surprisingly electric. The music was loud, violent and angry, and frontman Paul Fenech looked like he was covered in spittle and blood. The spittle was obviously from the audience, whilst his reputation for spitting chicken blood during his performances and the unplucked dead chicken hanging from the side of his guitar explained the rest. It was a scary place to be part of the crowd, and the prospect of actually appearing on that stage was even worse. When the time came, Mike decided to be as manic as he possibly could be. He thrashed around on his guitar, and eventually dropped it on the stage as the band walked off at the end of their set to increasingly loud feedback. The show was not as bad as they had feared, but Mike decided that it was not an avenue they should explore any further.

Although heavily involved in the playing side, Mike still liked to check out other bands, and a favourite venue was the Holte, a pub next to the Aston Villa football stadium. Once a month, the pub hosted a rock'n'roll evening with live bands that were invariably of a good quality. The Dynamite Band looked and sounded like Bill Haley & His Comets, and featured a very young Ray Gelato on tenor saxophone. Ray later fronted the Chevalier Brothers before eventually creating Ray Gelato & The Giants of Jive. The Blue Rhythm Boys featured Paul Ansell on vocals and well-respected Irish-born rockabilly guitarist Jim Carlisle. Restless had Mark Harman on guitar, and Mark remains a significant influence on Mike's own guitar-work. He also played guitar for Dave Phillips & The Hot Rod Gang, who had a huge rockabilly hit with their rocked-up version of the Northern soul classic, 'Tainted Love'. Mark had a style similar to Cliff Gallup of Gene Vincent's classic 1956 line-up, and this was to feature heavily later in Mike's career.

The Rockets played at the Holte a couple of times during the year, and they went down well with the knowledgeable Birmingham audience. This meant a lot, as the venue was always full of friends of the rock'n'roll genre, and as such their reaction was more important than at an ageing social club. With the Holte's stream of top-quality rockabilly performers it was important not to play too many of the same covers, and so the Rockets had a chance to experiment with some original high-energy songs such as 'Midnight Express' and 'Love Is A Drug', making full use of the Bigsby tremolo on Mike's guitar. They also mixed in a few unusual covers such as Hasil Adkins' 'Chicken Walk' and a neo-rockabilly inspired version of Engelbert Humperdinck's 'Please Release Me'. Mike's musical talent even extended to the banjo, and he picked up just enough to do a version of Elvis Presley's 'Just Because'. They also ventured into pure blues by covering the Link Wray version of Jimmy Reed's 'Ain't That Lovin' You Baby' featuring Ian on main vocals. The sound was magical, with Mike playing his beloved Antoria with the Bigsby tailpiece through a Watkins Copicat tape echo into a Music Man amplifier. It was not the Royal Albert Hall – that was to come later – but at the time it definitely rocked.

As the year progressed, the meetings with Andy and Ricky became more frequent and more meaningful. At first, it was simply about having a beer and a friendly chat about the music. They played songs and compiled sets to work on at rehearsals, and gradually the ideas started to form around a new band. Ricky had worked with drummer John Spinetto in the Icebergs and thought that he would be ideal for the new line-up. Ricky himself would alternate between vocals, tenor saxophone and blues harmonica, whilst Andy would be the lead guitarist.

Ricky describes how the band developed: 'Mike would also share the vocals and play some guitar, but when we found out about his skills on the piano, we started moving towards more swing-style rhythm & blues. It was a real voyage of discovery, with Andy and I searching out material, mainly by buying stuff from record auctions such as Red Lick Records and *Sailor's Delight*. Rehearsals were very exciting, because we were playing music that no one else was playing, and certainly not as authentically as us. Andy was now actively helping Mike develop his piano playing by turning him on to the likes of Amos Milburn and Charles Brown. He also helped Ian with his double bass playing, mainly from the point of view of accuracy and intonation. You can get away with murder playing rockabilly slap-bass, but not playing rhythm & blues!'

Ricky lived in the old centre of Bewdley town, and he knew of a cellar bar that was a part of the Thurston Hotel next to the River Severn. The landlord was happy for the embryonic band to use the cellar bar for rehearsals, and it was a small step to then turn it into a regular venue for them to try out new songs every Wednesday. The cellar bar was already an occasional venue for traditional jazz, usually featuring trumpeter Stanley Allsop's Jazz Band. Stanley was the father of Nick Allsop, Mike's colleague from school and founder of Rouen, who were still gaining success.

Ricky proposed that the band be called the Big Town Playboys after the most famous hit of Chicago blues guitarist Eddie 'Playboy' Taylor. This was agreed, but London promoter Steve Beggs, who had put on shows featuring both Ricky Cool and the Rockets, suggested that the name Ricky Cool should be included to maintain the considerable following that Ricky had already built up in the capital.

As Ricky recalls, it was not really his decision: 'We were not happy with the name, but went along with it on the understanding that, if we were successful in getting established, we would drop "Ricky Cool &". This was fine by me, because right from the start Mike did most of the singing, even if I did the between-song chat. We always thought of the band as the Big Town Playboys.'

It was Wednesday, 6 June 1984, when Ricky Cool & The Big Town Playboys performed their first live session at the Thurston, and although it was not particularly well advertised, word of mouth meant that there was a decent crowd to see the show. The Thurston became a regular gig, with the band playing virtually every Wednesday for almost two years, and the crowd were always appreciative of their local heroes.

The Rockets still played a couple of gigs every week, but compared to the new and exciting Ricky Cool line-up things were starting to get a little stale. Wednesdays at the Thurston were spent learning new songs and getting tighter as a band, whilst the end was fast approaching for the Rockets. Mike and Ian had to break the news to Tim that the Rockets would soon disappear, and he was naturally disappointed after the events of the previous three years.

However, the situation was a little more complicated when it came to Dual Management. The Rockets had signed a contract with the booking agency, but it actually proved to be relatively easy to get out of. Mike and Ian told them that they had had enough of playing dingy social clubs and that they needed to settle down into steady day jobs. It was a complete lie, but it worked. Howard Jones realised that there was no future for the band with Dual Management, suspecting that they were about to follow the path outlined to them by Ricky Cool, and so he allowed the contracts to lapse. It was an unfortunate ending to a relationship that helped to get the young musicians properly started, but there were no recriminations, and Mike will always acknowledge the role that Howard Jones and Norman Dickens played in his early career.

The Rockets still continued with Dual Management for a couple of months, including a memorable night when they supported the Steve Gibbons Band in Leominster and some shows at a number of US military bases, but eventually it came to an end. The Rockets' farewell gig was on 23 November 1984, appropriately at the Market Tavern in Kidderminster. There was a special guest appearance from Ricky Cool, and the audience was a sea of familiar faces and fans from everywhere. Although it was the end of an era, it was a good way to bow out, knowing that there were more exciting times ahead.

A week before the Rockets' farewell, Ricky Cool & The Big Town Playboys had already begun their regular trips to Fulham and Camden, with many other London shows booked for the months ahead. For Mike it was almost a rite of passage, leaving behind the band that was formed at school and starting down the uncharted path towards becoming a professional musician.

CHAPTER 5

Mr. Electricity

The early years of the Big Town Playboys honed Mike's musical career until eventually they became his band.

1984

Although the break-up of the Rockets closed an important chapter in Mike's life, it opened another that was a significant step forward in his musical career. Ricky Cool had once been Mike's schoolteacher and an early musical influence, and now they shared the same stage. Ian Jennings played double bass, whilst John Spinetto was a fixture on drums, but the dynamics of the band were constantly changing in those early days. Andy Silvester played guitar, so Mike spent more time at the piano. Ricky played tenor saxophone accompanied by Mike on the keyboard, then the bandleader would change over to harmonica with Mike on rhythm guitar and Andy on lead. They switched effortlessly from the West Coast rhythm & blues of Amos Milburn, Charles Brown, Roy Milton and Joe Liggins to the Chicago blues of Jimmy Reed, Little Walter and Eddie Taylor, and all within the same set.

Andy was a fantastic all-round musician, and he had a great ear for the piano parts on many of the tracks that the band were learning. They spent hours doing improvised sessions around the old piano in the George Hotel, with Andy leading the way on the black American rhythm & blues of Little Walter and Ike Turner. Mike was already an adept boogie-woogie player, and this gave him the ideal opportunity to perfect his left-hand riffs. Andy guided him through many of the intricacies, and Mike in turn went home and studied the new patterns. He was a keen student and soon got his fingers accustomed to the new rhythms.

David 'Rowdy' Yeats had been a friend of Andy Silvester since their time with the Sounds of Blue. Rowdy had been the lead vocalist in a band which also contained keyboardist Christine Perfect, who later became Christine McVie and joined Fleetwood Mac, and Chris Wood on saxophone prior to joining Traffic. By the mid-1980s, he had stopped performing and was working in A&R, as well as mixing for various record companies. Andy took him along to a BTPs gig, and he liked what he saw: 'I was very impressed. Right from the off, the live gigs were explosive. Ricky Cool was a showman, whilst Andy Silvester was a perfectionist musician. For him, if the original song was 2 minutes and 35 seconds long, then the Playboys' version of it also had to be 2 minutes and 35 seconds long. Mike played piano with them, and Andy was teaching him the nuts and bolts of how these ancient rhythm & blues songs were put together. Offstage, he was softly spoken and very likeable, but he had a wild side that came out onstage.'

From the early days of being a Big Town Playboy, Mike avidly learnt everything that he could about the wide range of music that was a constant backdrop to the band's life. Andy Silvester, in particular, had an extensive record collection on vinyl and cassette. Fans appreciated the variety, and sometimes the obscurity, that they produced and would send in rare rock'n'roll tracks for their entertainment, as well as inclusion in future sets. Warringtonian Dave Clarke, a good friend of the BTPs and part of a Northern collective of vintage blues and roots fans that included photographer Brian Smith and collector Tony Watson, converted thousands of tracks of obscure black rhythm & blues from the 1940s and early 1950s from the original 78s onto cassette tapes.

Dave recalls how he was reluctant to go to his first show: 'I was and still am a collector of American blues and rhythm & blues, and I was talked into going to see the Big Town Playboys, as I was told that Mike sounded like Amos Milburn. I was sceptical, but I went along to the International in Manchester and I was knocked out by them. After the show, I introduced myself to Rowdy Yeats and Andy Silvester, and we became good friends. I saw them many more times, and started dragging along other collectors. At the time, I was the cartoonist for *Sailor's Delight*, a magazine that was a vehicle for auctions of this kind of music. Rather than get paid, the owner of the magazine, Paul Vernon, allowed me to turn up at the end of each auction with an open reel tape and a turntable, and I recorded whatever I wanted from the auction. I started sending these to Andy Silvester, and many of them became a part of the Playboys' set. Sherman Johnson's "Red Hot

Mama" was one of the first that I ever sent to them.'

Brian Smith was one such music fan who accompanied Dave to the next show: 'Dave told me that they were my kind of band, and he was right. I saw them at Band On The Wall in Manchester, and I was hooked. After that, we saw them at every opportunity, including the Apollo and the Royal Albert Hall. I even used to record some of the shows on an old cassette player. Dave put together his tapes for them, and a huge amount of their repertoire was derived from these tapes.'

So what exactly was it about the Big Town Playboys that made them different? Dave explains: 'Many bands have tried to imitate vintage blues and roots musicians, but if you turned your back on the Big Town Playboys, you could be listening to the originals. I wrote articles for *Blues & Rhythm* magazine, which really was purist, and I came in for a lot of criticism when I convinced the editor to allow me to do a piece on the Playboys, explaining how authentic they were.'

Jonas Bernholm, in Stockholm, established Mr R&B Records and issued twelve-inch albums of the original 78s of many fabulous rhythm & blues collections, which Andy obtained through mail order. Even the labels themselves, such as Route 66, Saxophonograph and Jukebox Lil, evoked memories of the era that they brought back to life.

Mike devoured the music and read the album notes from start to finish, eager to know more about his new-found heroes. He took in Snader Telescriptions, which were videos of live performances from the 1950s, mostly from the *Live At The Apollo* series of shows, and his knowledge of the artists performing his kind of music expanded rapidly.

There is no doubt that, musically speaking, these were very much Mike's formative years, and he frequently acknowledges the great influence and direction that Andy Silvester and Ricky Cool provided in that early part of his career. Appearance, presentation, style, delivery, sound and classic entertainment were all developed, enhanced and fine-tuned by Mike under the watchful eyes of his two enthusiastic and experienced mentors.

Bookings proved easy to come by for the newly formed Big Town Playboys, with the cellar of the Thurston Hotel by the riverside in Bewdley becoming a regular Wednesday night gig. The attendance was always good, and it was the perfect time and place to experiment with new songs which they could then launch onto the tougher London audience at the weekend.

Ricky Cool's name and London contacts, including promoter Steve Beggs, ensured that they had a number of regular venues, whilst others, such as the Rock Garden in Covent Garden were new. Ricky and Andy were doing the management of the band, calling promoters and negotiating fees for gigs.

Ricky's fans became Big Town Playboys fans, and their gigs were played to packed houses. The London scene grew at a pace. The Dublin Castle in Camden became a regular venue, and it was a guaranteed sell-out every week. Ricky Cool had played there with several other bands previously and there was nothing quite like it: 'The atmosphere was electric, and we did their New Year's Eve show for a few years. This was also why we chose the venue for the first album, *Playboy Boogie!*'

The King's Head in Fulham, the Oval in Kennington, Dingwalls in Camden Lock, the 100 Club in Oxford Street and many others hosted the BTPs, who brought in the crowds every week. It was at the King's Head that saxophone player Martin Winning first saw the band: 'I just went along to see them and John Wallace introduced me. They were great, and I could see that Mike was the star. I was surprised that he was really quite shy, even though he was a fantastic showman. At the time, Ray Gelato was very big on the swing scene, but for rhythm & blues Big Town Playboys were the best.'

The band spent their evenings playing the revered London venues before crashing at a friend's flat. The afternoons would find them spending their hard-earned cash on vintage stage clothes, before it was time to travel to the next gig as darkness fell.

The physical appearance of the band was of great importance, and they wore vintage tweed jackets, fifties' trousers, black and white brogues and vintage silk ties to cultivate their image. Mike even grew a pencil moustache in the style of Little Richard to complement the image, and the musky smell of Sweet Georgia Brown pomade oozed from their hair.

Initially, Ricky set the playlist, and the band tried to add at least three new songs every week. The set rocked with the sounds of Amos Milburn, Little Walter, Roy Brown, Little Willie Littlefield, T-Bone Walker and other great musical legends from bygone decades. The punk era had by now been well and truly stifled, and the flamboyant New Romantics filled the charts, but for the London pub and club scene Ricky Cool & The Big Town Playboys were the only gig in town. They looked like no one else, and their rhythm & blues edge made them sound so different from the mainstream.

Occasionally, the BTPs came across bands who were similar in style, such as the Chevalier Brothers fronted by Ray Gelato, who was now singing as well as playing the tenor saxophone, and featuring Roger Beaujolais on the vibraphone. They played Louis Jordan-style swing and late thirties-style jazz, and received good exposure through frequent sessions on John Peel's radio show. There was also Rent Party, a lively jump blues and swing outfit; Sugar Ray Ford & The Hotshots, featuring Pat Reyford, who later became a good friend of Mike's; Juice On The Loose, including future Big Town Playboy Frank Mead on tenor saxophone; and the Balham Alligators featuring Geraint Watkins, bringing the Mardi Gras to South London, but no one was doing what Ricky Cool & The Big Town Playboys were doing. They were unique, and their fans cried out for more.

Their schedule was now hectic, with rehearsals on Mondays and sometimes Tuesdays at the Thurston, where they played on Wednesdays. Thursdays would see them in London, and they would stay in the capital for bookings on Fridays, Saturdays and Sundays, often with shows at lunchtime as well as in the evening. The week would usually start again with a set at the Wag Club, which was housed in the same building as the Flamingo Club made famous by Georgie Fame, and then it was back to rehearsals. Mike was buzzing with the new lifestyle and the thrill of playing to new fans every week, rather than the same faces they encountered at the Midlands venues.

The money started rolling in, but not as quickly as he would have liked. The Rockets had had the overhead of Dual Management, but the Big Town Playboys had bigger expenses, with sound engineers, promoters and several others who all wanted their cut. They kept costs down by crashing with friends in Islington and Camberwell, but by the time they had shopped for more stage clothes, there was very little left over.

1985

By 1985, the London club circuit had become very busy, and one night at the Dublin Castle Mike spotted a familiar face in the crowd. It was John Wallace, an accomplished tenor saxophone player who had previously found success with the Stargazers and JoBoxers. John made it known that he was available, and he joined the band a short time later. He initially played baritone sax, leaving the tenor roles to Ricky, though eventually he played tenor too, giving a different sound to the horn section. He was a real 'playboy' in every sense of the word, turning up to gigs in a pink Ford Consul with whitewall tyres. He always arrived late, long after the set-up had been done, and he was always the first to leave, usually with a car full of girls. To Mike, this was what success was all about.

The band's frequent trips to London and back home again, with rehearsals on the nights that they weren't playing live, could have become a chore, but they were in it for the fun, the music and the girls. Mike looked upon it as a boys' camping trip, with three or four of them crashing on a floor in sleeping bags, and after his years with the Rockets, it was good to at last find gainful employment.

The BTPs still found time to check out other bands in town, including a notable night at the London Palladium in February 1985, when R&B legends Little Willie Littlefield and Big Jay McNeely were on a star-studded bill.

Later that month, disaster struck as Big Town Playboys played one of their regular venues, the Grey Horse in Kingston upon Thames. Ian Jennings describes it as a 'terrible night', although most of the show went down well. Mike played keyboard for much of the evening, then picked up his beloved Antoria semi-acoustic guitar. When he plugged its lead into his amp, he noticed an odd buzzing sound. Ian explains what happened next: 'It was at the end of the gig. We normally finished the night with Mike switching to guitar for two numbers, "Hole In My Pocket" and "Shake Your Hips". There was a problem with the earth supply in Mike's guitar amp: the wire had come loose in the mains plug and touched the live or neutral wire. So, when Mike picked up the guitar and started to play he was OK, until he started to sing the first verse using the microphone. A circuit was formed with the amp and the PA system, with him in the middle. The mic stuck to his mouth, the strings on the guitar popped, and he flew into the drum kit behind him. Trix's fast thinking and action saved him. He grabbed the guitar lead and ripped it out of the guitar, burning his hands in the process, but it worked.'

Mike had received a severe electric shock, and although his eyes were open, he could not see a thing. The guitar strings had burnt through the skin on his fingers, but it was his thumb that sustained the worst damage, as the lesions went deep into his flesh. He blacked out and fell backwards. When he came round, he discovered that he had smashed into the drum kit, but at least he could see again. He was taken to Kingston General Hospital, where he was found to have an irregular heartbeat, and was kept in the intensive care unit for two days. On his first night in hospital, just as he was falling asleep, his heart monitor emitted a high-pitched monotone. The line went flat, indicating that he had died, and two nurses came rushing in from an adjacent room. Fortunately, it appears to have been a malfunction in the machine, rather than a worsening medical condition, and he somehow found the strength to stop the medics before they used the defibrillator on him.

Ian continues: 'The morning after the gig, Andy and Trix wanted me to call Mike's mum and dad to tell them what had happened. I didn't think this was a good idea, because if any mother gets a call from the friend of her son who says there's been an accident, she immediately thinks the worst, so we waited till we got to the hospital and Mike called her himself. We played at the venue again, but we all checked our gear and checked it again.'

Eventually Mike recovered, but it was a long time before he played the guitar again, and the scars that the guitar strings made across his fingers can be seen to this day. He still recalls thinking that, at least it was the end of the show and no one would ask for their money back. The event made headline news, including *Time Out* magazine as well as the London-based newspapers.

Stuart Colman had a show on Radio London, and also made reference to the incident: 'We were doing a live broadcast, and Rowdy Yeats brought Mike into the studio. I knew very little about him, though we introduced him as "Mr. Electricity". He talked about the dangers involved and told people to always check their amps before plugging them in. It was very relevant, as there had been a couple of deaths in the industry from electrocution.'

Colman was impressed by the larger-than-life character that he had interviewed and sought out more information: 'Soon after the Radio London spot, I saw Mike and the band live, and I was blown away – he was that bloody good. He could do things in the UK that no one else could do. In the US, students get given an instrument on their first day at school, and they learn rhythms and timings. That education doesn't exist in England. People go to their church for the music as well as the religion, and the way they play is just so different. Mike had that intuition, and more. You don't have to be a skilled musician to appreciate it. You could see his rolling eyes and his authentic body movement. It really made him stand out.'

The band were slowly gaining wider recognition and were featured in the leading musical press, including *New Musical Express* and *Melody Maker*. Rowdy Yeats was working hard behind the scenes to gain them further exposure: 'I was in London doing PR for anyone who would have me! The Big Town Playboys wanted publicity down there, and I was happy to assist. We got into *Time Out* magazine, and then there were two radio sessions, at Capital and London. I just rang the radio stations and told them I had a great band. It was a good time for me personally, as I was working with a hot act. I looked after them, but then quite often I would end up with six bodies on my floor if they had nowhere else to stay.'

In April 1985, the Big Town Playboys recorded their first video for the Channel 4 magazine show *Swank*. Success followed success, and in May they decided to record their first album. They used Vic 'Valves' Cleary as their sound engineer and recorded *Playboy Boogie!* over three nights at the Dublin Castle. Cleary was renowned for his sound-engineering skills, and his equipment of choice was an old reel-to-reel recording machine which the band had to carry down the stairs from his fourth-floor flat, which was in a building that had no lifts. Andy and Ricky thought that the valve equipment would give them a warmer and more authentic sound, but Mike feels it actually made very little difference. The LP was released on the Making Waves label owned by Barry Martin of the Hamsters. A three-track single was released to promote the LP, containing 'Down The Road Apiece' and two tracks that were not on the album, 'I Like It' and 'Gotta Do More For My Baby' (actually 'I Want To Do More'), both of which were recorded at the same Dublin Castle shows. Unfortunately the band saw virtually no money from sales of the album or its spin-off single, which remains the only 45 rpm recording that Mike has ever released.

Phil Carson of Atlantic Records owned the Heartbreak Hotel in San Antonio, Ibiza. Robert Plant, who was signed to Atlantic at the time, put in a good word for the Big Town Playboys, and in July 1985 they agreed to play a two-week residency at the hotel. Robert told them to go out and have a ball every night – and they fully intended to do so. Unfortunately, Ricky Cool could not make the trip due to his teaching and family commitments, and this was the beginning of the end for Ricky in the band as John Wallace assumed a bigger role. They played two one-hour sets every evening and then partied long into the night. They would eventually leave the club as the sun came up and fall asleep on the beach before recovering in time for the following night's shows. Mike even found time for romance with a Dutch girl who he was quite taken with, and he brought her along to the end-of-term party up in the woodland hills outside San Antonio. Unfortunately, John Wallace used his charms and seduced her, as he tried to do with so many others. After returning to the UK, they played a number of shows in Scotland, and, to add insult to injury, John travelled up not with the band, but accompanied by the Dutch girl, which alienated him from the other members.

After two weeks of solid back-to-back playing in Ibiza, the band were really tight when they returned to their home audiences. The London crowds noticed and showed their appreciation, and Ricky Cool was welcomed back for a prestigious gig at the Hurlingham Club, Fulham for the head of A&R at Island Records.

Earlier on in the year, Ted Carroll had brought pianist and singer Little Willie Littlefield across from the US. Littlefield was famous for being the first artist to record the Leiber & Stoller blues classic, 'Kansas City', in 1952, which he released as 'K.C. Loving'. A tour of clubs and pubs with the BTPs was scheduled for August 1985, and when Willie first met the band at the Dublin Castle, he was expecting to rehearse a few nightclub standards and country & western songs. Andy Silvester prompted the boys to break into 'I Like It', one of his originals from the 1950s. Littlefield was impressed, and for Mike it was the start of a friendship that lasted many years.

Little Willie was a great performer, and after the Big Town Playboys opened up the evening, he would come on for the main set with Mike watching from the wings. This was the best education that he could ever have hoped for, avidly studying Littlefield's playing as he hit the keys so hard that several times during the tour he broke the bottom C and G strings on the piano. Towards the end of the show, Mike would join the band onstage again, as Willie moved on to playing the double bass whilst still banging out tunes on the piano with his shoe and dancing for the crowd.

The Big Town Playboys were now well established, and their regular haunts such as the Thurston and the Dublin Castle were interspersed with newer venues such as the International in Manchester, *Basildon Blues Festival* and the Compasses in Ludlow. There were universities and colleges, a private event at Lord's Cricket Ground, and they finished the year off back at the Dublin Castle.

Musician Jim Merris describes the effect the band had on him: 'I saw them at the Thurston Hotel, and at the time I had just discovered the Blues Brothers. My best friend had told me about a great band, so we rolled up in a 1968 Pontiac Parisienne. I was dressed as Elwood Blues. The band struck up – it was the most dramatic moment. I saw the light! Chicago blues at its finest, with a sweating, gyrating massive-voiced man at the piano, looking like a throwback from the

1950s. Onstage he was sweat, sweat and more sweat. I had just started my own outfit, the Red Lemon Electric Blues Band, and we were invited to support the Playboys at the Thurston. They even asked me to guest on harmonica a few times, which was very generous, as I was not very good. From the outset, the influence that the Blues Brothers had on me was replaced by the Big Town Playboys.'

1986

The year 1986 was pivotal for Ricky Cool & The Big Town Playboys, and it started with the usual circuit of regular London venues and a few new ones further north. However, the highlight was a gig that they did not actually get paid for.

Robert Plant remained a fan of the band, and he was planning his line-up for a huge charity concert at Birmingham NEC in aid of *Heart Beat '86*. He contacted Andy to explain his ideas about the show, and shortly afterwards they arranged rehearsals at the Thurston Hotel. The Big Town Playboys including John Wallace, who was now a regular band member, were joined by tenor saxophonist John Wilmot and trumpeter Laurence Parry from Rent Party, as well as Robert himself. It was a prestigious event, and by far the biggest venue that Mike had ever played. Robert arranged a couple of warm-up gigs, at the universities of East Anglia and Leeds, and although these were not widely advertised, they quickly sold out as word spread about Robert Plant's 'new band'.

In mid-March, they spent two days at the NEC, rehearsing and doing soundchecks, until finally the day of the concert itself arrived. The bill included stars from the seventies such as Noddy Holder, Jasper Carrott, Roy Wood and Jim Davidson, as well as superstars of the rock world including ELO, the Moody Blues, UB40 and George Harrison. The event was televised by MTV, and Mike confesses that he was somewhat overawed by the transition from pubs, clubs and traditional festivals to this huge production, complete with cameras, film crew, an expansive stage and, most of all, a teeming, expectant audience. The charity concert was a huge success, with Roy Wood commenting that the Big Town Playboys were 'like a breath of fresh air'.

It appeared that they now had the world at their feet. However, four days later, on Wednesday, 19 March 1986, Ricky Cool played his last gig with the band. Fittingly, it was at the Thurston, where it all began.

CHAPTER 6

Fame!

When Ricky Cool left the band, Mike took over the frontman position.
There then followed a series of prestige gigs featuring Eric Clapton,
Andy Fairweather-Low, Mick Fleetwood, Robert Plant and Gary
Brooker.

1986

Promoters from as far away as the Netherlands and Norway had seen
the Big Town Playboys, and this led to them being booked to appear at
the *Amsterdam Blues Festival* in March 1986. This was their first
overseas gig apart from the residency in Ibiza, and Ricky admitted that
he could no longer juggle his commitments at home with life on the
road. With John Wallace in the line-up, his saxophone playing had
become less important, and the band decided that, musically, the Big
Town Playboys could do without him. Ricky agreed, and it was a
mutual separation with no ill feelings either way. It was a sad event for
Mike to lose one of his great mentors, but it gave him the chance to
remove the shackles and become the band's true frontman.

The Dickens in Southend was a regular venue for the Big
Town Playboys, and it was frequented by Procol Harum's Gary
Brooker. Gary became a big fan, and even offered to manage the band
for a while, but with Ricky Cool gone Andy Silvester took on this
responsibility alone. The gigs continued to roll in, alongside a
recording session for Paul Jones's radio show on BBC Radio 2, and
the filming of a short video, *Jive After Five*, by Canadian film-maker
Robert MacDonald. One of the radio recordings, 'Lowdown Dog',
was released later in the year on a BBC compilation LP called
Blues On 2.

May 1986 brought a performance with Little Willie Littlefield in Leverkusen, West Germany, as well as two shows in the Netherlands. The usual UK pub and club circuit followed, and then it was back to Europe for more shows in the Netherlands as well as Norway. The musical partnership with Littlefield blossomed in June, with rehearsals and gigs at the 100 Club, the Dublin Castle and *Hayfield Jazz Festival*.

Word was spreading around Europe, and towards the end of July the BTPs played the *Peer International Blues Festival* in Belgium. This included another set with Little Willie, and they also met Ed Mann, the drummer in Californian blues band, the Mighty Flyers.

There was a genuine sense of awe from the Big Town Playboys towards the Flyers, and Mike became besotted with their pianist, Honey Alexander, a beautiful, flirtatious blonde. Unfortunately Honey was in a long-term relationship with her partner, Flyers' frontman Rod Piazza, and so nothing came of Mike's infatuation. However, that was by no means the end of the BTPs' interaction with the band. Later that year Ed Mann wrote to them, simply saying, 'You guys need me,' and letting them know that he was on his way back to the UK to join them. An eventful weekend at Peer included John Hammond Jr, Buddy Guy, Junior Wells and many more, but it was the Mighty Flyers who left the biggest impression.

Gary Brooker stayed in touch too, and at the beginning of August he invited the band to an event at Dunsfold Village Hall in Surrey. Although this was a very small venue, the guest list was impressive and the main band featured Eric Clapton, Andy Fairweather-Low, Albert 'Mr Telecaster' Lee, Dave Bronze and Henry Spinetti.

Many of them were seeing the Big Town Playboys for the first time and the band made an instant impression. Andy Fairweather-Low describes them as 'unbelievable, fabulous', though it would be another ten years before he got the opportunity to join them.

Mike was concerned that John Wallace had failed to turn up at Dunsfold. John thought that, as it was just a small village hall, it was not worth the effort. They waited until the last minute – lateness was a well-known characteristic of his – but eventually they played without him. Afterwards, Andy Silvester explained to Eric Clapton that they normally had a saxophone player, but Eric was suitably impressed even without, and the chemistry between Mike and Andy would lead to him using the band on several future engagements.

As the evening progressed and they enjoyed a few drinks, Mike plucked up the courage to ask Clapton if he fancied a jam. Eric called his roadie, Lee Dickson, to set up the amps, and there followed an hour or so of impromptu playing around with a few old blues numbers. The Dunsfold gig was for charity, and the Big Town Playboys returned to this event several times, but that first appearance will be remembered for so much more.

A few days after the event, Eric Clapton's manager, Roger Forrester, called Andy to let him know that Eric wanted the band to play with him on a track for the Paul Newman film, *The Color of Money*. This exciting news was followed by more, as Eric also wanted them to open for him on his forthcoming European tour. The rest of August was a blur – the usual round of gigs was highlighted by shows in Belgium and the Netherlands – until finally the end of the month brought about their date with Eric at AIR Studios in Oxford Circus.

The chosen track was Bobby 'Blue' Bland's 'It's My Life, Baby', and the sound engineer was the legendary Tom Dowd, famous for engineering so many big hits for Atlantic Records including Clapton's *Layla* album. The band put in a good, solid shift, and the track was recorded in just a couple of hours. The studio was booked for the day, so Eric suggested that they could stay and record some of their own stuff. Mike felt that it was a real honour to work with Tom, and they spent several hours recording more songs, although none of these ever saw the light of day.

Autumn saw them extend their reach to Portsmouth, where they built up a loyal following, then to Edinburgh and Aberdeen. As November came around, Ed Mann appeared just as he had promised. Andy broke the news to John Spinetto that he was no longer required on drums, which came as something of a shock, as he had been with the band since its first appearance at the Thurston.

Ed was a tough character: a Jew from New York who put in powerful performances onstage. Initially, he scared the band with his demonstrative manner and Andy Silvester warned of the potential consequences, having spent time living and working in the US with American artists. Ed was intense in everything he did, and Mike admitted that they all learnt from him. Mann made his debut at the Rose & Crown in Kinver on 14 November.

John Wallace was becoming increasingly unreliable, and the day before they were due to embark on a three-week European tour he once again failed to turn up. Mike called him several times without success, and it was obvious that he was going to let the band down again. It was too much to take, and from that moment on Wallace was no longer a part of the Big Town Playboys. From being a heroic figure, his reputation had slumped as Mike realised that he was always looking after Number One, never so much as lifting a finger to help any of the other band members before or after a show. Mike revised his definition of success after this episode, and it was much later that he came to understand how to measure *real* success.

Wallace's departure was potentially a disaster, with their schedule in jeopardy, as well as Eric Clapton's tour that was due to start less than two months later. Andy Silvester took it really badly, and it seemed that the Big Town Playboys were about to unravel.

Gary Brooker came to the rescue, as he introduced them to Frank Mead, a tenor saxophone player from Juice On The Loose and a well-regarded session musician. Unfortunately, Frank was unable to go on the imminent European tour, but they still opened in Belgium as planned. From there, the tour moved on to Switzerland, the Netherlands, Belgium again, West Germany and Norway, where Jan Steele guested on saxophone at a couple of gigs. It was a fabulous time, with the European crowds even more receptive to the relatively unknown band from England who were willing to give everything onstage. The only sour note came from Little Willie Littlefield, who was disappointed that they had not managed to bring a sax player with them.

They returned to the UK to play a benefit concert at Stourport Civic Centre for Pictures In A Dark Room vocalist/bassist Johnny Pasternak. Well known and extremely popular on the local music scene, Johnny had suffered a fatal heart attack in October 1986. The benefit featured Robert Plant, Jimmy Page and many other stellar musicians alongside the Big Town Playboys.

The year finished with a return to Dunsfold Village Hall for another Gary Brooker charity gig. This regular show in the small Surrey village had now switched from a summer event to a Christmas party. The contact with Gary had unexpected benefits, as he was becoming increasingly involved in the band's management. He even took the trouble to travel with his wife, Franky, from Dunsfold to Bewdley to speak to Mike's parents to assure them that he was going to look after their boy. Gary's efforts also led to the BTPs' involvement in the Eric Clapton tour that consumed January 1987.

1987

The schedule began with two dates at Manchester's Apollo Theatre, followed by six nights at the world-famous Royal Albert Hall in London. The prestigious tour was a milestone for the band, although it was a little unusual. They were used to headlining and maybe playing two sets every night, but now they were required to play for forty minutes to an audience who had really come to see someone else. Despite this, they were well received and enjoyed the routine of playing big venues in big cities night after night. They subsequently appeared in the Netherlands, Belgium, France, West Germany and Italy, playing 19 major shows in just four weeks. The crowds were very different as they ventured from one country to the next, from the respectful and appreciative Germans, to the more unpredictable and occasionally violent Italians.

In Milan, the audience took to throwing coins and fruit to demonstrate their approval, with Andy standing in front of Mike to protect him, as he was an easy target at the piano. Even Eric was not immune from the barrage, and he was narrowly missed by an orange as he ended his set. This may have seemed like an indication of displeasure, but he was asked back for two encores amidst the hail of fruit. They finished the tour at the Palasport Arena in Florence and headed home exhausted but buzzing from the experience. They had gained many more fans across Europe, although they saw very little money after expenses were deducted.

With Gary Brooker at the helm and the Eric Clapton tour on their CV, the Big Town Playboys could reasonably have expected things to take off for them, but it failed to happen. The phone remained silent for a month, and so they took the decision to return to the UK rhythm & blues circuit. It was a disappointing spring without the star-studded tours and charity concerts, but they soon got back into their old routine. They were comforted by the rave reviews of their European excursions, and the promise from Eric that, if he ever recorded a blues album, it would be with the Big Town Playboys.

They toured Norway in May 1987, returning to the UK to learn that they would have to find a new saxophone player. Frank Mead was in demand for session work with Bill Wyman, Gary Moore and others, and Mike always knew that he would prioritise the big names and tours over the Big Town Playboys. They found Al Nicholls from Leeds

Music Studio, and he joined in time for the *Hayfield Jazz Festival* in June. They then returned to many of their well-established venues such as the Riverboat in Kidderminster, Basins Club in Portsmouth and the Dublin Castle in Camden.

In October, volatile drummer Ed Mann was compelled to return to the States for two reasons. Firstly, the band could no longer sustain his financial demands without embarking on another potentially money-spinning tour, and secondly, he was actually in the UK illegally, as he had no work permit. He played for the last time at the Arts Club in Dover Street, London, then headed back to the States.

Al Nicholls used his contacts at Leeds Music Studio and introduced Dai Powell to the band. Dai was from Abergavenny and had no real background in rhythm & blues, but with Andy's help he quickly learnt what was expected. He settled in well, and was a very happy and popular member of the band. He debuted at the Riverboat, and very soon the band were back to their best, playing to packed houses up and down the country.

Drummer Mark Morgan became a big fan: 'I'd travel many times all over the place to see them. They just seemed like the perfect rhythm & blues band. Great authentic approach and musicianship, and to top it all off, Mike fronting it. He was made for that style, and of course there have been many since that have tried to imitate, but failed to do it like he does. Unbeatable.'

However, there still seemed to be something missing, and so in December it was once again Al Nicholls who found another musician out of Leeds Music Studio. Paul Clarke played baritone sax, and he joined in time for another gig at the Riverboat. They saw the year out with two shows in Belgium.

1988

The international theme continued in 1988 with four nights in Helsinki, Finland. In March, they travelled to Italy to play the *Ravenna Blues Festival*, where Mike met one of his heroes, singer/pianist Rosco Gordon from Memphis, Tennessee.

At the end of the month, Mike also took a small but significant step in his own musical career when he started playing regular solo spots. This was at the Tardebigge in Redditch, a huge pub and restaurant that had once been a hospital for wounded soldiers from the First World War and seemed to have a haunted energy coursing through it. There was an ancient, run-down grand piano in the middle of the concert room, and with no PA system Mike had to perform acoustically. This was something that he was used to, having spent most of his early career on either upright or grand pianos, but he was always glad to get back to his electric keyboard.

The bar manager at the Tardebigge was Barbara Baylis, whom he fondly remembered as a pretty little girl from his high school days, and he had not suspected then that ten years later she would become his girlfriend. Mike used his solo bookings there as an excuse to spend more time with Barbara, although she was not really into the music or the musician's lifestyle.

In April 1988, Mike joined Paul Jones and Tom McGuinness at Raezor Studio in Wandsworth. Paul knew Mike from the 1986 radio session that the Big Town Playboys did in Manchester, and he asked him to play piano on a couple of tracks on the Blues Band's 'reunion' album following a seven-year recording hiatus, *Back For More*. Mike gave his usual consummate performance on 'Normal Service' and 'Can't Get My Ass In Gear', and they became good friends. Both cuts were recycled in 2004 on the Blues Band's BGO CD, *Be My Guest*, which featured a different guest or guests on each track.

In mid-April, Rowdy Yeats moved back up from London to his hometown of Kidderminster, and the Big Town Playboys were delighted to play at his wedding. Mike was still mixing solo appearances with BTPs gigs, and the Eric Clapton appearances were becoming a distant fond memory when an opportunity arose almost by chance.

It was May 1988 and Fleetwood Mac were playing venues such as Wembley and Birmingham NEC promoting their album, *Tango In The Night*. Andy Silvester was an old friend of Mick Fleetwood's and decided to get back in touch with him. He invited Mick, Christine McVie and guitarist Rick Vito to a BTPs gig at Dover Street Wine Bar in London.

Rick almost missed out, as he explains: 'I was not really keen on going for some reason, but at the last minute I jumped in a cab with them and, boy, am I glad I did. The Big Town Playboys were playing their own brand of jump blues, one of my favourite styles. The focal point of the band was Mike Sanchez, who seemed capable of channelling many of my boogie-woogie piano heroes, like Amos Milburn, Pine Top Smith, Johnnie Johnson and even Jerry Lee Lewis, all into one smooth and expertly delivered package. We all became instant fans, and we were so impressed that we invited some of the band to Wembley to lend their sound to our newest version of Peter Green's "Stop Messing Around", a tune that I sang. Mike, Andy and the band were truly a stellar lot.'

After the Wembley show, the BTPs returned to Mick's London hotel and discussed musical styles. Mick was evidently impressed, and invited them to perform at the end-of-tour party later that month. This was at the Roof Gardens in Kensington, where many famous artists and musicians were present. Mike developed a crush on Keren Woodward, the dark-haired singer from Bananarama, and convinced himself that the feeling was mutual. However, it was a short-lived fascination as neither of them did anything about it!

Mick Fleetwood then began to plan a US tour for the Big Town Playboys for the following year, and once again they felt that fame and fortune were just around the corner.

In June 1988, the band were involved in an extravagant present. Eric Clapton's management team, Harvey Goldsmith and Roger Forrester, invited them to play as a gift to Eric to commemorate his 25 years in the music industry, as at the time they were Eric's favourite band. Mike was on holiday in Spain when the request came in, but he had no hesitation in returning to take part in the memorable event.

The venue was a classic Victorian ballroom in the Savoy Hotel, where the majority of the 300 guests were household names. Mike had never seen so many well-known stars in the same room. The night ended with Steve Ferrone on drums, Chas Hodges from Chas & Dave on the piano, George Harrison on Mike's Telecaster, and Ronnie Wood on Andy's guitar. Mike will always remember George telling him that he loved the way the Big Town Playboys played with such passion. He also recalls Harvey Goldsmith and Roger Forrester having a few problems with the seating arrangements, as so many of the wives of the guests had previously been the wives of other guests who were there.

July saw another Gary Brooker charity event, this time at the Wintershall Estate in Surrey. It was dubbed *A Concert By The Lake* and featured Eric Clapton, Phil Collins, Mike Rutherford and Andy Fairweather-Low amongst many other stars. This opened the door to many high-society bookings, although Mike may have undersold the band. During the show, he was asked by a fan how much he charged. When Mike told him, the observer laughed: 'Ha, you've really underpriced yourself there. I would have paid you a lot more than that.' For Mike, it was a source of some regret, but it was quickly forgotten, as Mike maintains that he would not particularly have wanted to play for someone that arrogant.

Manchester had a strong blues scene around this time, and the Big Town Playboys got the opportunity to support John Lee Hooker at the Free Trade Hall. It was a different audience for them, but they did their usual set and welcomed the applause from the appreciative and knowledgeable crowd.

August saw the band embark on a short tour of Finland, including Tampere, where US Vice President George H.W. Bush drove past the gig on his way to a meeting with various world leaders later that evening.

During the autumn, Mike's solo gigs became weekly, alternating with Big Town Playboys shows at their regular haunts. There was also a two-day blues festival in the Netherlands and a gig at Newcastle Playhouse, where they backed Oklahoman blues legend Lowell Fulson, though the latter proved a little frustrating. The booking agent gave them an idea of the songs that Fulson might want to play, most of which originated in the 1950s and had careful and intricate horn arrangements which Al Nicholls and Paul Clarke had prepared. However, when it came to the gig, he just wanted to play newer stuff, and so it turned into a bit more of a jam session than a live show. At times when the phone did not ring and there were no confirmed bookings, Mike continued to use the Tardebigge to fill in the gaps.

Another personnel change saw Dai Powell leave the band, to be replaced by professional session and band drummer Clive Deamer. Clive explains how he got involved: 'There was a guy in Bath, Richard Hutchison, who let me know that the Big Town Playboys were auditioning drummers. He said they were going to do some shows in the States, but I wasn't supposed to know that. I got sent a cassette tape with their music on it and I thought it was great. There were some songs that I knew and some that I didn't. I went to audition in Stourport, but I remember that my car broke down on the way. We went through the songs and it progressed from there.

'Mike and Ian would make up cassettes, so that I could play them in the car. I had never met a bunch of guys so knowledgeable about that kind of music. They were *totally* into it. They introduced me to a lot of new stuff, like Howlin' Wolf, and I learnt a huge amount from my time with them – especially from Andy Silvester. Andy was an authority on that kind of music, and he was also into drumming. It was through him that I began to learn the significance of people like

Earl Palmer. Despite being serious musicians, it was still fun. Mike and Ian had such a great sense of humour.'

Clive played his first gig at the University of Birmingham in November 1988. With Mike, Andy and Ian joined by the horn section of Al Nicholls and Paul Clarke, he completed the jigsaw that came to be generally regarded as the Big Town Playboys' best and most stable line-up. They were perfectionists, and Clive thinks that this sometimes went too far: 'We were trying to play in the spirit of the original tracks, though sometimes it became obsessive. I was asking whether we should include the mistakes from the originals, and it could be like a bit of a prison trying to play like someone from forty years ago.'

Gigs were coming in thick and fast, and they were good gigs. December saw the BTPs play for the SAS at their headquarters in Hereford, as well as performing at the iconic Claridge's Hotel in Mayfair. Gary Brooker's supergroup of musical friends assembled once again just before Christmas to play the Dunsfold Village Hall charity gig, and it had become a regular event that they all looked forward to.

The boys saw out the year on a Thames barge at the Watermans Arts Centre, but there was no time to recover from the festivities, as the following day they were at the Dublin Castle and the merry-go-round started again.

1989

Mike's solo appearances continued alongside the Big Town Playboys' schedule which included a reunion with Little Willie Littlefield at the inaugural *Burnley National Blues Festival* at Burnley Mechanics in March 1989. They played their own set, as well as two more backing Little Willie and New Orleans blues pianist Champion Jack Dupree. The following night, Mike played a solo set on the Burnley Mechanics stage to an affectionate audience that would welcome him back many times as their event grew into the *International Rock and Blues Festival*. Live recordings of two of the BTPs' numbers, 'Baby Please' and 'Red Hot Mama', were included on the 1989 JSP CD, *The First Burnley National Blues Festival*, as well as two of them backing Little Willie Littlefield and one with Champion Jack Dupree.

Roger Eagle of Eagle Records was well known on the blues circuit, as he had been responsible for bringing many of the leading US blues artists across from the States in the 1960s. He put together a number of promotions in the North-West, though some were more successful than others as photographer Brian Smith explains: 'Roger would come up with a bizarre series of gigs, such as rock'n'roll in Alderley Edge on Tuesday nights. He would always get the Big Town Playboys to do the first night, as that ensured a successful launch, but after that they could become financial suicide without the big-name attraction.'

In April 1989 there were overseas trips to Switzerland and Amsterdam, and upon their return from the Netherlands, they played the 100 Club in London, where they bumped into Ted Carroll of Ace Records. They discussed the possibility of recording an album for Ace, and it was scheduled for the following month. With the thought of the recording still buzzing around their heads, the band then played possibly two of their strangest-ever gigs.

They were booked for a private event at the Natural History Museum and set up on the expansive staircase. The guests seemed to be miles away from their lofty perch, and it was not a particularly enjoyable experience. Two weeks later, the 1989 *Red Balloon Ball* was also held at the museum, and the performers included Gary Brooker, Joe Brown, Chris Rea, Mark Knopfler, Sam Brown, Gary Moore and Dave Gilmour. This time, the stage was set up beneath the head of a giant diplodocus – a much better position than the staircase – and Mike has returned to this historic venue several times since.

They also played at JB's in Dudley, where Roy Williams was the sound engineer. Roy knew Andy Silvester from his days with Chicken Shack, and he loved the sound of his new band. At that point, he did not know that he would soon be engineering that sound himself.

At the start of May 1989, the Big Town Playboys supported Chicago blues guitarist Lurrie Bell, who was appearing with his father, the renowned blues harmonica player Carey Bell, at the Newcastle Playhouse. The Newcastle scene was one of hardcore blues, and a real change from the celebrity charity gigs. Mike slipped in another solo gig at the Tardebigge, then joined up with the rest of the band to concentrate on the recording for Ace.

Hope Bagot Village Hall, near Cleobury Mortimer, had been converted into a recording studio, and the old building produced a good organic sound. Al Nicholls' friend Dave Baynton-Power came in on the recording and also played conga, eventually staying with the band as sound engineer for over three years. After a week of rehearsals, they were finally ready to lay down the tracks and the Zipper Mobile Unit was brought up from London. They spent four days in the converted village hall, but in hindsight Mike admits that they could have spent more time on it and chosen better songs. The tracks all came from their current set, including 'Hungry Man', 'Baby Please' and the instrumental 'Doopin'' – all original compositions by Andy and Mike.

The day after the recording session finished, they played at a wedding party at Widecombe-in-the-Moor in the Dartmoor National Park, Devon. It was organised by actor and director Peter Richardson, most famous for his role with *The Comic Strip Presents...* series. Peter was a big name in television comedy, and the wedding was attended by Robbie Coltrane, Adrian Edmondson, Rik Mayall, Dawn French and Jennifer Saunders, but Mike rarely got time to watch TV, so was not really a fan!

Another celebrity charity event followed at Stocks Country Club in Hertfordshire, where Eric Clapton, Bill Wyman, Gary Brooker, Andy Fairweather-Low and Ronnie Wood were amongst the many star names in the audience. Three days later, they met up with Peter Richardson again, this time at a show at Westway Studios in Shepherd's Bush for the Models 1 agency, home to Yasmin Le Bon and many other A-list models.

Peter was by now a confirmed fan of the Big Town Playboys: 'I first saw them at a swanky event at the Savoy, and I thought, *Wow, incredible*. I then went to see them several times with Jeff Beck in Camden. They were such great performers. We were at a wedding party and things threatened to get out of hand, but then the Big Town Playboys got up and instantly the mood changed.'

Their live performances were starting to gain recognition with a wider audience, and when the *Sunday Express* magazine ran a feature entitled 'Who to Book for Your Society Wedding', it was no surprise to see the Big Town Playboys high up on their recommended list.

At the end of May, Mike got a call from long-time girlfriend Barbara Baylis who sounded so cold on the phone. She ended the relationship there and then, with no explanation, and that put a temporary end to his solo gigs at the Tardebigge. A couple of years later, he bumped into her in a music shop and it was as though nothing had ever happened. Mike used this experience as the inspiration for one of his original songs, 'Rock Me Again'. The gaps left by the lack of solo gigs were filled with more Big Town Playboys shows, including a performance at Hough End Hall near Manchester that was recorded for Granada Television.

Mike needed his freedom, and as his father's plan to rent out rooms had come to nothing, he decided to move into one of his dad's properties in Kidderminster. He paid a reasonable rent to cover the mortgage, and eventually ended up owning the house outright.

At the end of June, the BTPs spent time in London overdubbing and mixing their forthcoming second album, but would have to wait several more months for it to see the light of day.

The *WOMAD* festival in July saw them sharing the bill with Buddy Guy, Junior Wells and Clarence 'Gatemouth' Brown. Then Andy Fairweather-Low asked Mike to play piano in a rock'n'roll supergroup for a charity event at the Metropole Hotel in Brighton. This type of gig was normally reserved for Gary Brooker, but as he was unavailable Mike was more than happy to fill in. It was a prelude to what would eventually follow with the Rhythm Kings, and the all-star ensemble spent two days rehearsing at the farm estate of the Beatles' producer, Glyn Johns.

In early August, the BTPs were adopted as the house band for the *Southbank Blues Festival* in the Queen Elizabeth Hall at the Southbank Centre in London. They backed their old friend Little Willie Littlefield, as well as Texan guitarist Joe Hughes. Also on the bill was Jimmy Nelson, a traditional blues shouter, who put in a great performance on the opening night. Unfortunately, he lost his voice after a few too many vodkas and was unable to sing on the second night. They then embarked upon a brief tour of Denmark including the *Skanderborg Festival* – the Danish equivalent of Glastonbury – then returned to play the *Edinburgh International Jazz Festival* before taking the next significant step on their road to stardom.

In late August, the Big Town Playboys jetted off to the US for the tour promoted by Mick Fleetwood. After staying at the Century Plaza Hotel in Los Angeles, they had a meet-and-greet session followed by rehearsals in the Trancas Club at Zuma Beach, Malibu, where Fleetwood brought along Billy Burnette and Rick Vito. After two days of rehearsals, a limousine took them from their hotel to CBS Television City, where they guested on the *Pat Sajak Show*. This was a very popular late-night talk show on the CBS network, and it afforded the band some great publicity prior to their tour. They performed 'Down The Road Apiece' and 'Red Hot Mama' with Mick Fleetwood on drums, and the set ended with the show's host walking across to Mike and wiping the sweat off his brow with a towel. He was not used to seeing such an energetic performance under the hot studio lights, and he chatted to Mick and Mike about the tour. The show aired to around 15 million viewers across the US, and it was undoubtedly the biggest exposure that Mike has ever achieved.

They flew on to Boulder, Colorado, approximately 5,400 feet above sea level, playing the Boulder Theater with oxygen tanks next to the stage as a precaution, due to the altitude. From there they travelled to the ski resort of Aspen and two more shows, followed by gigs in Steamboat Springs and Evergreen, before descending upon San Francisco. It was a hectic tour, and there was a potentially tragic incident at Los Angeles Airport when Al Nicholls collapsed. He was taken straight to hospital, where he remained for two days, though the initial diagnosis of a suspected heart attack was revised to acute mountain or altitude sickness. In best showbiz tradition, the band played on and performed at the Palomino Club without their tenor saxophonist. Mike prefaced the show with an emotional speech about Al and his condition, as at that stage they really did fear the worst.

The gig itself went down well, with Mick Fleetwood on drums and Fleetwood Mac guitarists Rick Vito and Billy Burnette joining them onstage along with Christine McVie. Rick Vito, in particular, was thrilled with the show: 'Man, we rocked! I really loved it. Afterwards, I was just hoping that more opportunities would come up where we could play together.'

The entire tour received rave reviews, and Mike thought that it might lead to a lot more work. The B-52's loved the band and wanted to use them as their support on a forthcoming tour, but it never happened. The BTPs returned to the UK tired, but anticipating more US engagements. Fortunately, Al recovered in time for the flight home, suffering from nothing more than US medical costs.

Autumn 1989 was filled with their regular gigs plus a few additional bookings, but never the phone call that their US tour deserved. The Californian limousines were replaced by battered old vans, and on one occasion Mike drove himself home to Kidderminster from a show in Aberdeen, spending a solid eight hours at the wheel. After playing the CBS/Fox Video Christmas party, as well as a private event at Elstree Studios, the Big Town Playboys got to meet up with their old friends again at the Chiddingfold Club, Surrey, which alternated with Dunsfold Village Hall as the venue for Gary Brooker's annual charity event.

The following year was already looking promising, as they were once again booked to play as Eric Clapton's support at the Royal Albert

Hall, and although the band had retained the same line-up for over twelve months, the new year saw a change to their sound engineer. Dave Baynton-Power left to play drums for James and subsequently featured on all of their hits. He had really wanted to stay on until after the Royal Albert Hall gigs in February, but the band decided that Roy Williams should take over. This did not feel quite right to Mike, and it is one of his few regrets that they did not give Dave the chance for a big finale, but Roy had worked with many big names including Robert Plant and was an ideal replacement.

1990

January was a relatively quiet month musically, but Mike met his first serious girlfriend since Barbara Baylis. Athene Parker was a fan of the band, and they got together after a gig at the Aztec Room in South Norwood, London. She was just seventeen when they started a relationship, but she was very streetwise, having grown up with older Jamaican friends in Stockwell and Brixton. After her parents moved to Sidmouth, Devon, she took the opportunity to shack up with Mike at his home in Kidderminster. She was the first woman that he had ever lived with, and everything was fine for over a year, but eventually her obsessive jealousy drove them apart. The beginning of the end came one evening at a gig when she was sitting with her friends. She had ignored Mike all night, and he had no idea why, so he went across to her and very gently poured a full pint of beer over her long hair. Needless to say, their relationship did not survive much longer and within a month she had moved out.

When Eric Clapton decided to play a series of *Blues Nights* at the Royal Albert Hall, the Big Town Playboys were the natural choice for support act. Buddy Guy and Robert Cray were also part of the star-studded show, and Cray was so impressed that he asked the band to play at his wedding at the Grand Hotel in Leicester a week later.

After the Clapton shows they went to Thames Television studios for rehearsals, following which they performed Jimmy McCracklin's 'The Wobble' on *The Ronn Lucas Show* which was broadcast on 21 February. It was considered to be a very middle-of-the-road programme, but with a good audience, and once again the band hoped for more success from this different exposure. Peter Richardson invited them to play *The Comic Strip* end-of-filming party at the

St Moritz Club in Soho, and although there were numerous stars in attendance such as Motörhead's Lemmy, Robbie Coltrane, Dawn French, etc, Mike's favourite recollection from the evening is that Kate Bush told him that he had really great charisma.

Shortly afterwards, Peter met up with his friend, Jeff Beck, and inevitably the conversation turned to music, as Jeff recalls: 'I said I'd just seen the best band in the world, the Giants of Jive at Ronnie Scott's, and he said, "No, no, I had a party at my house with the Big Town Playboys and Mike Sanchez, and they are the best band in the world." So I decided to go and see them too. It was at the Country Club up in Hampstead, and I watched them. Amazing. Then I went to see them at the 100 Club about four or five times in a row, and they got better. They might have had a slight member change, a different guitarist or a different sax player, but each time Mike was the one who stole the show. He was amazing. He glued everything together. I became friends with Mike, Andy, Ian and Clive, and when Clive left to join Portishead, they got another drummer and Mike kept it all together. He is like a Spanish Little Richard. He is *our* Little Richard, with a bit of Jerry Lee Lewis thrown in.'

The BTPs' eagerly anticipated second album, *Now Appearing,* was finally released in early 1990 on the Ace Records subsidiary, Blue Horizon. Although they were very excited about it – not least because of the additional publicity it would attract – it turned out not to be quite the grand event that they hoped for. Sales were never discussed, and Mike still has no idea how many copies it shifted.

In an attempt to get the band even more coverage, the BTPs spoke to a number of people regarding PR, including promoter Steve Beggs, but they were never short of bookings. They made their second television recording of the year in April, when they played 'Red Hot Mama', 'The Wobble', 'My Girl' and 'Safronia B.' for Anglia TV.

Another TV appearance followed in May, when they recorded 'Sea Cruise', 'Baby Please' and 'Red Hot Mama' for Jools Holland's *Happening,* though this may have had an adverse effect on Mike's future episodes on the small screen. Many artists and friends of his believe that Mike's powerful performance as a singer and pianist overshadowed Jools, which led the ex-Squeeze keyboard player to exclude him from future shows, even though he remained a fan.

By this time, Roy Williams had spent a few months working with the Big Town Playboys, and even he was surprised at their musical talent: 'I was really into their musical genre, but I learnt a lot from them. Mike used to help me out sometimes, as he used to sing slightly off mic when he was playing the piano. The gigs were great, though. We just used to get in the van, go to the venue and have a laugh. The Royal Albert Hall shows were good, but they were such a great band that the venue didn't really matter. They turned it on wherever they played.'

The highlight of their summer appearances was on the acoustic stage at Glastonbury. Despite the name, this was an electric performance which brought out the best in the band. Mike counts it as one of his favourite gigs. Drummer Clive Deamer explains the appeal: 'It was so authentic and such a lot of fun. I saw real, serious musicians at the side of the stage watching us, and they were blown away.'

They also played a gig at Marble Arch, in a club run by future band member Rohan Thee Man. In July, Mike and Andy Silvester were interviewed by Helen Mayhew for Jazz FM, and the following month they were involved in a promotional tour for Heineken lager. The *Heineken Music Big Top* started with a fantastic show in Bradford in August and continued throughout the summer. It was a series of large, free events staged in a touring circus tent, where the audiences ran into thousands, and they shared the bill with top acts like Dr Feelgood and the Tom Robinson Band. Mike saw this as an honour, as he was a fan of the Feelgoods in particular and their big hit, 'Milk And Alcohol'.

In October 1990 they appeared at Ruby's Dance Club on Carnaby Street as part of the *Soho Jazz Festival*, before performing in Oxford at the wedding of Stephen Woolley, co-producer of *The Pope Must Die*. There was another wedding in October, at the Natural History Museum under the head of the diplodocus again. This was for the daughter of Bill Curbishley, producer and manager of many rock legends like the Who and Robert Plant. Show followed show, but their diary was always their rock. Once a show was in, it could not be cancelled. This hard and fast rule never changed, and they once had to turn down Stella McCartney's wedding as they were already booked.

The Big Town Playboys played the Wembley Conference Centre in November, but this was far from a big-name stadium gig. It was actually arranged by BBC West Midlands news presenter Bob Warman, who had become a big fan of the band, and the occasion was a florists' convention that he also compèred.

December featured two memorable Gary Brooker charity gigs. The first of these was the *Red Balloon Ball* at Alexandra Palace, where they opened the show. They were followed onstage by mother-and-daughter combination Vicki and Sam Brown, Chrissie Hynde, Dave Gilmour, Jools Holland and many more big names. The second was their annual reunion, this time at Chiddingfold, where the usual supergroup once more came together.

1991

By January 1991 Peter Richardson had become more influential in the lives of the BTPs, and arranged a jam with his friend Jeff Beck at the Town & Country Club in Islington. This was a highlight for Mike and eventually led to the *Crazy Legs* album in 1993.

Mike was busy enough with the Big Town Playboys, and then promoter and musician Martin Pryce filled in most of his spare dates with another band.

Mike Sanchez and the Hoola Boola Boys were a seemingly random bunch of musicians thrown together for a birthday party. However, their first engagement was very well received and they never looked back. In the following months, Mike played around a hundred gigs with the band, mainly in pubs around the Welsh border. Many of these probably contravened the local music licence laws, but the Hoola Boola Boys were a fun-loving band who steered clear of the vintage sound. Their standard was to play well-known rock'n'roll classics and to make them nice and loud, which was not really Mike's style. Musically, however, he got on very well with sax player Ted Bunting, and they encouraged each other to stay with the band. The line-up even included Robert Plant on occasion, but the pressure of balancing the Hoola Boola work with the Big Town Playboys' commitments caused a considerable amount of conflict, and Mike believes that this ultimately led to the most challenging change in the BTPs' cast list later that year. All of the Big Town Playboys' gigs came in via Andy Silvester's phone, and Mike admits that the rest of the band only ever gave their numbers out to girls. Sometimes Andy would get a call at the last minute, and eventually schedules clashed. Mike was due to play a Hoola Boola gig at the Salwey Arms between Ludlow and Hereford, but Andy told him they had a BTPs booking. He had to let the Hoola Boola Boys down, and things were never quite the same afterwards, but he also thinks that the conflict may have niggled Andy too.

Meanwhile, the start of February saw the band get involved with Peter Richardson again. He was putting together the soundtrack for a film he was directing, *The Pope Must Die*, starring Robbie Coltrane: 'I loved their music and I asked the band if I could use their songs "Hungry Man", "Baby Please" and "In The Middle Of The Night" to supplement other music on the soundtrack that was provided by Jeff Beck.' In addition to contributing the three album tracks, they went into Angel Studios in Islington to assist Jeff and Anne Dudley from Art of Noise with the background music and sound effects.

After that, they had time to fit in a couple of other gigs, including a date at the Rendezvous Club in Chester for Roger Eagle, before once again jetting off to Los Angeles at the request of Mick Fleetwood.

This time, the BTPs were there for a residency at the launch of Fleetwood's L.A. Blues Club on Santa Monica Boulevard. The opening night on 12 February 1991 saw a motorcade of limousines laid on for Madonna, Terence Trent D'Arby and many other household names from rock and pop. The Big Town Playboys were the house band, and backed veteran blues piano man Floyd Dixon, Bo Diddley and Mick Fleetwood's own blues band. John Lee Hooker also got up to provide a few numbers, and throughout the whole evening the stage was almost one big happy family of the world's best blues artists.

Mike felt comfortable with all of these stars, partly because he had the talent to play alongside them, and partly because he was so easy to get along with. He was their equal, and they treated him as such. For the next month the BTPs played four nights a week at the club, and they had a great vocal group called Flawless who opened up each night, and who guested with them, which gave them a fuller sound than they were used to.

Rick Vito remembers the opening night well: 'I was chatting with Mike about all our mutual blues and rockabilly favourites. My wife and I were thoroughly delighted with Mike's enthusiastic and totally believable performance each time we saw him live or on TV.'

The *Los Angeles Times* was also gushing in its praise, highlighting Mike's trademark big red suit as something that Jerry Lee Lewis would have been proud of, although they did make the mistake of referring to the band as the Big Town *Players!*

The BTPs spent around a month in LA, and Mike was glad to get back on the plane to the UK. He was starting to feel homesick for the land he knew – a land far removed from Los Angeles, which somehow did not feel like a real place. His parents back in Bewdley were happy to hear from him once a week or so, but there was no denying that he was missing his home.

Ironically, their return to the UK was followed almost immediately by a festival booking in the Netherlands, where they shared the bill with blues regulars Dave Peabody, Bob Hall and Johnny Copeland. A week later, they played Up The Creek in Greenwich, which was often frequented by Jools Holland, who lived close by. The sound and style of the band had always appealed to Jools, who was a big fan, and he later booked them for his 40th birthday party.

Throughout the spring of 1991, the Hoola Boola Boys played more gigs than the Big Town Playboys, though the BTPs did put in a notable appearance at the Brean Sands *International Rock'n'Roll Festival*, where they shared the bill with Johnny Burnette's son Rocky, as well as Dave Phillips & The Hot Rod Gang. *Langbaurgh Blues Festival*, Redcar, saw them backing Little Willie Littlefield once more, but Mike followed this with three more Hoola Boola Boys shows.

On Friday, 10 May 1991, they played a private party for Gilly Wheeler, an equine trainer and performance specialist, and this is where Andy Silvester announced that he was planning to leave the band. It was a monumental event in terms of the BTPs, as Andy had not only been a founder member and very influential regarding its musical direction and the integration of new members, but also, away from the music, ran many of their affairs including bookings and transport.

Fortunately, it was not an immediate departure. Andy wanted to help them to find a replacement and in the end he stayed on for four months following his announcement, but even so Mike was very concerned for the future of the Big Town Playboys. Andy had been with the band for seven years, and Mike was convinced that no one else could do what he could do.

A week after Andy's announcement, they played at Carmen Plant's wedding to Charlie Jones, and then Mike found solace in yet more Hoola Boola Boys dates, including rehearsals with Robert Plant for his appearances with the band. Robert took to the stage with them at JB's in Dudley and they rocked the place.

Kevin Gammond, a friend of Robert Plant's and a tutor at Kidderminster College, arranged for Mike to do an interview and performance on the piano for the students. They were naturally astounded by his talent, and who knows how many he may have inspired to try to make their name in the music industry after this lesson?

The Pope Must Die was released at the end of June, and the BTPs played at the premiere in the Crypt at St Martin-in-the-Fields in

Trafalgar Square. It was another star-studded event, but one that ultimately failed to propel them further along the road to stardom. The film went on general release a few days later, and although it was not generally well received, this had nothing to do with the pumping part of the soundtrack that featured Big Town Playboys.

They still played plenty of dates for Roger Eagle, including the historic Bodelwyddan Castle in Denbighshire, Wales, where art designer Chris Wroe wanted to do some filming: 'I met Mike a few years earlier at the Jazz & Roots Club in Shrewsbury, and we discussed the possibility of recording a show. Although I worked for Central TV, there was a problem with the availability of cameras. I had a couple of Super 8s that I decided to use, but it was a disaster. After that, I started taking photos instead, though we always thought that we would go back to the films.'

Mike was as busy as he had ever been, juggling his commitments to two bands with rehearsals with Jeff Beck in Gary Brooker's barn and at Jeff's house in Wadhurst. These were usually arranged by Peter Richardson, and Jeff was happy to mix his traditional style with the vintage shuffles that the BTPs were familiar with, whilst his partner, Sandra Cush, ensured there was an endless supply of tea and cakes.

The Big Town Playboys played through the summer of 1991 with the spectre of Andy's departure hanging over them. The Heineken promotion that had been so successful the previous year was repeated in Nottingham, Manchester, Swansea and Portsmouth. The boys enjoyed playing all of these events – not least because they were well paid!

At the Nottingham gig in Wollaton Park, bass player Nick Whitfield was in the audience: 'I remember being totally blown away by the show, and the *Now Appearing* album on Ace Records was on sale. I joined the queue to buy my vinyl copy after what was one of the most eye-opening performances I'd ever seen. Mike was dressed in a big red suit, clambering all over his piano with a stage presence that just demanded your attention. It was a killer show, the real deal, and I'd never before witnessed a live rhythm & blues band of this particular style and authenticity.'

At the show in Swansea, the search for Andy Silvester's replacement began in earnest when Pete Matheson joined them onstage as a second guitarist. Unfortunately, this did not really work out, and the departure of Andy was growing ever nearer.

The Portsmouth event was the biggest and best of the Heineken series, and to this day Mike's fan base in the naval town remains substantial.

Mike did more impromptu sessions with Jeff Beck, although at this stage they did not really know what they were working towards, as *Crazy Legs* was still more than a year away. Meanwhile, they rehearsed with Newcastle upon Tyne blues guitarist Paul Swaddle – another potential replacement for Andy – at the Old Plough in Kinver, and although he stayed around for a couple of months, he was still not quite right.

Robert Plant's birthday party at the Old Plough was followed by a set backing Andy Fairweather-Low at the Roof Gardens in Kensington, then there were dates in the Netherlands and Italy, where they returned to the *Ravenna Blues Festival*. Mike played a solo gig at the Stourbridge Lion and coupled this with a get-together at Robert Plant's to try out some new songs.

Kidderminster Town Hall was a venue as close to a home as the Big Town Playboys could get, and it was fitting that this is where Andy Silvester played his farewell gig with the band on 30 September 1991. Ricky Cool MC'd the show, and he also joined them for a few songs, as did Robert Plant. It was an emotional night, and afterwards Mike considered that this should really have been the end of the band. However, Ian Jennings was still there, and he and Ian had been together since school. It would be hard, but it was up to the old schoolmates to keep their musical partnership together, and so Big Town Playboys began a new era, with Ian taking charge of the band's affairs and Mike leading the musical direction.

CHAPTER 7

Train Keeps A-Rollin'

The 1990s saw a considerable amount of change within the Big Town Playboys, though they still drew huge audiences and released a number of albums. These included Crazy Legs *with Jeff Beck, a collection of Gene Vincent songs.*

1991

Andy Silvester's departure was made worse by Al Nicholls leaving at the same time. Paul Swaddle, who officially joined the day after Andy's last gig, was the first attempt to replace him, and the line-up was completed by Rohan Lopez aka Rohan Thee Man on tenor saxophone.

Rohan was renowned for his deejay nights on the London scene, and had a great taste in hardcore rockin' music, as well as a visual style and look that made him stand out from everyone else in the capital. He was a dancing, screaming, one-in-a-million character who was much adored by all who met him on his crazy nights of rockin' roots music. Rohan had been a friend and fan of Mike's since he first saw the BTPs in their early days, and he had been learning to play the tenor saxophone. He was still very raw and never had the musical education of players such as Al Nicholls or Paul Clarke, who qualified as teachers of their instruments.

When Rohan found out that Al was leaving the band, he asked to join and Mike could not refuse him. For the short time that Rohan shared the stage with the BTPs, it was as if a wild animal was with them. When it was his turn to solo, it was like hearing a punk rocker with a saxophone in 1950, and often enough it was his exuberant passion that transcended his inability to play fluently. Together with

Ian Jennings, Clive Deamer and Paul Clarke, the Big Town Playboys were now a six-piece again.

Mike and Ian were joined by sound man Roy Williams for a trip to London to speak to the Alan Robinson booking agency in the hope that they would take over the band's management. Robinson was a blues booking agent with an office in Putney. He liked to book authentic blues bands, and Mike, Ian and Roy thought that he would be able to get them slots on European tours and at some of the bigger blues festivals. They did secure a few additional gigs through the agency, as well as gaining exposure to a wider audience and other agents, but the events were not great payers.

In November 1991, Roy Williams wanted to arrange a benefit gig at Birmingham Town Hall, and he put together his own supergroup of Birmingham-based musicians. These included Mike, as well as Steve Gibbons, Jim Hickman, Trevor Burton and Kate Pereira. They called themselves 'The Journeymen' and played occasional gigs through to the following July.

At the end of 1991 Mike bade farewell to the punishing Hoola Boola Boys schedule and concentrated on stabilising the Big Town Playboys, as well as his solo gigs. Adrian Utley, a long-time friend of Clive Deamer, came in on guitar to replace Paul Swaddle. Clive and Adrian previously had a Bristol-based swing-jazz band called the Glee Club in which Clive had been the singer and drummer. However, the BTPs' line-up continued to change on a frequent basis.

1992

Rhythm & blues is popular all over the world, and Greece is no exception. Even Athens had its own promoter who regularly booked blues bands, and so it was that the Big Town Playboys headed for the Greek capital. At the end of February 1992 they played consecutive nights in Athens and Thessaloniki, after which Rohan left the band. His saxophone playing could definitely be replaced, although his energy and charisma would be missed. Big Town Playboys fans will always remember his brief time with the band as being crazy, happy and exciting.

The band returned from Greece and changes were made. London session musician Pete Long joined on baritone saxophone, whilst Leo Green, son of jazz musician and author Benny Green, played tenor. Leo was just sixteen when he joined the Big Town

Playboys, but he had already developed a honking Big Jay McNeely style and had done some successful try-outs prior to the fateful Greek odyssey. Chris Wroe arranged for them to do some filming for Central Television at Ronnie Scott's in Birmingham, with himself as the cameraman.

Pete Long was only with the band for a short time, and he was replaced by Nick Lunt on baritone saxophone. Nick, who had first seen Mike when he was with the Rockets, credits the band for his switch away from drums: 'I saw the Big Town Playboys in the '80s, as I was into the jump jive scene. I got to know them, and just listening to them inspired me to take up the saxophone. I just loved the sound of it being played by first Al Nicholls and then Paul Clarke. I got a call to audition and I thought it would be a bit scary. I was a little intimidated, but I needn't have been. We just played through some tunes and that was it. There were no egos – in fact, Mike was and is a real gentleman.'

With Nick in place, the band once again seemed settled. There were plenty of solo bookings for Mike along the way, and the rehearsals with Jeff Beck had finally found an outlet: Jeff had always been a big fan of Cliff Gallup, guitarist with Gene Vincent, and one particular session turned into a Gene Vincent jam. Jeff played the intro to 'Crazy Legs', and Mike and Ian remembered it from their days with the Rockets. They played a few Johnny Burnette and Eddie Cochran tracks, but kept returning to Gene Vincent.

The following day, Mike got a phone call from Jeff, telling him that he wanted to record an album of Gene Vincent covers, and they started rehearsing in earnest at the beginning of March 1992. The whole Gene Vincent catalogue from 1956 and some of his 1957 tracks were up for inclusion, with the exception of 'Be-Bop-A-Lula', as Mike considered that they could not improve on the original, and Jeff agreed.

Jeff explains why the project was so important to him: 'I wanted to pay tribute to Cliff Gallup, the guitarist in the Gene Vincent band, as nobody else was. It was all Eric Clapton and Jimmy Page and Jimi Hendrix, but these guys were doing it in '56 in a way that we couldn't even shake a stick at. When I was younger, I learnt to play exactly like Cliff Gallup. There was no film of him. I used to go home from school and implant this stuff in my head, even though I couldn't play. I just remembered every single note, and then when I picked the guitar up I could do it. Mike's band, the Playboys, were the perfect foil for me to do *Crazy Legs*. It was the best thing that I could do for Cliff, even though he had died. People die without anybody knowing how great they were, and I didn't want that with Cliff. That was the reason I did *Crazy Legs*.'

Clive Deamer was hugely in favour of the Jeff Beck collaboration, and not just because he was a fan of the guitarist: 'Doing the Jeff Beck album was a massive thing for me. It was so interesting, and I latched onto it and chased it. I pushed so hard, but I thought that it could spread our reputation a lot further, rather than just getting more of the same.'

Rock'n'roll enthusiast Pete Anderson has an unusual background in that he comes from Latvia, but he clearly recalls his first encounter with Mike: 'I had lived all of my life in the Soviet Union and I thought that I would never be let out of that evil country, but miracles do happen, and when the regime collapsed it changed forever. I had already been out of the country at the beginning of Gorbachev's *perestroika*, and I had toured Sweden and Denmark with my band, Pete Anderson & The Archives. I was even lucky enough to perform at the Brean Sands weekender on the same bill as Bill Haley's original Comets.

'In 1992, I had a short vacation, which I decided to spend in London and explore the rock'n'roll, rockabilly and rhythm & blues scene, visiting numerous clubs and gigs. It was on one of these evenings when I happened to see a flyer somewhere in a music store which advertised the upcoming show of the Big Town Playboys at the 100 Club on Oxford Street. I liked the name of the band and the short description saying that they play jive, swing and rock'n'roll. It sounded promising, and I thought that I just had to be there, 'cos these are all among my favourite styles of music!

'I was stood in front of the stage impatiently waiting for the band to show up. As soon as they started to play and the piano man opened his mouth, from his very first syllable the enormous thrill and excitement overtook me! There was a certain magic, some hypnotic wonder that came from that frontman, who reminded me a bit of a young Richard Penniman. His raw energy, his devotion to the music, his wild grin and crazy eyes grabbed my attention. His piano playing was miraculous. I've never seen any performer from modern times like him before. I stood there stunned, flabbergasted and shocked. During the break I went to talk to the guys, bought their 1990 *Now Appearing* LP, got it signed, and finally got to know the name of the wild singer and virtuoso piano player – Mr Michael Sanchez. I still have that great LP in my collection along with all of the other albums of the Big Town

Playboys, and of Mike as a soloist.

'I also had a little chat with the upright-bass guy, Ian Jennings, and guitarist Andy Silvester. I asked them half-jokingly if they would be interested in coming to Latvia to play some day. They were very enthusiastic and confirmed their wish to come over whenever it would be possible!'

In April 1992 the Big Town Playboys returned to the *Peer International Blues Festival* in Belgium, whilst Mike also played a few shows accompanied by just Ian Jennings around the West Midlands. The Fox in Stourton, where Mike had previously played solo, was a particular favourite with their local fans. Things were starting to happen again, and the band set sail for Bremen in Germany, where their show was accompanied by a radio interview. Before they returned home, they also played dates in Amsterdam and Antwerp.

Mike concentrated on the busy BTPs diary throughout the spring of 1992. At the end of May, they shared the bill with the Five Blind Boys of Alabama and James Hunter and his band at the Catfish Club in Brighton. The sublime performance of the blind gospel singers is one that will remain with Mike forever. They followed this with an appearance at Gassy Jack's in Cardiff, where ex-Amen Corner saxophonist Allan Jones was the promoter. This went down extremely well, and Jones later booked them for a residency in Tenerife.

Tony Coni caught the band at the Robin Hood in Merry Hill, Dudley and revised his opinion of Mike: 'He totally blew me away. The gig was rammed, and he commanded the whole place. Everyone was stood up and dancing where they could. I didn't even know he could play piano until then.'

The start of June saw the Big Town Playboys join Jeff Beck at the Nomis Studios in Olympia for more rehearsals for the *Crazy Legs* album. Chris Wroe took several photos of the process, and he was enthralled by what he witnessed that day: 'I just sat there and watched. It was amazing. For Mike to go in there and hold his own with Jeff Beck just shows what a talent he is.'

The album was to be produced by Stuart Colman, and the BTPs spoke to him about the possibility of recording other songs. He was well known for producing hits for Shakin' Stevens, the Jets and Little Richard, and loved the prospect of working with the band. They cut some demos at Workshop Studio in Redditch, but again these did not really go anywhere. This happened many times, as the band spent fortunes on studio time and often did not even listen to the recordings afterwards. Rehearsals with Jeff Beck intensified, whilst Big Town Playboys also played a number of festivals including *Birmingham Jazz*, Bradford, Sheffield and *Glasgow Jazz & Blues*.

In July 1992, they completed their final *Crazy Legs* run-through in Olympia the day before going into Townhouse Studios in London for the recording of the album. Stuart Colman was joined by sound engineer Leif Mases, well known for his work with Led Zeppelin, Black Sabbath, ABBA and many more, and they spent four days trying to recreate the original sounds.

Colman was not expecting an easy ride: 'I had heard that Jeff could be difficult to work with because he is a perfectionist, but with this it was different. Mike had done so much preparation on his vocals, he virtually did it live. There was so much energy and rhythm in his voice, it was as though it was an instrument in itself. As soon as I turned the mic on, it sent shivers down my spine. Sometimes a producer has to work really hard with a vocalist, as they do no prep and can be egotistical, but not on this. Everyone worked well together, and we actually recorded two extra tracks that are not on the album, just for the hell of it.'

Mike took time out from the session to share a coffee with Sting, who was in an adjacent studio at the time, but then it was back to the band for the final touches. *Crazy Legs* was unusual in that only Jeff played an electric instrument, and he had to scale down his usual power to fit in. This helped to ensure that the tracks were as authentic as they could be. Beck was indeed a perfectionist, and he continued to work on the guitar tracks after the BTPs had departed. It was an exciting project, and after three days of vocal overdubs about a month later, the work was done; they just had to wait patiently for the release.

The summer of '92 continued at a frenetic pace, with Ted Carroll's birthday party, a tennis party at Jeff Beck's house, and two sets at the *Great British R&B Festival* in Colne (one by the Big Town Playboys, the other a solo appearance by Mike) amongst the regular BTPs gigs. They played the *Bremerhaven Festival* and six other shows in Germany, and then it was back to the Nomis Studios in Olympia for more rehearsals with Jeff Beck. This time, they were preparing for the tour to accompany the release of *Crazy Legs* that was scheduled for the following spring.

Chris Wroe and Jenny Moore had been close friends for many years, and the Big Town Playboys performed at their wedding at the beginning of October 1992. There were more festivals, rehearsals with

Jeff, duos with Ian and a four-date German tour. During the latter, the promoter asked Mike to go into the Fairland Studios in Bochum, where he recorded four solo cuts which appeared on the German 1993 compilation CD, *The Blues According To...*, released on Valve Records.

Later in the month, Mike met Tracey Murray, a psychiatric nurse from York, and they started a relationship that would last for over two years.

1993

1993 started slowly, but with the worldwide release of *Crazy Legs* to look forward to. The BTPs played in Austria and Greece, and returned to a photo session in Notting Hill with Jeff Beck.

Towards the end of April 1993, Sony hosted a launch party for *Crazy Legs*, which was released both on LP and CD in the UK: they flew their A&R team over to Paris for a showcase performance at La Cigale by Jeff Beck and the Big Town Playboys. They played every song from *Crazy Legs*, as well as BTPs favourites 'Lonesome Train' and 'The Train Kept A-Rollin'', and a few Jeff Beck standards such as 'Going Down'. They switched styles throughout the show, and Mike believes it was the most stressfully energetic performance of his career. There was the challenge of playing a two-hour set with Beck, who was fanatical about the music and particularly the guitar, together with the pressure of performing in front of potentially influential Sony executives. Unfortunately, Sony did not really see the commercial possibilities beyond the Jeff Beck project.

In June 1993, Mike took a complete two-week break from his UK work. He flew to Los Angeles to work on Mick Fleetwood's blues rock band project, Blue Whale. They began rehearsals with American guitarist Ron Thompson and recorded enough tracks to fill an album at Paramount Studios in Hollywood, but it was never released.

Mike stayed at Mick's house and had the use of his daughter's car for sightseeing. It was such a relaxing time away from the pressures of managing his commitments in the UK, and he spent many long hours just travelling the criss-crossing flyovers of LA for no reason in particular.

After one recording session, Mick received a call asking him to play a part in a movie. Mike asked if he could come along for the experience, and when the director spotted this larger-than-life character, he ended up giving him a part as an extra, arguing with a woman over the use of a telephone. There was the very real possibility of Mike staying out in LA to live and work, but ultimately his commitment to the Big Town Playboys, and the stability that that brought to his life, persuaded him to go back.

The Blue Whale project may have been put on hold, but it was not too long before Mike returned to the US.

At the end of June, the Big Town Playboys flew to New York for a residency at Tavern On The Green in Central Park. The booking was arranged by Jeff Beck's management at Equator Music on the back of the *Crazy Legs* album, and once again there was the possibility of bigger and better times ahead.

They stayed on Columbus Avenue and spent the daytime as regular tourists, visiting the place where John Lennon was shot and the Empire State Building, and Mike even had a picture taken of himself on the rooftop of one of the Twin Towers at the World Trade Center. At night, they played the rather plush Tavern that was so unlike most of their UK venues. Yoko Ono and her son, Sean Lennon, were just two of the celebrities that came to see the show, as did Mike's niece Sarah Bastida, who flew in with her boyfriend. The BTPs put in good performances night after night, but the management team of Ralph Baker and Ernest Chapman did not really know how to handle such a purist band, though to their credit they stuck at it for four years.

The return to the UK in July 1993 saw a tumultuous time for the BTPs, with Adrian Utley and Clive Deamer both announcing their departure. They went off to join Bristol-based band Portishead, and Clive later also played with Robert Plant in Strange Sensation. Even so, he still has a huge respect for Mike: 'The passion that he has for the piano playing and vocal styles of his favourites such as Charles Brown and Amos Milburn set him apart. You might get a piano player who can't sing, or a singer whose piano playing is a bit flaky. To get the two things together is unique.'

Tenor saxophonist Leo Green also left, so Mike and Ian found themselves virtually starting from scratch. Mike thought back to the time of Andy Silvester's departure and again wondered whether he should have called it a day back then, but Ian remained a solid performer and a long-time friend, and so the BTPs continued.

The band played Gary and Franky Brooker's 25th wedding anniversary, and then at the end of July Mike got the chance to meet one of his musical heroes when Charles Brown played five consecutive nights at Ronnie Scott's in Birmingham. Mike was a huge fan of

Brown and went to four of the five nights. He considered it an honour to meet his hero afterwards, and the photo that Andy Silvester took of Mike and Charles together still has pride of place on the wall at Mike's home. He was thrilled that Brown commented on his 'handsomeness', and still tells the story twenty years later.

Towards the end of July, the search for new members began in earnest. Mike bumped into Tony Coni again in Stourbridge and did not quite get the outcome he was expecting, as Tony explains: 'He was looking for a guitarist at the time, so we went to his basement in Kidderminster and he introduced me to some early blues, jump, swing that I had never encountered before. Unfortunately, I was working as a graphic designer on some children's books, so could not spare the time, but then he said he was also looking for a drummer. I had played in a band with Mark Morgan before, so I suggested him. Eventually, I fell out with the guy I was working with on the kids' books, but by then he had got Steve Walwyn in the band.'

The search for band members continued into August, with the possibility of a tour on the back of the release of *Crazy Legs*. The album reached No. 171 on the *Billboard* chart and remains Mike's most successful project. Rehearsals and auditions took up most of their time, with the acquisition of a drummer being the top priority.

They spent a day at the Old Plough in Kinver listening to and playing along with a number of different candidates. Adrian Badland was followed by Brendan O'Neill and Rob Tyler, who showed some promise. Then came Alan 'Sticky' Wicket and finally Mark Morgan. Mark had played with Birmingham-based Wicked Whiskey and was a true rock'n'roll and rockabilly drummer. He had seen the Big Town Playboys on many occasions and so had the advantage of knowing their repertoire, though he was a little in awe of them, as he explains: 'I was a huge fan of the Big Town Playboys, and I'd actually not been far away from Mike in a crowd on many occasions previously, but never had the guts to go up and say hello. I guess it felt like poking Elvis on the shoulder or something. Mike was kind of how I expected, a striking, larger-than-life individual with the same aura offstage as on. I believe this is what makes him the performer he is. Over time, I realised that Mike didn't always have this side of him switched on, though, and he can be a regular guy that you can have a good one-to-one conversation with.'

Mike and Ian were almost certain that Mark was their man, and two days later they took him to Jeff Beck's house to run through the

Crazy Legs set. Mark was already a fan of that era, but he was still nervous at rehearsals: 'I had grown up listening to a lot of rockabilly, and was even in the Gene Vincent Fan Club in the early 1980s, so I kind of knew the material back to front anyway. Early rehearsals were enjoyable but nerve-wracking, as I still didn't know if I was going to be in the band or not! Once I got into some sort of comfort zone, I asked if we could do some Big Town Playboys stuff as we'd played the Vincent songs to death, with Mike playing lead guitar, which he does really well. He politely switched to piano, and that is when the hairs stood up at the back of my neck and I thought, *I've arrived!* Ian Jennings jested, "Mark knows the set better than us!" Shortly after, I was offered the position.'

Mark was very familiar with the local rockabilly scene, and his involvement brought the band closer to some of their original fans. These included Little John Cowan, who had first seen Mike in the Rockets. He became the band's roadie, as well as helping out selling CDs at gigs. They still played plenty of shows, but without a regular guitarist, and so the search continued. Paul Rose, a rock guitarist from Newcastle, helped out on three dates, and then they returned to the Old Plough to audition Steve Walwyn.

Steve had been with Dr Feelgood for many years, until the long-term illness of frontman Lee Brilleaux brought a temporary break to their performances. He had seen Mike and the BTPs before, so he knew what they were all about: 'A friend of mine told me that I just had to go to see Mike, as he was just brilliant, so I did and he was. It was at Hinton's in Leamington Spa. After that, we played the Heineken gigs with them when I was with Dr Feelgood. I just stood at the side of the stage and watched and thought, *Whoa, what a great band!* I met Mike, and we got chatting, and it was great.

'After Lee Brilleaux became ill, I joined a couple of bands but I was at a bit of a loose end, and Mike's sound engineer, Roy Williams, who I had also known for a long time, called me up and said that the Big Town Playboys were looking for a new guitarist and would I be interested. I didn't know what I wanted at the time, but I called Mike, and he told me to come along the following day. We played all afternoon, just running through stuff that we mutually knew. I must have passed the audition, as he asked me what I was doing that night. I had planned to go home, have dinner with my family and put my feet up, but he said "Fancy a gig?" and I said "Go on then." '

Steve was not really the vintage 1940s and 1950s guitarist that the BTPs were looking for, but he did have stage presence and energy, and perhaps they were trying just a little too hard to find another Andy Silvester when one did not really exist. Mike was saddened by the deteriorating condition of Lee Brilleaux, but he was excited to get Steve Walwyn. He needed support out front on the stage, and Steve could definitely provide that. He debuted immediately after his audition at the Old Plough, and that was the last time he can remember doing any rehearsals with the band: 'If we wanted to learn a new song, we just went away and listened to it. Next time we did a soundcheck, we would run through it, and then it would be included in the set. We rarely got together in the same room to practise, as we all lived in different places and it was a logistical nightmare to meet up, apart from at the gigs.'

Frank Mead returned on tenor saxophone, and then it was straight back into the big time, with another Gary Brooker event. This was at Cowdray Ruins in West Sussex for the King Edward VII Hospital charity concert, with Queen, Phil Collins, Genesis and Pink Floyd also on the bill.

The band were settled again, with Nick Lunt and Frank Mead providing the horns to complement Mike, Ian, Mark Morgan and Steve Walwyn. Mark felt that he had found his ideal role: 'The marriage between Mike and Ian as friends and musicians showed, and I basically learnt to groove properly with them. It was my first pro gig, and I was going to enjoy it! With this kind of music I believe playing live is the best experience. The early gigs for me were fantastic, as I was hungry for it – sometimes a bit over-eager – but it worked out. The band were playing lots of festivals and doing tours abroad: it was a far more hectic schedule back then. Mike was so professional around gigs. He would only ever drink water before going onstage.'

As new musicians joined the band, rehearsals could have been tense, but Nick Lunt found the opposite to be true: 'It was all very laid-back. Mike was writing quite a bit, but even when his ideas were overtaken by others, he just got on with it. He was part of a band, and they were all really good players in that genre, so it was just accepted.'

The Big Town Playboys decided that the time was right to release another album, so they once again went to Ted Carroll's Ace Records. The production of *Hip Joint* began in the summer of 1993, though it was not actually released until 1996. It was a gruelling experience, with limited time available in the studio to lay down a mixture of originals and covers, and they spent over thirty hours recording before embarking on the long drive home.

Steve Walwyn used to visit Mike occasionally, and they would sit around listening to music. They also started writing songs together as Steve recalls: 'We would just kick ideas around. Sometimes they would be his, and sometimes they would be mine. We would play around and see what came out. One of the songs, "Sweet Louise", I eventually recorded with Dr Feelgood, but it was originally done with the Big Town Playboys.'

October 1993 should have seen the band's debut in Russia, but a stand-off between the president and parliament led to borders being closed and travel plans cancelled. Later that month, they played at the *Starlight Foundation Ball* at the Hilton Hotel in London. They performed on their own, as well as backing soul singer Kym Mazelle. Kym's repertoire was quite far removed from the BTPs' regular set, so they rehearsed a few songs that she was comfortable with and it was a great success. For Mike the evening had added significance, as it was the first time he met Bill Wyman and they had quite a chat about musical styles.

The gigs came in quick succession once again as they managed to fit in BBC's *Children In Need* in Nottingham, at which Nick Whitfield's own rockabilly band, Skinny Bop Trio, opened the show. Nick could see that Mike was suffering: 'It was an open-air event for *Children In Need*, and it was a cold winter's night. Backstage in the marquee it was clear that Mike was very unwell with flu: he was sat with his head in his hands and wrapped in towels. You wouldn't have known that he was ill by the show he gave a few minutes later: another 100 per cent performance.'

The year finished with the annual Gary Brooker charity event at Chiddingfold and the *Capital Radio Christmas Party* in Battersea Park.

1994

The beginning of 1994 was filled with many rehearsals, as well as hours spent recording demos in a new studio at Kidderminster College. As with many of their recordings, these original compositions were left to gather dust after completion. Steve Walwyn also took time out to play with Dr Feelgood in what turned out to be the final two concerts for Lee Brilleaux.

The BTPs played the usual round of gigs around London, the Midlands and beyond, and then put on a show at the Gainsborough

House Hotel in Kidderminster to celebrate Mike's 30th birthday. This was a BTPs gig; however, Mike, Ian Jennings and Mark Morgan decided to do an additional set to open the evening. They played in balaclavas and military gear and called themselves Forced Entry. Mike's brother announced them onstage with the completely fictitious news that they had just signed a massive deal with Sony, but it certainly got the crowd on their side. Following this, they played a brief tour of Norway and increased their time in the Kidderminster College studio to around three days per week.

Mark Morgan noticed the difference between their European and UK gigs: 'On the continent, the crowds seemed healthier and more up for it, which gives you something to bounce off. You also get treated better. When I went to Norway for the first time, I experienced enthusiastic and quite drunken audiences!'

Mike's long-term girlfriend Tracey Murray became pregnant, and both agreed that they were not really ready for the responsibility of parenthood. With her connections at the hospital, she managed to arrange a termination quite quickly, and the same night she was back to normal enjoying a drink in their local pub. A short time later, Mike had a very vivid dream in which Tracey was in bed with someone else. He described the house, the trees and even the partner to her, and she confessed that the dream was actually true. This was quite a shocking revelation, both in terms of the betrayal itself and the way in which it had appeared to Mike, and they deduced that the unborn child which had been aborted was not Mike's at all. It was an event that the relationship could not overcome, and they parted in mid-April 1994. The split was particularly upsetting for Mike, as he had always considered Tracey to be a lovely person, even though at times he found her a little difficult to handle.

This upset was quickly forgotten as the BTPs launched into a phenomenally busy period. It started at the end of May with a residency at the Coconut Grove Hotel in Playa de las Américas, Tenerife. Promoter Allan Jones made all of the arrangements, which included Mike doing an interview for Tenerife-based Radio Bahia. Tenerife had not seen such a band before, and very quickly musicians and public alike flocked to the club to see them play. One evening, comedian Roy 'Chubby' Brown got himself invited up onstage. Brown had a property near to the venue and was keen to get involved with the BTPs, so Mike announced him to the mainly British audience, who greeted him with a chorus of his anthem, 'You Fat Bastard'. Suitably welcomed, Chubby took the drumsticks off Mark Morgan and played a couple of rock'n'roll numbers surprisingly well.

The reaction of the audience to the BTPs' onstage performances gave them a lift, and they returned to the UK a much stronger and tighter outfit for the experience. They played the *Bergen Jazz Festival*, and there followed interviews with Paul Jones for Jazz FM, as well as another for BBC Radio Hereford & Worcester.

The Journeymen resurfaced for a charity event in aid of cancer research, and two weeks later the Big Town Playboys played at Jeff Beck's 50th birthday party. This was one of the highlights of Steve Walwyn's time with the band: 'It was a surprise party for Jeff. He had been sent out for the day on a ballooning trip or something like that, and we came along and set up. He knew nothing about it. He started telling me about all of the work that he's been doing on his house, and I was doing work on mine at the time, so we were comparing notes about guttering and stuff. It was surreal. Then, all of these rock stars and celebrities started turning up: Brian May, Kate Bush, Paul Rodgers – and Brian's wife, Anita Dobson, who started dancing in front of us. So, we were set up in Jeff Beck's front room, and Jeff came in with a bottle of champagne. I remember thinking, *Jeff Beck is just sat watching me play*, and then he took me upstairs and showed me his guitar collection. It was a real thrill.'

Brian May was evidently impressed, as he asked the band just how they managed to *feel* the music and make it rock the way they did. For Mike, it was an easy question to answer, as he had been doing that for his entire career. A day later, they were in Gateshead for *National Music Day*, sharing the bill with guitarist Mick Taylor, Then Jerico, and Nine Below Zero.

In July, the Big Town Playboys played at the Dog Inn in Harvington for old mate Will Wakefield's birthday. This was followed by a weekend at the Alexandra Hotel in Molde, Norway, where Mike met Tormod Bugge, who became a good friend. Tormod helped out at many of the Norwegian blues and rock'n'roll festivals, often picking up bands from the airport in his big black Cadillac. He introduced Mike to Norwegian beauty queen Anette Rødal, and they began an ill-fated and often scary relationship. She was an exquisite-looking woman: seductive, tanned, with gorgeous black hair. They kept in touch over the phone, and eventually she came across to live with him in the UK. To Mike it was an idyllic relationship, as it seemed that all Anette wanted to do was to cook for her man and keep him happy.

At the end of July, the Big Town Playboys played Dave Gilmour's wedding in Twickenham. The guest list included Bob Geldof, Paula Yates and Michael Hutchence, as well as Jeff Beck and Kate Bush, who seemed to spend more time with the band than with the wedding guests.

The following day, there was a party for Robert Plant and his family, and then it was back to the regular gig circuit including five days at Ronnie Scott's in Birmingham. Work on *Hip Joint* for Ace Records continued, and there were festivals in Colne in August and Monaghan in September.

In mid-October they embarked on their first tour of Spain, arranged by Barcelona-based booking agent Alfonso Sánchez (no relation). They played a total of six gigs in six days across the country, and it was a gruelling schedule with a lot of travelling.

Mike could often be laid-back and even a little careless, and in Spain this proved to be very costly as Mark Morgan explains: 'After the final gig, Mike went off partying. I always put my stuff away neatly, but Mike relied on others to do that for him, including his Telecaster guitar. We got to the airport, and he thought that the guitar case seemed a little light, but there was definitely something in it that was rattling around. He opened it up, and his guitar had been replaced by a champagne bottle!'

Upon returning from Spain, Mike got involved with Ricky Lee Brawn and his Big Six project. Bass player Anders Janes explains how it came together: 'Ricky had kept in touch since our days with the Stargazers, and he had this idea of putting together an all-star band. Mike was such an incredibly dynamic performer that I remembered from way back when he was in the Rockets, and he joined on piano and occasional vocals. Al Nicholls was on tenor sax with Nick Lunt on baritone. 'Sugar Ray' Pat Reyford played guitar and provided the vocals. We got together to record the first album, *Ready To Rock*, at the Priory in Bedfordshire. There were no rehearsals, we just got there and recorded it.

'We only did a few gigs with Mike, including our debut at Ealing Town Hall in January '95. He thought that Big Town Playboys were his main project and the Big Six were diluting his presence on the scene. He was also concerned about fans being confused when they saw him in two bands.

'*Ready To Rock* was released on both CD and LP on the Vinyl Japan label, and our version of the T. Rex song, "20th Century Boy", was chosen to be in the film, *The Truman Show*. Vocals on that song were shared between Mike and Pat Reyford. I actually filmed it with a camcorder at Ealing Town Hall, and you can still find it on YouTube.'

With a varied set that concentrated on the 1970s, the Big Six grew in popularity, particularly with the neo-swing scene emerging in the US. Unfortunately, Mike only played a handful of live gigs with the band due to his other commitments, but he still occasionally gets asked to do Big Six reunions. It is a testament to his influence that, although he hardly ever appeared onstage with the band, he is still considered to be one of the founder members. Mike himself has fond memories of the band – with the possible exception of the big, loud tartan zoot suits.

In the middle of November 1994, Mike did the final overdubs for *Ready To Rock*, and then transferred to the Zella Studios in Birmingham, owned by local rock stars Magnum, to continue with *Hip Joint*. Stuart Colman and Roy Williams were brought in to improve the sound prior to the album's release, and Colman was amazed at what he saw: 'On *Hip Joint*, Mike was very, very good. Seeing him live onstage is one thing, but that doesn't mean you can cut it in the studio. He can do both. He is unique in that. Mike and a piano go together like ice cream and a cornet. He is very good on guitar, but with the piano it's as if the instrument is a part of him.'

Mark Morgan recalls Colman's influence on the proceedings: 'Mike was very professional in the studio, and he put himself on a level with the rest of us. When Stuart came in, he listened and he was open to new ideas. He is very fast as well. He performs in the studio the same as he does onstage. The first half of *Hip Joint* was done very quickly, but the second half went a bit hairy, as there were a lot of distractions. He needs a good engineer or he can get distracted. Sometimes he needs to be guided and pushed.'

1995

There were not many live shows at the start of 1995, as Mike split his time between rehearsals with the Big Six and recordings and overdubs for *Hip Joint*. The Gainsborough House Hotel in Kidderminster again played host to Mike's birthday party, and the BTPs played the following night as a special benefit. Tenor saxophonist Frank Mead was in urgent need of a new bridge for his teeth, so the second show was effectively a Frank Mead fundraiser.

At the end of February, Mike went to Peckham to once again

put on a loud Big Six suit, this time for a photo session. Later that evening, Mike, Ian and a host of other professional musicians went to the luxurious flat of fashion designer Peter Golding in Chelsea, to discuss a recording project with him. Golding, who created the first-ever stretch denim jeans, is also an able musician and wanted to put together a promotional CD called *Stretching The Blues*. Sessions were duly arranged for April.

In March, the Big Town Playboys got the chance to repay a kindness from ten years earlier. Brian Curran had helped them out by letting them stay at his flat in London during the Ricky Cool & The Big Town Playboys days, and they agreed to headline at the *Daffodil Charity Ball* in Ilkley, which he was organising. Later that month, they played another residency at Ronnie Scott's in Birmingham, followed by an interview for BBC Radio WM and an appearance on the BBC magazine show, *Pebble Mill At One*. The host was Gloria Hunniford, and they played the original composition, 'Hungry Man'.

April began for Mike with a solo residency at the Stefanie Piano Bar in Arendal, Norway. There then followed a series of different recording projects, starting with *Stretching The Blues* at the Nomis Studios in Olympia, but in Mike's own words, 'the less said about that the better'.

The Big Town Playboys then went into the Angelshare Studios in North Wales to progress the recording of *Hip Joint*, while Bill Wyman asked Mike to assist on a recording session with guitarist Terry Taylor and sound engineer Stuart Epps at the Mill Studios in Cookham.

Bill explains why he wanted Mike: 'I first saw Mike at a charity event at the end of the '80s. It was just him at the piano and I was very impressed. I then saw him at another charity event with the Big Town Playboys in October 1993[*], and again I was very impressed. I had some ideas for the Rhythm Kings – just recordings – and on and off I'd do two or three days' recording per month. I needed a vocalist, and thought it would be nice to use him and his style. I just wanted to hear what he sounded like. He did his stuff and I really liked what he was doing.'

Whilst all of this recording was happening, Mike fitted in an appearance with the Big Six at the National Film Theatre sponsored by the BBC, as well as a regular BTPs gig at the 100 Club.

After festivals in the Netherlands and Spain in May 1995, and

---

[*] *The Starlight Foundation Ball.*

another session at the Angelshare Studios for *Hip Joint*, Mike played at a Dr Feelgood memorial concert in Southend just over a year after the death of Lee Brilleaux. With Steve Walywn's encouragement, Mike had actually auditioned to join the Feelgoods as their frontman, but it was not quite right for either side. It was fun doing the run-throughs, but Mike knew he could never be a Lee Brilleaux. However, Steve decided that his future lay with the Feelgoods, who were now re-forming permanently, and the BTPs had to prepare to replace him.

Steve's style was made for Dr Feelgood, but he will always remember his time with the Big Town Playboys: 'I spent two years with the band, and Mike and myself had a great rapport onstage. It was a bit different for me, as with the Feelgoods I had to play all of the time. When Mike is on piano, I can take a bit of a break. I love to play with Mike whenever I can.'

On 21 May there was another memorial, this time for Alexis Korner at the Buxton Opera House in Buxton, Derbyshire. Korner, who was revered as the founding father of British blues, had died eleven years previously, and the concert featured Mike playing solo, as well as sets from Norman Beaker, Paul Jones, Jack Bruce and many others. Three of the songs that Mike performed, 'Be Careful', 'Reconsider Baby' and 'Down The Road Apiece' were included on the 1996 CD, *Alexis Korner Memorial Concert (Volume 3)*, released on the Indigo label.

In June, Mike played the first of several solo appearances at the tiny Basement cellar bar in Leamington Spa, organised by promoter Phil Dunn. He regularly enjoyed these nights, as it was close to home and always filled with his friends and fans. Another advantage was that the bar always seemed to employ attractive waitresses, which appealed to Mike's flirtatious nature. The BTPs played the Pyramids Centre in Southsea, where guitarist Otis Grand and Jools Holland & His Rhythm & Blues Orchestra were also on the bill, as well as spending two more days in the Angelshare Studios, as *Hip Joint* was nearing completion. When the recording finished, Mike met up with Andy Silvester, and it seemed that Andy was willing to help out the band on guitar for a while. The following night, they played the *Blues On The Farm* festival near Chichester, with Andy on guitar and Nick Payn on baritone saxophone.

However, Andy was not a permanent option, and in July they auditioned Birmingham-based bottleneck guitarist Stuart Ford. Stuart played just one gig with the band, at a large open-air concert at

Titchfield Abbey, but his different sound did not really fit in.

Mike took the opportunity to take a break by attending the *Molde International Jazz Festival* in Norway. The highlight was the American soul, funk and rhythm & blues group the Neville Brothers, and when Aaron Neville began to sing, Mike could not prevent the tears from streaming down his cheeks.

The mixing of *Hip Joint* continued into August as the BTPs went through a series of guitarists, each of whom played just one gig. They were generally discovered at the last minute, taken through some hurried rehearsals, and then thrust onto the stage. The exception was Ian Hatton, an old friend also known as 'Tat' who used to sell amps at Sean Dee's music store. Ian had been the guitarist in Weapon of Peace, a Midlands-based reggae band that built up a good following in the 1980s with Roy Williams as sound engineer. More recently, he had joined his friend Jason Bonham (son of Led Zeppelin drummer John) in the rock band Bonham, who also gained a measure of success with performances that were broadcast on MTV.

In September 1995, Tony Coni joined the band. Tony was an old friend of Mike, Ian and Mark Morgan, and when Steve Walwyn left, Mark recommended him. The work at Angelshare Studios took an interesting turn as Mike decided to replace Steve with Tony on a couple of tracks. He said that it would not take long, but Tony recalls that the reality was very different: 'It was mad. We drove down there so that I could play guitar on "Ain't No Big Deal". At four or five in the morning we were still there, so we slept on the studio floor for a few hours and then carried on after breakfast.'

Rehearsals with Tony continued throughout the month, and he made his debut at the 100 Club, but it was a real step up for him: 'Previously, I had been in non-professional bands, so this time there was pressure, but Mike was so easy to work with. If you mess something up, he just laughs it off – which is unlike most other bands.'

Chris Wroe was called upon to produce the album cover for *Hip Joint*, and he describes some of the complications he had to overcome: 'At one point, the cover was completely redesigned, making it more bluesy and removing the picture of an actual hip joint that was not quite right. Eventually, I shot Mike against a white van with a cheap Fender Squier guitar, but when I came to do the sleeve, I altered the image to show him against a brick wall. I then took the head of a Fender Stratocaster and replaced the inferior Squier with it. It looked so much better, and Fender actually sent Mike a new guitar as a thank you for the publicity, even though the image was made up.'

Mike's parents sold their home in Bewdley and moved some of their possessions to the house next door to their son's in Kidderminster whilst they planned their retirement and a new home back in their Spanish homeland. Mike's mum would often go across to his house to use the washing machine, and she frequently saw his girlfriend, Anette, getting dressed up before getting into a car with another guy whilst Mike was away. However, at this stage she kept the secret to herself. Mike's father was unaware of it, and loved the idea that his son was finally settling down with a beautiful woman who seemed to just want to cook and clean for him.

His parents had set their hearts on settling back in Spain, and were having a house built in El Tiemblo, in the hills outside Madrid. In mid-September, they finally drove their car across as it neared completion, and as the weather was not too cold, they stayed in a caravan whilst the building work was being completed. When they considered it habitable they sent out lots of house-warming invitations, even though the builders had only just installed the floors and the windows and the Spanish terrace was far from ready. Mike and Anette went along as a happy couple, but that would change soon afterwards.

In October, the BTPs shared a double bill with swing and rhythm & blues outfit King Pleasure & The Biscuit Boys at the Pyramids Centre in Southsea. King Pleasure finished his set, but before the BTPs could take to the stage, Frank Mead slipped a disc, leaving him in excruciating pain. The band were in a panic and asked the Biscuit Boys' tenor saxophonist Martin Winning to play through their set. Martin explains what happened: 'Frank Mead was on his back in the dressing room, and I had to jump in and play with the great Mike Sanchez. Nick Lunt helped me out, and as I was playing with them, I noticed just how good they were. I saw how everything seemed to fit together, and so it was easy to slot in.'

This was the first time that Martin played with Mike – an engagement that he was to fulfil many times in the future.

Rockabilly fan James Steel opened a bar called James in Bewdley, and this became a regular haunt for Mike. It was a new place to socialise, as well as a great venue for solo and duo performances. These gigs started in mid-October and were followed by a special night at the 100 Club backing legendary US rock'n'rollers Don & Dewey. The Americans were somewhat obscure, but they played high-energy rock'n'roll. The BTPs were a perfect fit, and the expectant audience did

Big Town Playboys at the Riverboat, Kidderminster, July 1988.
Left to right: Paul Clarke, Al Nicholls, Andy Silvester, Dai Powell, Ian Jennings and Mike.

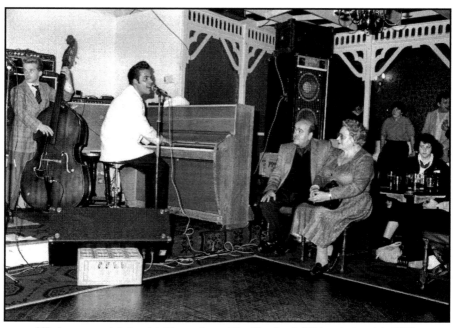

Mike's mum and dad watch him perform at the Riverboat, Kidderminster, July 1988.

The Riverboat, Kidderminster, July 1988.

The BTPs at Yesterdays, Alderley Edge (Roger Eagle promotion), February 1989.
Left to right: Al Nicholls, Andy Silvester, Clive Deamer, Mike and Ian Jennings.

Rehearsing with Joe Hughes, *Southbank Festival*, August 1989.
Left to right: Joe Hughes, Andy Silvester, Mike, Ian Jennings and Clive Deamer.

Photo by Paul Harris

Ian Jennings and Mike at Bodelwyddan Castle, 23 June 1990.

Looking suave on this poster for a gig in Chester, February 1991.

At Fleetwood's L.A. Blues, Santa Monica, California, February 1991.
Left to right: Andy Silvester, Mike and Mick Fleetwood.

Charity gig with Gary Brooker, Chiddingfold, December 1991.

Rehearsals for *Crazy Legs* with Jeff Beck, June 1992.
Left to right: Adrian Utley, Mike, Ian Jennings, Clive Deamer and Jeff Beck.

Mike rehearsing with Jeff Beck, Nomis Studios, London, June 1992.

Publicity shot, 1992.
Left to right: Adrian Utley, Ian Jennings, Leo Green, Clive Deamer and Mike.

Mike meets blues piano legend Charles Brown, Birmingham, July 1993.

Publicity shot, ca. 1993.
Left to right: Mike, Ian Jennings,
Mark Morgan and Steve Walwyn.

EASTER RHYTHM & BLUES PARADE!

featuring **BIG TOWN PLAYBOYS**

"PIANO-POUNDING, SAXOPHONE HONKIN' 40's & 50's RHYTHM &
BLUES DANCE CLASSICS FROM THE MUSICALLY & VISUALLY
STUNNING COMBO, RATED AS ONE OF THE UK'S TOP LIVE BANDS."

plus **JAMES HUNTER & THE JOKERS**

"BLUESY, OFTEN SOULFUL, R'N'B FROM THE FORMER HOWLIN'
WILF & HIS JUMPIN' POWER-PACKED BAND."

DJ / Compere Steve Beggs

SATURDAY 2ND APRIL '94

DOORS OPEN 7.30 : LIVE SHOW STARTS 8.30
£5 BAR CLOSES MIDNIGHT **£5**
R'N'B DANCE COMPETITION AT 8pm

at **THE BOTTOM LINE**

(NEXT DOOR TO THE OLD BBC TV THEATRE)
SHEPHERDS BUSH GREEN • LONDON W12 8QE
TEL. 081 746 0255 / 081 740 1304
(3 MINUTES WALK FROM THE SHEPHERDS BUSH & GOLDHAWK RD. TUBE STATIONS.)

**DRINKS AT PUB PRICES :
BIG DANCE FLOOR :
AIR CONDITIONED**

Headlining at the Bottom
Line, April 1994.

The Big Six sport a natty line in threads, January/February 1995.
Left to right: Ricky Lee Brawn, Mike, Al Nicholls, Anders Janes, Nick Lunt.
Front: Pat Reyford

Breakdown en route to Jersey, August 1996.
Left to right: Will Wakefield, Mark Morgan, Roy Williams and Mike.

Backstage at the Royal Albert Hall, February 1996.
Left to right: Mike, Frank Mead, Mark Morgan, Eric Clapton,
Tony Coni, Ian Jennings and Nick Lunt.

Mike puts in a typically energetic appearance at the *Guildford Free Festival*, August 1996.

The Big Town Playboys play the 100 Club, London, July 1996.
Left to right: Ian Jennings, Mike, Andy Fairweather-Low and Mark Morgan.

Party at Peter and Marta Richardson's house, Camberwell, July 1997.
Left to right: Mike, Jools Holland, Mark Morgan and Andy Fairweather-Low.

Getting ready to go solo:
1999 publicity shot for
Just Can't Afford It.

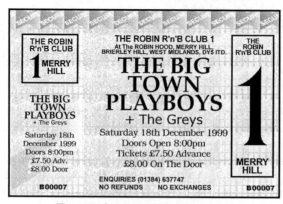

The end of an era: Mike's last gig with
the Big Town Playboys, 18 December 1999.

not leave disappointed. A week later the BTPs played a session for Paul Jones's BBC radio show, and then Mike did his final Big Six show at Thames Valley University.

November was taken up by the BTPs' longest tour, as they took to the road with well-respected San Diego rockabilly band, the Paladins, led by guitarist Dave Gonzalez. They played Belgium, France, the Netherlands, Germany and Norway before catching the ferry to Newcastle. It was a wild time, with both bands sharing a tour bus and living and breathing a rock'n'roll lifestyle. By the time they played their first UK date at the Front Page club in Carlisle, the Californians were getting homesick. The cold venue and British November climate did nothing to cheer them, though they did complete their remaining UK dates.

At one of these, Nick Whitfield reacquainted himself with the BTPs: 'There had been some changes in the line-up since I last saw them in Nottingham. Mark Morgan, a good friend of mine, had replaced drummer Clive Deamer, and Antonio Coni was on guitar instead of Andy Silvester. I was lucky to catch two dates of the joint-headline tour of the Big Town Playboys and the Paladins. These were two bands that were covering all aspects of what I love about the blues – the perfect combination. I distinctly remember the London show at the Borderline: the Big Town Playboys opened up on this particular show and I was stood at the front, when all of a sudden Mike jumped off the stage and slid along the floor on his knees. He stopped at the feet of a girl stood just in front of me, and he was gazing up to her and serenading her mid-song. He still does this kind of caper today, just not on his knees!'

Drummer Mark Morgan considers this to have been his best tour with the BTPs from a musical perspective: 'With the Paladins, it was kind of a friendly rivalry, and I think we certainly had to up our game. I learnt so much from that trip, and we were very tight as an outfit by the end of it.'

It was a baptism of fire for new guitarist Tony Coni, but he took it all in his stride: 'Every gig had a great vibe. Playing with Don & Dewey was a killer gig, and the Paladins were fantastic – especially the show in Holland on my birthday, that was really special. It was also good to hang around with Mike. He is a rare breed, and always thinking musically. He always wants to share his music and spread the word because he gets so much joy out of it. It's like a big musical spliff, and he just wants to pass it around. It was great fun.'

After the Paladins tour ended, Mike got the first indication that things were not quite right with Anette. Although at that time it was nothing more than a hunch, he noticed that she had developed a rather friendly relationship with a local guy who ran a ladies' hairdressing salon. Despite this, she was busily planning their wedding, which Mike let her get on with, as it kept her happy. Meanwhile, the Big Town Playboys continued their regular shows, including a return to Chiddingfold for yet another Gary Brooker Christmas party.

1996

January 1996 saw Mike invited to be the special guest star of the Storyville Big Band at their New Year concerts at the Kino in Molde. They did a couple of rehearsals before the shows at which Mike's girlfriend Anette, as a former Norwegian beauty queen, was the host and presenter.

A six-night residency with the BTPs at Ronnie Scott's in Birmingham followed, and then the band once again prepared to support Eric Clapton. This began with a number of radio interviews and a one-off show at Manchester's NYNEX Arena, before they moved on to the Royal Albert Hall for twelve shows in fifteen nights.

Nick Lunt considers these to have been the best he played: 'When the Big Town Playboys opened up at the Albert Hall, the sound was just amazing. Mike was such a good frontman, and he's never played a duff gig, but these were special. He is so good at the roots stuff, and that's why the stars love to play with him.'

Mark Morgan thought that the Royal Albert Hall shows were a mind-blowing experience, but he knew that it could not always be like this: 'My parents and sister came down on one of the nights, and I hope they were proud, even though they probably also saw me playing in the Bucket & Ferret pub a few weeks later! That's the nature of the game: big gigs, small gigs – it's all part and parcel of being a working musician.'

The Big Town Playboys were very much Mike's main focus, but he also had other projects to work on. The rest of the band likewise began to look elsewhere, and five minutes before setting foot onto the Royal Albert Hall stage, Tony Coni announced that he intended to leave. Ian Jennings and Mark Morgan were involved in a band called Mitzi, and Tony decided that he wanted to go in that direction full time. Mike initially resented this collaboration, but he began to realise that perhaps they were just looking out for themselves whilst he was off doing other things.

Tony admits that leaving the band was a tough decision: 'I was involved in other projects which were stretching my musicalities, and it was clashing with the Big Town Playboys. Mike was upset and so was I, as we had become really close friends. But there was an atmosphere, so I said, "I think you should find yourself another player," as I didn't want to upset the Playboys. I told him that I would do as many gigs as he wanted me to until he found another guitarist.'

Local newspaper the *Kidderminster Shuttle* did an interview and photo session in the aftermath of the Clapton shows, and Ian and Mark remained with the band, but Mike's main concern was to find someone to replace Tony. After playing another *Daffodil Charity Ball* in Ilkley, he visited Andy Fairweather-Low at his home in Rhiwbina, Cardiff.

Tony continues: 'About a week later, he got Andy Fairweather-Low to cover for me. I didn't expect it to happen that quick. We gave each other a big hug and that was it. It was sad, because neither of us wanted to part from that music. I felt like I was to blame for the bad atmosphere, and everyone could feel it.'

Andy had been working with Eric Clapton as his second guitarist on his world tours and most notably on best-selling albums such as *Unplugged*, and Mike had become friendly with him over many years, particularly at the Dunsfold and Chiddingfold events. His work with Eric had recently ended as the guitar star took a break from recording and touring, and Mike offered him the chance to join the Big Town Playboys, which he readily accepted.

Mike was pleased with his new line-up, and he considered it an honour to have Andy Fairweather-Low in the band. He was a great guitarist and a close friend, and he made his first appearance at the Knights Variety Club in Kidderminster on 23 March 1996. Andy fitted easily into the BTPs' set, and after a few rehearsals they had a full diary of bookings.

Andy enjoyed the relaxed atmosphere with the BTPs: 'The rehearsals were fun, fun, fun, and the gigs were fun, fun, fun. There was a lot of travelling to and from gigs, but it felt like one big party.'

Four dates in Bremen were followed by another *Alexis Korner Memorial Concert* at the Buxton Opera House. This time, the line-up included Fleetwood Mac founder Peter Green, playing live for the first time in many years, and Mike has fond memories of playing Peter's 'Love That Burns' with Andy Fairweather-Low on guitar and Peter watching from the side of the stage. Festivals and charity gigs came in quick succession, and although Andy was a true guitar legend, he was just another member of the BTPs. Occasionally promoters would increase the fee because of Andy's name, but he was happy to just be a part of the band.

Audiences varied, and at the 100 Club in May 1996 Peter Green, Jeff Beck and various members of Iron Maiden were in attendance. However, Andy Fairweather-Low remembers a much more low-key appearance earlier that month: 'We played a private gig at Highclere Castle in Berkshire. It's now famous and on TV every week, as *Downton Abbey* was filmed there. We set up in the library, but they were worried that the sound would damage the old books, even though there were never more than a handful of people in the room at any one time. Mike still managed to make a show of it. Five minutes in, he was on the floor at the feet of a woman in a red dress, singing to her, whilst the rest of the audience – just two men – looked on amused.'

Sound engineer Roy Williams continued to entertain the notion that Mike should step outside the authentic rock'n'roll genre and try something different. He arranged some rehearsal sessions at the Sound Station, Birmingham and Ice House, Stourbridge studios and brought along American jazz and blues guitarist Mickey Baker and bass player Steve Dolan to help out. They ran through a few original ideas, but it never really worked out. Mike told Roy: 'I'm Mike Sanchez. I do boogie-woogie, and I do rhythm & blues. That's me.'

At the end of May 1996, a BBC GLR radio interview and session for Bob Harris were followed by the long-awaited release of *Hip Joint*, which featured two guitarists who had long since departed the Big Town Playboys. The album was officially launched at the 100 Club, and although they had spent a lot of money over several years in its production, they managed to sell plenty of copies on the night and were very pleased with themselves.

However, Ace Records owned the rights, which meant that the band saw very little from sales, and they soon realised that they would have been much better off releasing it themselves and keeping it under their own control. They would then have been free to sell the album at shows and through mail order. Mike was not happy with the quality of the recordings, mainly due to the guitar sound. Onstage, Steve Walwyn's style had really complemented Mike's playing and his frontman image, but on *Hip Joint* his guitar was too 'electric' for the authentic sound that the album required.

There followed another Jazz FM session for Paul Jones, and then Mike embarked on a number of solo and duo gigs. Towards the end of June 1996, he played in a four-piece at the Royal Pump Rooms in Leamington Spa – with Andy Silvester on guitar for this one occasion, as Andy Fairweather-Low was unavailable. Although everything was going well with the latter, it felt good for Mike to play with his old mentor once again.

Throughout the summer of 1996 the gigs once more flowed into each other. There was also a photo shoot for *Steppin' Out* magazine, and many more interviews, before another six-night residency at Ronnie Scott's in Birmingham at the end of August. September saw more dates in Norway, including the *Hell Blues Festival*, where Mark Morgan spotted another band with talent. He urged Mike to go to see Knock-Out Greg & Blue Weather, a Swedish outfit who were playing close by. Mike was immediately impressed by their vintage blues sound and bought a couple of albums which they had released through Håkan Forshult's Last Buzz label.

The Swedes also remember that night well, as guitarist Anders Lewen explains: 'It was in Stjørdal, Norway. We had finished our gig, and Dr Feelgood were on after us, but Steve Walwyn recommended that we went to see the Big Town Playboys, who were playing just a few blocks away. I think the whole band went, and we were all just totally knocked out immediately! Not only by the music, but also by Mike's incredible charisma! At that time, we hadn't yet seen the filmed material with Amos Milburn at the Apollo, but seeing and hearing Mike was just like being in that movie. It was like an awakening for our band. Being Scandinavians, we knew how to play in the old style, but Mike really showed us how important it is to visualise it as well. It's just as important being an entertainer as well as a musician when you're fronting a band. Hearing Mike as a vocalist and piano player was just as breathtaking as the visual parts of the show. We were inspired by some of the same things as Mike: Amos, Floyd Dixon, Charles Brown, T-Bone Walker, Billy Emerson, Slim Harpo, Howlin' Wolf, etc., but we had never seen or heard anyone play it as great as Mike and the Playboys did.'

Greger Andersson agrees: 'I was really blown away by his stage appearance and great vocals. He had a really powerful impact when he performed and acted wild onstage. I thought he would be a really tough guy with a short temper from what I could see. I realised that nothing could be more wrong. I thought, *Wow, this is the closest I will ever get to seeing Little Richard perform in the late '50s.'*

After returning from Norway, Mike had a visit from Peter Green. His Splinter Group had played several nights at Ronnie Scott's in Birmingham, and at the end of the residency, the band called round to Mike's house. Mike made them pizza and salad, whilst Peter drifted off into a happy sleep flicking through Mike's extensive music collection.

Roy Williams thought it would be a good idea to try to take some of the burden off Mike and Ian, so he suggested that his friend Trevor Long should take over the management of the band. This was a well-meaning act that brought with it a lot of problems. Mike had always considered Ian to be tight with the band's money – probably because there was never much of it around – but that was nothing compared to what lay ahead, and it was ultimately Trevor Long's involvement that led to Mike leaving the band.

In October 1996, the Big Town Playboys played a gig in Austria, and another at the *Leverkusen Festival* as part of an extensive German tour. Nick Lunt shares an insight into their life together on the road: 'It was great fun getting in a van and travelling around. There were no egos, and everyone just got on great. Mike is quite shy and introverted offstage, with quite a sensitive side. He is totally different when he is up there performing. Occasionally there were problems though. Mike snores like a warthog and sleeps really deeply. This even caused him to miss a flight.'

An interview for the BBC followed, then the BTPs continued their gigs through to the end of the year. Mike also managed to fit in a solo appearance at the Railway Bell in Kidderminster, where he was joined onstage by Robert Plant.

1997

There was a fresh start for Mike in 1997 as he started working on his first solo album, *Just A Game*. It was inspired by one of his musical heroes, Little Willie Littlefield, and all of the tracks are originals. For Mike, it was also a welcome change to the group collaboration, where things often did not get done. He again went into the Angelshare Studios, with Kevin Tonner as sound engineer. He released the album himself, getting just one thousand copies pressed. Once they were sold, that was it, and he consigned the record to history.

After another appearance at Chiddingfold, Mike spent most of February 1997 in various recording studios. The following month, Hugh Phillimore, who later became Imelda May's manager, arranged for the Big Town Playboys to play at Mark Knopfler's wedding. Mark asked the band to play a few Ray Charles numbers such as 'What'd I Say', as well as their usual set, and they went down well with the celebrity audience.

Andy Silvester returned for a gig at the Brook in Southampton, and then Mike, Ian and Mark Morgan went to Wool Hall Studios near Bath to help out on a number of Van Morrison recordings. Former Big Town Playboy Leo Green was his band organiser – a job that Mike was offered on two separate occasions, but which he turned down, as the Irishman could be rather difficult to handle. Mike was more than happy to be involved in these sessions, however, which featured versions of many of Van's favourite rhythm & blues numbers from the 1940s and early 1950s, though as was typical of many Morrison sessions over the years, the album remains unreleased.

The *Burnley National Blues Festival* was a highlight of spring 1997, and then there was a gruelling day on 4 April during which the band rehearsed and recorded a live double album. It started with them setting up at the Robin Hood in Merry Hill, Dudley. There were soundchecks and rehearsals as the Fleetwood Mobile unit was set up, and then the gig itself, with the whole process of recording live putting a different edge on the performance. The album was mixed in a couple of days towards the end of the month, and Mike's friend Chris Wroe produced the cover design. The result was the 2-CD, *Off The Clock... Live*.

The BTPs were proud of their work, especially Andy Fairweather-Low: 'I am glad that somebody recorded my involvement with Big Town Playboys. It was me learning from them, rather than bringing anything new to the band. They knew what they were doing, and they were doing it well.'

The band paid for all the recording and production expenses, and got some CDs pressed up to sell at gigs. Trevor Long then sold the album to Eagle Records with a view to getting it into record shops, but this turned out to be a mistake. The band members received a minimal amount from the sale, and in accepting this, gave up the rights to sell it themselves, which would have made them a lot more money.

Meanwhile, Mike's girlfriend, Anette Rødal, was becoming more of a problem, progressively replacing his furniture with hers when he was out on the road. There were baroque-style seats, large gold-framed mirrors, statues, vintage Norwegian lamps and chandeliers, and Persian rugs. It seemed as though she was intent on turning Mike's house on Comberton Road, Kidderminster, into a mini-Graceland.

On one occasion, he was putting rubbish in the dustbin outside when he noticed a bunch of his old photographs that she had thrown away. When he challenged her about it, she started to have hysterical temper tantrums, slamming doors and shouting at him. Every time he enquired about missing items around the house, she had fits of rage and would lock herself in a room for hours. She would often take long, lonely walks in the middle of the night – but all of the time she was planning the wedding. She had decided that the main ceremony would be in her hometown of Molde and that there would be a blessing at the Parish Church of St Leonard's in Ribbesford. She sent out all of the invitations, and even arranged for Roy Williams to be the best man. Mike had originally agreed to everything, based on how well the start of the relationship had gone and how keen Anette was to be settled down and married, but it all started to feel very wrong as the tantrums and the rages increased, and she continued her involvement with the guy from the salon who lived a couple of blocks away from their home.

Mike felt a degree of guilt, as he felt responsible for having brought this woman to his home from another country, and he needed to ensure that the ending of the relationship went as smoothly as possible. During a trip to Jersey, he reached breaking point and he told her that there would be no wedding. A few days later, she arranged for her new boyfriend to collect all of her things from Mike's house. Mike was overjoyed, and even helped to load the van, shouting 'Freedom!' as they drove away and out of his life.

More solo gigs followed the split, and after another studio session with Van Morrison, the Big Town Playboys embarked on a brief tour of Germany and Switzerland.

Andy Fairweather-Low loved the touring: 'It was hard travelling and hard partying. We were travelling on a train from Germany to Switzerland, and there had been a lot of drinking. Ian had his double bass, I had my guitar, and it was difficult to move about the carriage. A German guy was sat in our seats, despite them being pre-booked, and he refused to get up. We even got some people who spoke German to intervene, but he was not for moving. I went to find Mike, and for some reason he was in the next carriage putting on red lipstick!'

The BTPs played the *Breda Jazz Festival*, followed by another live session and interview which Mike did with Paul Jones at the BBC's Pebble Mill Studios.

Mike was also becoming increasingly uncomfortable with Trevor Long's involvement, and so took on even more solo bookings. He still appeared with the BTPs, and at the *Leominster Fringe Festival* in June 1997 he introduced his new girlfriend to the band. Britta Medeiros was from Stuttgart, and she became a very good friend and confidante. She was of Mexican extraction and extremely good-looking with long, thick black hair and tanned skin. She had her own band, Pumping Special, who played rock'n'roll covers, and she also became an occasional singing partner for Mike, gaining his respect and affection in everything that she did. Inevitably, Mike spent time in Stuttgart and performed shows with Britta and Pumping Special at the start of July.

In July 1997, there was a surprise party for Peter Richardson's wife, Marta, in Camberwell, attended by the *Comic Strip* team as well as Jools Holland. Peter loved to have Mike at his parties – and not just because of his musical ability: 'When the Playboys played at my flat, it was fantastic, but we had to put mattresses up against the windows to cut out the noise. Mike has a wonderful energy and is a fantastic live performer. When he plays, it's impossible to not want to get up on your feet and dance. He's also a really nice guy: at one anniversary party, he was playing with his left hand and taking pictures of me and my wife on the dance floor with his right.'

London Zoo was an unusual venue that hosted the BTPs for a private event, and then they travelled to Finland to play the *Pori Jazz Festival* in mid-July. This was a five-day event during which they shared the bill with American gospel group the Dixie Hummingbirds, as well as sharing time, pizza and whisky with Stray Cats guitarist Brian Setzer. Brian was staying at the hotel next door, and Mike felt quite flattered that he actually knew who he was.

The weather was hot and sunny throughout the event, and for one of their three shows the BTPs played outdoors on a stage by the side of a river to an audience of thousands. Unfortunately, one of the crowd fell into the river and a commotion ensued. Mike saw the ambulance but thought that it must have been heat exhaustion or something similar, and so the band played on. Sadly, the victim had drowned – the only known fatality at a Big Town Playboys gig.

In August, Mike played the *Notodden Blues Festival* in Norway, where he performed with Knock-Out Greg & Blue Weather for the first time, and *South Blues Festival* in Belgium. In September, there was a trip to Italy for the *Milan Blues Festival*, followed by two dates in Germany.

Upon returning to Kidderminster, Mike got some much-needed assistance at home. Lynne Phillips had been made redundant from the local bus company, and she responded to an ad from a recruitment agency: 'They wanted someone to produce a newsletter for a jazz musician. I rang the number and Mike answered. When I went round to meet him, the place was full of handwritten envelopes. He told me that, when he sent one newsletter out, he immediately started writing the envelopes for the next one. I did his newsletter, and then I set a database up for him with contact details and categorised it for each person.'

In October, Bill Wyman released his first Rhythm Kings album. *Struttin' Our Stuff* featured Mike's vocals on 'Jitterbug Boogie', a track he had recorded with Bill two years earlier. Another album that was less popular with the Big Town Playboys was the CD reissue of *Playboy Boogie!* with three bonus tracks, 'I Like It', 'I Want To Do More' and 'Well Oh Well'. The original record label, Making Waves, had gone into liquidation some years earlier, and the rights to the material were sold without the BTPs getting the chance to acquire them. Ian Jennings, in particular, has always maintained that it is a bootleg, and it remains a sore point.

Andy Fairweather-Low was nearing the end of his tenure with the band, as Eric Clapton was planning to resume touring in 1998. His replacement had to be chosen within days, as a European tour was fast approaching. Roy Williams suggested Trevor Burton, who had previously played with Steve Gibbons and the Move, and although Trevor joined them there were still some doubts as to his suitability. However, the band simply had no idea who knew how to play guitar in the vintage styles required. Trevor proved to be loud and blues rock-orientated, and the Big Town Playboys struggled to get him to adapt to their style. It led to a difficult few months ahead.

1998

Mark Morgan encouraged Darrel Higham to audition for the Big Town Playboys in mid-January 1998, and although he looked and sounded great, they had already started to use Trevor Burton. Higham had a rockabilly style that was much more akin to what the BTPs were playing. In addition, he idolised Eddie Cochran and modelled his appearance on his iconic fifties' hero. He even co-wrote a book about him with Julie Mundy – *Don't Forget Me: The Eddie Cochran Story* – and also travelled to the States to visit Cochran's mother, where he sat and played Eddie's Gretsch guitar.

Jools Holland booked the band to play at his 40th birthday party at Up The Creek in Greenwich, with Andy Fairweather-Low on guitar and Eric Clapton in the audience. Holland had always been a big fan, and the guest list for the event was a who's who of comedians and other television celebrities. The BTPs played a number of gigs in early February, which gave Trevor Burton the chance to practise with the band and to try to blend in with their style prior to a major European tour. Andy Fairweather-Low still helped out occasionally, but they needed a more permanent arrangement and so persevered with Trevor.

In May 1998, Eagle Rock Entertainment, the parent company of Eagle Records, staged a three-act promotional night at the Shepherd's Bush Empire to boost record sales for new albums by Mike Peters, ex-frontman of the Alarm, Then Jerico and the Big Town Playboys. This may have increased sales of *Off The Clock...Live* and the label's profits, but it did little for the BTPs themselves. After just a couple of years, Eagle, who were involved with many other artists, made a decision to delete it, and so all the Big Town Playboys' hard work in creating this landmark double album eventually felt like a waste of time, even when it became a rare and collectible recording several years later.

A few days later, Mike and Frank Mead featured on the NBC *VIP* prime time chat show. Mike had been watching the show for a few months and quite fancied the host, Catrina Skepper. When he arrived at the studio in Great Russell Street, Bloomsbury, he hadn't realised that she would be doing the interview. He could do little more than sit staring at her, and when he did get to speak, it sounded as though he had put on a different voice, but it was all a result of the attraction for Catrina that he had developed over the previous weeks.

Meanwhile, back onstage the guitar playing of Trevor Burton was getting no closer to the Big Town Playboys style, and the tour of Austria, Switzerland and the Netherlands in May 1998 was particularly difficult. His reluctance to adapt to what the audiences were used to was threatening to turn off many of the BTPs' fans. In mid-June, Mike had finally had enough and he asked Trevor to leave. Mike once again thought back to the time when Andy Silvester quit, the time that he should perhaps have wound up the Big Town Playboys for good.

Darrel Higham fronted his own band, the Enforcers, as well as being a regular on the European rock'n'roll circuit, but he was certainly interested in working with the Big Town Playboys. His great style and looks were perfect for the BTPs, and he arrived just in time for a busy summer. They played the *Bishopstock Blues Festival* near Exeter as well as *Blues On The Farm* near Chichester. The Eagle Rock PR team got the Big Town Playboys involved in a bikers' festival in Bilbao in the Basque region of northern Spain, for which Andy Fairweather-Low returned.

There were several Spanish radio interviews, including National Radio 3. One of these did not go exactly as planned, as the presenter asked Mike for his opinion of Frank Sinatra, who had recently passed away. Forthright as ever, Mike said he was more of a Nat 'King' Cole fan and that Nat did not get the same exposure that Frank did as he was not white and did not have the support of the Mafia. The radio station cut him off mid-interview.

Mike committed another faux pas in Bilbao when he sang a Mexican-style bolero in Spanish and structured it to his own style – the fiercely independent Basques were not impressed. It was a mistake that he repeated in Barcelona, where he announced to the Catalans that he was Spanish with a mother from Malaga and a father from Madrid. However, the Catalans are so proud of their heritage, they simply did not want to hear this.

After Bilbao there was a brief trip to Amsterdam, where the Big Town Playboys supported Jeff Beck at the Paradiso as a prelude to a week-long tour later in July. They played the *Falmouth Festival*, famous for its tall ships, before flying to Sharm el-Sheikh in Egypt for the opening of a new Hard Rock Café, which was thankfully air conditioned. They then travelled to Germany for six more dates with Jeff Beck, for which Darrel Higham returned on guitar. The audiences were avid Beck fans, but they appreciated what the BTPs were doing, and the shows went down very well. There were more festivals in Norway and Denmark and an open-air gig in Sheffield city centre with Andy Fairweather-Low, after which Mike decided to take a break.

Mike often made the time twice a year to visit his parents, who were now settled into their new home in the Sierra de Gredos mountains, an hour west of Madrid, though on this occasion he flew back to London to play a duo with Ian Jennings at the Royal College of Art in South Kensington. This was for the launch of best-selling horror

in Berlin. Frank Mead had always been a powerful musician, and though his tenor saxophone playing could be described as 'angry', his original influences were based more on the modern alto sax players such as David Sanborn, rather than the vintage styles of Maxwell Davis, Lee Allen or Big Jay McNeely. Frank made up for this by being a great stage performer, and Andy was always happy to provide his views about how to improve the arrangement of a particular song, putting a smoother touch to parts of the set. Rehearsals were used to refine the sound and style, but once they were on tour it was more difficult to fix, and frustrations could boil over. There were nights when Frank's saxophone playing was too loud and impatient, and Andy gently reminded him of the arrangements that they had agreed earlier.

That night in Berlin, Frank was once again prompted about his playing, but this time he was exasperated and stomped about childishly. Mike had never been one to tolerate embarrassing egos from anyone onstage, and by the time the band reached the end of their set, he had already decided what must be done. As they waved to the audience and headed back stage, he calmly but clearly explained to Frank just how upset he had made him and why. Mike then told Frank that he was no longer in the band, before they returned to the show for the encores. Fortunately, Al Nicholls was available to replace Frank, and suddenly the Big Town Playboys were one big happy family again. The tour continued on to Denmark and Sweden, where they did a television appearance, and finally to Norway.

Promoter Mike Hamblett opened the Robin 2 in Bilston, and as the Big Town Playboys had played many times at the original Robin Hood in Merry Hill, it was fitting that they played the new venue. There followed a whistle-stop tour of the Netherlands, Belgium and a blues festival in Germany, and Mike continued to fit in plenty of solo gigs in and amongst.

In late May 1999, Paul Jones presented the *Glasgow Rhythm & Blues Festival* for BBC Radio 2, which included a live performance by the Big Town Playboys. On this occasion, the line-up featured both Andy Silvester and Andy Fairweather-Low, and they were a huge success, playing several numbers live from the Renfrew Ferry bar in the heart of the city. The BTPs once again played the *Bishopstock Blues Festival*, with Mick Fleetwood as their special guest. The following weekend, Mick came down to Kidderminster, together with a film crew, to discuss a project with Mike, Ian and Andy Silvester. The proposal was a large-scale television and Internet show, but it never came to fruition. In hindsight, it was probably ahead of its time, and Mick returned to London with the idea on hold.

Meanwhile, tensions with manager Trevor Long were continuing to rise, as the band were not happy with the way things were going. However, Long was an imposing figure, and when he spoke people tended to listen. Ian defended him, arguing that he was good with contracts, but dissent was burning within Mike. The Big Town Playboys continued to perform throughout June 1999, but by July Mike had finally had enough and decided it was time to leave the band.

They were playing on the MV *Savarona*, the world's largest non-Royal yacht, at an event organised by Hugh Phillimore in honour of fashion designer Tommy Hilfiger. The Temptations and the Supremes were also on the bill, and the guest list included Sylvester Stallone and Mick Jagger. After the gig had finished and the band were taken back to their hotel, Trevor ended up in a ditch, very drunk and unable to walk unaided – as Mike recalls he quite often was at the end of shows.

Mike looked at the finances and could see that they were not really making any money. When the phone did not ring, they earned nothing and when they did play, they saw very little.

Mike told Ian that he had no intention of staying within Trevor's reach. Ian continued to support the manager, which frustrated him even more. He felt that he was losing control. He was the red-suited frontman that everyone wanted to see, yet the band was being managed by someone he could not trust. Mike did not have any tangible disagreements with Ian, but he thought that they were heading in different directions. There was a genuine love and respect for his schoolmate, but their involvement in the band was tearing them apart. Ian had become the level-headed businessman, whereas Mike was the dedicated entertainer who made a point of washing all of his stage clothes after every gig. For Mike, the prospect of a solo career was not such a bad thing. At least he would regain control of his musical direction, as well as his freedom.

The summer of 1999 continued with an increase in solo gigs as Mike grew apart from the band. At the start of September, he played the George Hotel in Lower Brailes, a village pub in Warwickshire. The local promoter was Tim Porter, who became a close friend. Tim had played blues harmonica in various bands on the local pub circuit and drifted into promotion almost accidentally. It started when he was asked to run a festival at the George, following which he organised regular music events at local pubs. He then moved on to the *Banbury Blues Festival*, the *Gloucester Rhythm & Blues Festival*, *Shipston Proms*, and his latest venture, *Blues at Broom Hill*.

He explains how he came to book Mike: 'I'd seen the Big Town Playboys a few times and was impressed with their authentic style, and particularly Mike's presentation and playing. When I was looking for new acts to introduce to the area, a friend of mine, drummer Chas Chaplin, recommended Mike Sanchez, as he knew him through his association with Steve Walwyn. I went to a duo gig he was doing with Steve in Leamington Spa and was introduced to Mike. I was impressed by his charismatic showmanship and his knowledge of the history of boogie-woogie and rhythm & blues. I booked him for a solo gig at the George, and I realised the power he could command over a crowd with mixed musical tastes. We then progressed to band gigs, and I built up a big audience for him. It wasn't long before he was doing quite a lot of work for me at various events both in south Warwickshire and in Gloucester. I booked his four-piece and bigger outfits, with the great horn players he attracts, and of course Imelda May. Mike also met Sarah, now his wife, at one of my shows.'

There were still plenty of BTPs performances, including the *Silk Ball* in Clerkenwell for the NSPCC, the *Beersel Blues Rock Festival* in Belgium and the *Darlington Rhythm & Blues Festival*. They also played at the 60th birthday party of old friend Geoff Goodwin, brother of Tony, whom Mike had first met so many years previously in Huw Benjamin's living room. Geoff was a trombone player, and his own band played the first set, before he joined in to jam with the BTPs.

In late September and early October there was a brief spell in Norway, but back at home Mike was making plans. He was at the pre-production stage for his second solo album, *Just Can't Afford It*, having borrowed a double bass from Andy Silvester. By mid-November, he had recorded all of the tracks at Sonica Studios in Brixton, helped by long-time friend Rowdy Yeats. Rowdy, who also did the cover notes, recalls just how much of a solo effort it was: 'He recorded the basic rhythm & blues tracks and played all of the instruments himself – except for the drums, where he used Mark Morgan. The guitar, piano, bass and vocals were all his. I made a few suggestions, but it was all his own work. There was even a Spanish track on the album, which was controversial, but it was what he wanted to do.'

Mike did a photo shoot with Gordon Ayres and got the cover design completed by Chris Wroe. It was ready to go, but with very little money and a great deal of uncertainty ahead the release was delayed until the following year. Mike is now a little embarrassed by some of the tracks, but it was a brave attempt to create a genuine Mike Sanchez album.

There were many solo spots in the run-up to Christmas 1999, as well as an appearance at Chris Wroe's 50th birthday party. Finally, on Saturday, 18 December, Mike played his last gig with the Big Town Playboys at the Robin Hood in Merry Hill. Despite the historic nature of the gig, it was not a particularly emotional occasion, but word had got around that Mike Sanchez was leaving the band. Fans turned up from as far away as London to pay their respects and to see the last of the BTPs in their current form. The band continued after his departure, though several ex-members, including Tony Coni, thought that this was wrong. For Mike, there was the prospect of a new album and a solo career to see in the new millennium. He says the emotions he felt on leaving the BTPs were similar to the relief he experienced when Anette Rødal moved out.

CHAPTER 8

Going Solo

Mike was committed to making a success of his solo career, but he also put together his own band which included a lot of his favourite Playboys.

2000

The split with the Big Town Playboys was final, but it was not the end of Mike's involvement with many of the musicians. Ian Jennings continued with the band, as did Lee Badau. Several other members of the BTPs privately agreed that it was time for Mike to move on, and they also told him that they wanted to come along too.

His brother, Juanjo, knows that Mike must have been pushed too far: 'It does take an awful lot of needling and pushing to get him in a stroppy mood. He has always been willing to accommodate other people's views, and he would much rather have a reasonable conversation than get into an argument. I think there must have been a level of rivalry within the group with other people thinking that he was getting too much attention – but he was the frontman!'

Mike now had full control over his own destiny, and Nick Lunt could see the change: 'In the earlier days, he got involved with managers that split the band. He was much happier doing his own thing and not being railroaded by these characters. When it became Mike's band, the band were happy to do it. They knew that they were Mike's band and that's what they wanted too. The vibe was much better.'

Andy Fairweather-Low agrees: 'People were just as happy with Mike on his own as with the rest of the band. He is the driver, and everyone else just gets on the road with him. He has that natural talent. It's like me and Eric Clapton on guitar. We play the same instrument, but it sounds so different. There is no comparison, and that's true with Mike. Like John McEnroe at tennis or David Beckham at football, Mike has that on piano.'

Trevor Long continued to promote the Big Town Playboys, but often failed to tell venues that Mike Sanchez was no longer in the band. As a result, Mike had numerous conversations with disappointed punters over the next few years, having to explain that it was not really his fault.

Mark Morgan continued with the BTPs, but he also played with Mike: 'I tried to do the right thing with Ian as well as Mike. They had both been my mentors, as the Playboys had been my first professional job as a musician. I missed the early togetherness of touring with the Big Town Playboys, but I knew Mike had his reasons for leaving and I couldn't really blame him. He wanted to make his own decisions. I would have liked the Playboys to go on for another five years or more, but there was trouble with the politics and ever-changing guitarists. Personally, I would have loved to just work with Mike. After the split, we started to play under Mike's name, and it was good to have Andy Silvester back again.'

Despite all of the big names, the prestigious gigs and the CDs, Mike never managed to make much money during his time with the BTPs. January 2000 continued in the same vein as previous years, but now he was on his own. He finally released *Just Can't Afford It*, so he had a product to sell and a new hunger to perform, but he was not about to sit around and wait for things to happen. He had always feared earning more money for record executives after he was dead, than for himself while he was still alive, and now he was absolutely free from that prospect. He could concentrate on pleasing no one but his public and himself.

Although Mike was still a relative novice when it came to computers and the Internet, his assistant, Lynne Phillips, helped him out: 'He decided that he needed to learn how to use a PC and run his website for himself, and I already ran some evening classes on the subject, so I invited him along. I helped him out with a few other things, and then got him a more modern computer. He was going on tour and needed a laptop, so I went to a local dealer in Stourbridge and got him a brand new Toshiba. I couldn't really go to Currys, as I had a credit card with the name "Mike Sanchez" on it. The local dealer didn't mind.'

Mike also found that solo gigs were much easier to arrange all round. For a start, there was only himself and his equipment to worry about. Will Wakefield had moved on to other jobs and was often in the wrong part of the country to help out, so Mike regularly used Tim St John, a mate of Will's and a good, reliable driver. More often, however, it was just himself. He still kept in touch with Rowdy Yeats, and as Rowdy lived just down the road, he was an obvious choice for refining liner notes and other pieces of text.

Then there was the money. While larger venues that hired bands had to pay for a music licence from the Performing Rights Society, smaller ones who engaged solo performers did not. By going solo, Mike was able to open up a whole new market for himself. He may not have earned as much on his own, but equally there was no one that he had to split the cash with.

It was such a liberating feeling. If he spent his money badly, he had only himself to blame, and if he wanted to record something, he would simply go ahead and do it. There was no debate, no diaries to check, and the freedom felt wonderful.

Although he had a reasonably full schedule, Mike still found time to spend a week with his parents in Spain, as well as taking a break with his old friend Tormod Bugge in Molde. It was such a refreshing change to not have to arrange these little breaks around four or five other people, and he felt enthralled by the opportunities.

Mike had never been really happy with the quality of the recording on *Just Can't Afford It*, so he started to plan another solo album, *Blue Boy*. He also talked to Chris and Jenny Wroe about the possibility of recording some of his live shows. With a CD on the way as well, it started to turn into a busy time.

James Steel had become a good friend over the past few years, and he still ran his pub, James, with his wife in Mike's old hometown of Bewdley. James wanted to sing and play the double bass, and he often asked for advice from Mike, who still performed there. They spent many fun nights just hanging out, playing duos to cramped audiences of friends. It was one of the first times that Mike was able to feel normal in and around pubs, as, since he had been old enough to drink, most of his time in bars had been spent setting up, rehearsing and performing. He was finally getting a social life that did not involve putting on a show and driving home late at night.

He could choose where and when he played, and he chose lots of local venues in Kidderminster and around the West Midlands. One of these was the Railway Bell at the end of February 2000, just six doors down from his home. An exception to the local gigs was the Hereford Sub Aqua Club, where, for the first time since going solo, he put together a four-piece band.

Five weeks later, Mike embarked on another holiday, this time spending two weeks with his father's sister in Seattle. Auntie Angela had separated from her husband, but not before they had produced Marcus, Mike's cousin. Angela had then met her second husband, Steve, and they settled in Seattle, where they ran a jewellery shop. Mike's mum and dad had visited Angela, Steve and Marcus prior to their retirement in Spain, and they loved being shown the sights of Kitsap County, Washington, as well as a trip to Las Vegas that Angela had arranged. Mike's mother always had her video recorder by her side, and she showed Mike the hours of footage that she had taken on this trip. It was the only time that his parents ever ventured to the US, and they were so happy for the incredible experience. Mike decided that he wanted to see what all the fuss was about, and he was not disappointed. Angela and Steve had a wooden home by the water in Port Orchard, a small city to the west of Seattle. Every day, they travelled on two ferries to reach the port close to Seattle, and the contrast was marked.

Mike thought that Port Orchard was a beautiful place to live, but what he saw of Seattle made him want to leave as quickly as possible. He frequently came across heroin addicts and homeless people, and he did not feel safe walking around the streets. On one occasion, he heard a pumping bass coming from the subwoofers of a car several blocks away. As the car came into view, he saw that it was a stunning early 1960s vintage model with a gang of black guys inside. He remarked to his aunt about the merits of the car, but she told him to look away before he got himself shot.

However, there was one bright spot. Angela and Steve arranged for Mike to do an open-air solo concert in the middle of downtown Seattle. They even had a huge banner made displaying the legend *'Seattle welcomes the fabulous Mike Sanchez'*, which the local authority permitted them to display above the monument where Mike was to play. He picked up a digital piano and a sound system from a musical equipment rental company, and he was ready to go.

Mike has always considered that it was a brave thing for his aunt to do, but together with Steve they pulled it off. It was a lot of fun for Mike, as dozens of families, shoppers and business people on their lunch break gathered around the stage and enjoyed the English man in a bright-red suit performing blues, boogie-woogie and rock'n'roll beneath the hot afternoon sun. Some had a little knowledge of the music he played, whilst others had a sense of disbelief that he could have remained hidden from them for so long. Eventually, Mike's time in Seattle ended and he headed back to the UK and more shows.

April's prestigious *Burnley National Blues Festival* was followed by a week in Norway, where he played with Bergen-based blues band Good Time Charlie. On the final night of the *Bergen Blues Festival*, at Rick's Club, Mike met a girl named Iren Hjønnevåg. There was an instant rapport, but this was the end of the tour, so any thought of a liaison had to be put on hold.

May 2000 boasted a wonderful variety of gigs that summed up Mike's new lease of life. He played the Jazz & Roots Club at the Buttermarket, Shrewsbury with his four-piece band, followed by a solo engagement at an Indian restaurant in Leamington Spa. The 7th *Alexis Korner Memorial Concert* was again held at Buxton Opera House, and this time the bill included Paul Young. Mike then headed north to play a piano-bar-style nightclub in Manchester called the Living Room. This was noted for having a VIP area for local football and music stars, but Mike recalls that when he played there it was full of drunken, half-naked Mancunians – and he was booked in for two nights! The month ended with a wedding for rock'n'roll fans Rusty and Ali Rookes, at which he performed several songs in the church and several more on a barge, before finishing off at a rather grand hotel.

At the Little Civic in Wolverhampton, bass player Al Gare and his wife, Saffron, came along to see the show. Mike had contacted Al about joining up with him and considered that they had a lot in common. Mike had spent fifteen years with the Big Town Playboys, and Al had been with King Pleasure & The Biscuit Boys for a similar period. Al was younger than Mike, but he had a vintage outlook and was a celebrity waiting to happen. He resembled a character out of a 1950s *Tom & Jerry* cartoon, and he had the sharp and enthusiastic wit of a classic music hall comedian. Above all, he was a great bass player, and Mike was thrilled when he joined his fledgling band.

Mike's brief encounter with Iren Hjønnevåg in Bergen took an unexpected turn when she wrote him a letter. She had found his contact details on the *Just Can't Afford It* album, although it was just a PO Box. Mike was impressed that she had taken the opportunity to review virtually the entire album in very good English. He was intrigued, and responded with a handwritten reply asking for a photo, in the hope that this 'Iren' was the same girl that he had spoken to after the show at Rick's in Bergen almost two months earlier. Her picture arrived, showing her sitting on a Harley Sportster motorbike, and Mike was instantly hooked. The relationship started slowly, with letters and messages exchanged by email, but that in itself brought excitement.

By June it was time for another break, and he combined another trip to Molde with a few shows in nearby towns. Mike once again visited Tormod Bugge and took in the breathtaking scenery of what to him was one of the most beautiful places on earth.

His return to the UK saw a gig at the Sands in East Finchley, a club run by rockabilly singer Paul Ansell. Mike had been a fan of Paul since his days with the Blue Rhythm Boys, and he still took pleasure in hanging out with musicians whom he had admired and respected for so many years. In Paul's case, the feeling was mutual: 'I'm a big Amos Milburn fan, and I'd never heard anyone doing it as well as Mike Sanchez did. For an English band to get the nuances of that American sound really blew me away.'

It was now time to get serious with his latest album, and Mike started to book recording time and suitable musicians. Michael Wigfall was the sound engineer, and Mike's old friend Rowdy Yeats once again helped with the production. Logistically, it proved to be a lot more relaxed without the constraints of the band, as get-togethers and ideas sessions tended to be impromptu affairs, rather than having to be squeezed in when time permitted between Big Town Playboys gigs.

In the middle of June 2000, Mike put together a four-piece band for a free concert at Shipston-on-Stour. He was particularly pleased to have Anders Janes on bass, as Anders had become a good friend during their time in the Big Six project. However, this event also turned out to have a much greater significance, for in the audience was Sarah Wynne. The show was on an open-air stage in the market square, and Sarah watched from a second-floor flat which overlooked it. She recalls that this was the first time that she ever saw Mike, although on this occasion he did not see her: 'He jumped off the stage and started pretending to look up girls' skirts. I was very young – too young to get drunk – so I stayed far away.'

After a private event in Paris and a festival in Brussels, it was time for another holiday, so Mike and his current girlfriend, Nadine Edwards, took off to Fuerteventura.

The first steps on the road towards *Blue Boy* were taken at Sweet Georgia Brown's studios in Islington, where Mike bumped into old friend Paul Ansell, who happened to be recording there at the same time. Paul later joined the BTPs, but ran into the same kind of problems that Mike was all too familiar with: 'I played with them for about a year, and it was the most unpleasant experience of my life. I almost left a number of times, and it was all down to Trevor Long.'

As July wore on, Mike headed for Molde again to play the jazz festival there. On this occasion, he performed solo, sharing the bill with American neo-swing band Big Bad Voodoo Daddy at the Alexandra Hotel. The following afternoon he played another solo set, this time on a concert grand piano on the huge open-air stage under the hot summer sun. Legendary jazz keyboard player and composer Chick Corea was amused and intrigued by Mike and his rather basic music, but as usual the crowd loved it.

Holidays were becoming more of a priority for Mike, and less than three weeks after returning from Fuerteventura, he went to Spain to spend two weeks with his parents.

Back at home, his long-time assistant, Lynne Phillips, had a bad accident and almost lost her leg. She had finally introduced Mike to cyberspace, and she recalls that he used it to stay in touch: 'He emailed me every day, telling me that it should not have happened to me. We had become really good friends, and he is such a sincere person. People were quite in awe that I knew Mike Sanchez, but I just thought, *You've not seen him in his T-shirt and track pants*. He is a lovely guy and a different person at home.'

Nadine had gone through a series of jobs, including working at a chemist's in Droitwich and as a rep for a car company. Mike would often get home from a gig as she was going off to work, and he found himself noticing other girls whilst she was out. He realised that he was not really being fair to her, and so he brought their relationship to an end in July 2000.

In August, guitarist Ian Hatton from rock band Bonham was getting married to Katrina Chester, and they asked Mike to play at their wedding in the Mill Hotel, Alveley. Katrina's father was Gary Chester, the legendary American session drummer who played on many soul and pop hits from the 1960s and 1970s. The event was a nostalgic one for Mike, as not only did he renew his acquaintance with Robert Plant and his family, the venue was actually the same hotel that his dad had worked at for many years before he retired in the early 1990s.

Mike now had his own set of regular shows and regular clients. He flew off to Malaga for a solo gig at the Sotogrande estate of banker and rock'n'roll fan Olaf Rogge. At the *Coventry Jazz Festival*, he shared the bill with Al Nicholls' swing outfit, Blue Harlem. This was followed by the *Great British R&B Festival* in Colne and more sessions at Sweet Georgia Brown's.

September saw another trip to Norway to play with Good Time Charlie again. Mike also performed on the scary-sounding *Hell Station Blues Cruise*, which was actually just getting on a boat and playing whilst everyone else on board drank to excess, before returning home to a hectic time in the UK.

He was still working on *Blue Boy*, and then got involved with another Mick Fleetwood project. This one was to mark the launch of Mick's new Internet auction site, **FleetwoodOwen.com**, and also involved Mick on drums, Andy Silvester on guitar and Anders Janes on bass. Rehearsals were followed by a show at Harrods, with the prospect of an auction of Beatles memorabilia a few weeks later. Anders was delighted to be involved: 'It was a very memorable occasion when Mike asked me to be in a band with Mick Fleetwood. It was a real thrill to play with Mike and Mick.'

In October 2000, Mike guested with Billy Bowel & The Movements, featuring Andy Silvester, Robbie Blunt, Johnny Bryant and Ian Hatton, before a one-off gig with the Big Six. More recording time ensured that *Blue Boy* remained on schedule, after which Mike played another solo gig for Tim Porter at the George Hotel in Lower Brailes.

This was the night before he headed off to London for the memorabilia auction in the Hard Rock Café on Piccadilly, and as Tim recalls, the solo gig was not exactly the best preparation for it: 'He did the show for me in order to shorten his journey from Kidderminster, as Brailes is about an hour nearer to London, and he booked a room at the George to ensure he could get there early the next day. After the gig, we cleared the gear away and had a nightcap, and as Mike was heading for his room he suddenly realised he didn't have an alarm clock. He had to be in London early for the soundcheck, so the landlady produced an absolutely massive Bart Simpson children's clock – apparently the only available timepiece with an alarm. The clock failed to go off, and Mike woke up late. He hurtled off to London, concerned that he was going to miss this auspicious occasion. As it turned out, the soundcheck had been delayed, and all was well.'

The evening of the auction began with a procession of bikers on Harleys and choppers outside the Café. The centrepiece was the upright piano that John Lennon used for 'Imagine', and Mick had only asked Mike the night before if he would play the song on it during the auction. This was real pressure, as Mike had to quickly find the correct chords, fingering and lyrics for this iconic moment. The Hard Rock Café was filled with dozens of potential bidders with open laptops and cameras, and it was a nerve-wracking event. They were not there to see Mike perform, and that seemed to add to the pressure. Once the auction was finished, it was business as usual and Mike and the band played a good, rocking set into the early hours.

The auction was typical of the events that Mick Fleetwood got Mike involved in. They had a mutual love and respect, though Mike often found that, when Mick got a project in his head and started to focus on it, the whole scenario could be quite intimidating. However, he rarely said 'No'.

At the end of October 2000, Mike travelled to Hanover to meet up with Gabi Schwanke. Gabi had been very helpful and became a good friend through their involvement with Steve Walwyn and Dr Feelgood. She had also created websites firstly for the BTPs, and more recently for Mike himself. It gave him the opportunity to take a break from the UK for a few days and spend time with a like-minded soul. It was a confirmation of the freedom that he now had, as he did not need to ask for anyone's permission to disappear.

His return from Germany saw several line-ups put together, both four- and six-piece outfits, and, without the democracy that was prevalent within the BTPs, he had full control of just who was in each one. Anders Janes remembers a duo that he played with Mike at the Jam House, a restaurant in Birmingham: 'It was a little bit odd to play in a middle-of-the-road restaurant, especially as Mike was a fairly big name. It was unusually low-key, and when we got there, it was very, very empty. There were no Mike Sanchez fans, just regular people who were out having a drink and a meal. No one was particularly interested in us. Mike started playing, which was always great fun, and he was putting on a show as ever. In front of us was a small dance floor surrounded by tables and chairs. Only one table was occupied, and that was by a group of young ladies. They didn't look in our direction. Mike was getting a bit fed up, so he started having a bit of fun. He started playing guitar on one song, starting on his feet, then getting on his knees and finally on his back. He crawled across to the girls, almost getting under their table whilst still playing, and then he wriggled back again. They didn't even bat an eyelid!'

As the winter took hold, Mike's budding relationship with Iren became something more tangible as they moved on to telephone calls, and for the first time they could hear each other's voices. Mike wanted more, but it would be another couple of months before he finally got to meet up with her again in person.

The regular Gary Brooker event at Chiddingfold took place in November 2000, although this time there was an exciting addition. Gary and his wife, Franky, usually came backstage at the charity events, and this time Gary had news. Gary had been fronting Bill Wyman's Rhythm Kings alongside Georgie Fame, Albert Lee and Beverley Skeete for a number of years, but he had been offered some substantial tours with his old band, Procol Harum, and this eventually led to a clash of dates. Therefore, Gary needed to find a replacement for his seat in Bill's band.

He suggested that Mike would be the man to sit in for him on the Rhythm Kings' tour, starting in May, but it was not just Gary's decision, as Bill Wyman explains: 'Me and Terry [Taylor] thought that Mike would be suitable for the Rhythm Kings, to take over from Gary. Gary recommended him, but we had already made up our minds. He ended up staying with us for three and half years, and it worked really well.'

Mike was both excited and stunned at the prospect of playing with Bill Wyman and his cast of all-star musicians. He had no idea what it meant in the short term, or what would happen when Gary Brooker came back. He had been an admirer of Bill and Albert Lee for many years. Would he now really get the chance to play alongside them? A sleepless night followed as he thought about the possibilities, but for now there was work to be done closer to home.

The finishing touches to *Blue Boy* were done before the end of November, and in December Mike made his first return to the 100 Club since the split with the BTPs. This was with his six-piece outfit, and they stayed together to play a private event arranged by Hugh Phillimore. The impresario had always been a big fan of the Big Town Playboys, arranging a number of bookings for them, and he remained a fan of Mike's.

The year ended on a high for Mike, with a tour of many of his favourite venues in Norway, together with the news that he had been given the 'UK Keyboard Player of The Year' Award by *Blues in Britain* magazine – a title he was to hold for four consecutive years. It was something of a surprise to him, as he had always considered himself to be a singer who played piano, rather than a keyboard player per se.

2001

Blue Boy was almost ready for release, and in January 2001 there were two photo sessions and more visits to the studio. At last everything seemed to be complete, and Mike rewarded himself with another week-long break to see his parents in Spain. The following month he was in the air again, heading to Greece for four dates. This was a brief tour arranged by promoter John Angelatos, during which Mike was reunited with bassist Anders Janes.

In February 2001, Mike headed for Norway with two intentions. The first was to play at Tormod Bugge's 40th birthday party, and the second was to spend some more time with the lovely Iren. The party went well, as did his trip to Bergen, where he and Iren really got to know each other. Tormod had a friend in Bergen, and she helped Mike to get a solo show at the Radisson Blu hotel bar, which presented live blues and rock music. All that Mike required was free accommodation at the hotel for a few days. Iren acted as a tour guide and showed him all of the sights of her beautiful city, and they became very close companions.

Mike returned to the UK, but there was very little time for anything before he flew out to Belgium, where he played a number of solo gigs around the country. Towards the end of March, he finally got to spend some time at home, which coincided with the completion of the artwork for the cover of *Blue Boy*. There was no accompanying publicity when the album was released, but such was the quality of it that word of mouth ensured good sales. It was also played regularly by deejays at rockabilly weekenders.

Mike is justifiably proud of *Blue Boy*, and it's also one of Mark Morgan's favourites: 'It was really fun to do with Andy Silvester on guitar. It felt like a family creating music together, rather than people coming in just to do their part.'

Mike also had a dream, which was to imitate the 1950s rhythm & blues caravans of Johnny Otis and Alan Freed, with himself leading the show and introducing a succession of special guests. It would be his very own rock'n'roll revue, encompassing rockabilly, blues, ballads, boogie, jumpin', honking, dancing and harmonising. Towards the end of March 2001, he started to bring this dream a step closer to reality.

Michael Wigfall, who played bass with Darrel Higham & The

Enforcers, suggested that he should consider asking Darrel's wife, Imelda Clabby, to join the band. Imelda had enjoyed success on the Irish rock'n'roll circuit before moving to London in 1998, where she was soon singing with Al Nicholls' band, Blue Harlem. It was an obvious choice. She was such a dynamic performer and very confident onstage. She was physically alluring, with luscious brunette locks and stunning good looks, and she used this sassy sex appeal to her advantage. Her vocal performance had been perfected over a number of years, and she attacked each song with gusto. She first appeared as a guest singer with Mike at the 100 Club, and the following day they went into Backstreet Studios for a full rehearsal.

They were joined by London-based doo-wop trio the Extraordinaires, whom Mike had first seen in the 1980s. They were visually stunning and unique outside the US, and from the first rehearsal it was obvious that Mike had something exciting to take on tour. Imelda was everything that he had expected. She had an aura about her, coupled with a wonderful and consistent voice. The ensemble had energy, variety and chemistry in abundance, backed up by an exceptionally talented group of performers. Dave Priseman was a trumpeter who had played with Blue Harlem at the same time that Imelda began to emerge. He often joined Al Nicholls on tenor sax and Pete Cook on baritone, and they were collectively known as the Harlem Horns. Then there was Mark Morgan on drums, Andy Silvester on guitar and Al Gare on double bass. Mike Sanchez & His Band were now billed as 'The Mike Sanchez Rhythm & Blues Revue'.

After another brief trip back to Norway for a couple of shows and some more quality time with Iren, it was back to an old haunt to try out some of their new sounds. Imelda and the Extraordinaires both featured at the Robin, and with this rehearsal out of the way they were ready for the *Burnley National Blues Festival* in April.

Nobody had seen anything quite like the Mike Sanchez Rhythm & Blues Revue, as Mike introduced his special guests Imelda Clabby, Paul Ansell and the Extraordinaires, and the show received rave reviews. Mike was quite nervous about the whole evening in case anything went disastrously wrong, as the introductions between the acts were unrehearsed, but it all went remarkably well. Even long-time fans like Brian Smith were impressed: 'I have seen Mike in various incarnations, with his four-piece, six-piece and, of course, solo, but the Revue was him at his absolute peak. He did the whole night at his own pace, and it was just marvellous to watch. The show proved that he is one of *the* great British performers, and he has in no way been suitably credited for it.'

The event was also filmed by Chris Wroe, who had already shot some footage of Mike at other gigs: 'I got a few bits at a solo in the George in Brailes. I got a grant, so gradually acquired more equipment, and by the time we got to Burnley there was proper sound and three or four cameras. We were continuously improving, and when it came to the finale, "Ramblin' Boogie", we were upping our game and getting really good results. The best footage is from the 100 Club. It's a bit rough and ready, but it epitomises what the gigs were like. Mike was such a natural. When you put a camera on him, he looked straight down the lens at you. It felt like he was just singing directly to you. I put all of the parts together for the *Red Hot...Live!* video, which Mike mainly sold at his shows, but we also shifted a few on Amazon.'

CHAPTER 9

Rhythm King

Mike initially joined and ultimately fronted Bill Wyman's Rhythm Kings, whilst still producing solo material and touring with his own band.

2001

The dream of the Rhythm & Blues Revue was gaining credibility, but Mike had another commitment that was about to get in the way. Towards the end of April 2001, he received a call from tour manager Tony Panico, confirming that he would be filling in for Gary Brooker on the forthcoming Bill Wyman's Rhythm Kings tour. It was only going to be for three weeks, and he arrived at the Nomis Studios in Olympia where he was met by Bill, Albert Lee, Beverley Skeete and former Big Town Playboy Frank Mead.

Albert had heard the name Mike Sanchez through his friend Frank Mead, and he knew of the Big Town Playboys, but he did not know what to expect at that first meeting: 'He was this larger-than-life character and instantly likeable. I didn't realise how good he was until we started playing together. I just love it when people appreciate all of the nuances of what they are trying to play. Really he didn't need a rhythm section. If ever there was such a thing as a one-man band, it was him. He was such a natural performer.'

It was also the first time that Mike had seen Frank Mead since his sacking from the BTPs, but there were no hard feelings. They both realised that they would be performing and living together for several weeks, so they had a laugh and a hug, and from that moment on they got on really well. After four days of rehearsals they were ready to go, but there was still just over a week until the tour was due to start.

Iren flew over from Bergen for a brief visit, during which the

Mike Sanchez Rhythm & Blues Revue got together again at the Guildhall Arts Centre, Gloucester. It was another good performance, but for Mike the anticipation of the Rhythm Kings tour overshadowed any plaudits that came their way.

After travelling to Denmark on 10 May 2001, Mike watched the Rhythm Kings perform in Copenhagen before Gary Brooker left to join Procol Harum. Mike took over at the next show two nights later in Hamburg, and despite his nerves he received congratulations from the rest of the band, recognising his contribution. They continued the tour with dates in Italy, Croatia and Austria. In Zagreb, the show was filmed and distributed around the world, and Mike was pleased to hear from fans from as far away as Russia who had seen him perform.

It was a brief but exciting journey across Europe, and there were many more dates lined up for their return to the UK. There were grand old venues such as Aberdeen Music Hall, the Theatre Royal in Bath and Sheffield City Hall, as well as more modern arenas like St David's Hall in Cardiff and the Bridgewater Hall in Manchester. It was a different world to running his own band, and even to the Big Town Playboys. There were as many as twelve band members, several roadies, a tour manager, two buses and a great variety of venues. Mike felt that he would have to be on his best behaviour, and he also found there was very little time to relax. They would check in at a hotel, travel to the gig for a soundcheck, play to a full house and then get back to the hotel. The next morning, they would be on the road again, heading for the next town. He had to juggle his time at the microphone with Georgie Fame, and although he sang a larger percentage of the songs than the rest of the vocalists, he had a familiar feeling of not really being in control of this huge production.

Guitarist Albert Lee noticed the difference with Mike in the band: 'I was so fortunate to be on the same side of the stage as him. It was the perfect place for me, as we had the nucleus of the band on our side: we were the engine room. Offstage, he was so easy to get along with. We would be on the tour bus listening to music and swapping songs, and he introduced me to a lot of stuff that I had never heard of. He had such great knowledge of that kind of music.'

In early July, the Rhythm Kings flew to Switzerland, whilst Mike took a short but lucrative detour to Germany. He got permission from Bill's office to play the *Gaildorf Festival* with Swedish outfit Knock-Out Greg & Blue Weather, as long as he was back in time for the soundcheck at the *Montreux Jazz Festival* the following day.

Montreux is the second largest jazz festival after Montreal, and brings together musicians from around the world. The 2001 event included a tribute to the stars of Sun Records and featured rockabilly legends Sonny Burgess and Billy Lee Riley. Robert Plant and Jimmy Page also performed at the festival, with Ian Jennings playing double bass on their set. Unfortunately, there was only time for a quick hello before the Rhythm Kings flew back to the UK.

They then departed for Madrid, where Mike played his final gig on this particular Rhythm Kings tour. They were joined onstage by Gary Brooker, who had finished his stint with Procol Harum. It had been an exhausting but exhilarating schedule, and afterwards Mike was confirmed as a longer-term replacement for Gary on future tours – a fact Gary cheekily reminded him of the next time they met.

Bill Wyman subsequently compiled recordings of the Rhythm Kings' live performances in June and July into an 'official bootleg' album, *Travlin' Band*, which was released the following May. Mike plays piano on all but one of the tracks, and provides the lead vocals on 'Chicken Shack Boogie', 'Jitterbug Boogie' and 'Tell You A Secret'.

Mike decided to spend a few days in Spain relaxing with his parents before returning home to get his own band back together again, starting with a rehearsal at Backstreet Studios. They played at the 100 Club, and then it was on to the *Nice Jazz Festival*, where Bill Wyman, B.B. King and Van Morrison were amongst the headline acts. Martin Winning was playing with Van Morrison, and enjoyed meeting up with Mike again: 'I've always had a lot of time for Mike, as he carries a torch for rhythm & blues. I have a lot of respect for the guy. At Nice we shared a bus, and we didn't say much as he really is quite shy, but then up on stage he came alive. On the stage, you get a vibe for how good he is.'

In August, Mike went to Sweden to meet up with Knock-Out Greg & Blue Weather once more. They had previously shared a stage on a few occasions, but this was the first time that they had officially performed together. Anders Lewen recalls that it was a big event for them: 'Greger Andersson contacted Mike through Kjell-Inge Brovoll in Hell, Norway, and some gigs were booked with us as his backing band. We were all very nervous, but we had practised and done our homework, so everyone knew the songs quite well. When we met Mike, I remember thinking that this is a true English gentleman with a dangerous touch! He was very humble and kind, and had a lot of patience with us when we were unsure about some of the song arrangements, but onstage he could look really mean, especially when he did "I'm Mad". He also looked like that whenever a drunk from the audience interrupted the show, and he would start singing the Rivingtons' "Papa-Oom-Mow-Mow", looking like the maddest, baddest guy in *The Sopranos*! I was already into many of the top names in rhythm & blues, but Mike introduced me to so many more. I guess he appreciated how all of the different styles of T-Bone Walker, Willie Johnson and Jimmy Rogers, etc., came together in my playing.

'It was so much fun and so educational for us, and Mike always delivered 100 per cent, even when there were few in the audience. When they didn't pay attention, Mike just worked even harder. The first gig that Mike and Blue Weather did at a restaurant called Akkurat in Stockholm, Sweden, was a legendary one. It was one of those nights where Mike and everybody in the band were just into the music with heart and soul, and the audience were just rockin' with us. We probably played for two and a half hours, but it felt like twenty minutes. We could have gone on all night, but it was Sunday, so they had to shut the place at 1 a.m.. People still talk to me and ask about that gig, it was so special.'

Greger Andersson also remembers that night: 'He put on a real killer show. He was sweating like hell and did all of his tricks. The audience were going crazy. It was a great moment to be able to bring such a great performer to our local club, and all of our friends came out to support us.

'We did not rehearse much. He would send us CDs with tunes he would like to do, and we turned up to shows well prepared. We would just run through the most difficult ones during soundcheck. Mike is always really easy to follow onstage as he starts playing the piano. It's like boarding a train with you just riding along. Sometimes the shows were really wild, with Mike crawling on the floor in front of all of the girls. He never complained about anything like lame sound engineers, shitty loudspeakers, terrible food, rain or snow. He would always put his suit on and put on a great show. One of the most easy-going guys I've ever played with. I remember him telling me about his mother and how she made his suits for him. They were made to go in the washing machine, and he would bring one for each show. At the end, all the suits were so soaked like he'd been swimming in a pool, and he would just put them in a big black plastic bag that he was dragging around. After six days there were six suits in it, and they were all just a mess.'

They played three gigs, with Iren constantly by Mike's side, but then his plans were thrown into disarray. Gary Brooker was still with the Rhythm Kings for a tour of the US, but Georgie Fame was unable to travel to Canada for two shows in Ontario, and so Bill Wyman once again called for Mike. Mike had planned to spend most of the summer with Iren, so when the Rhythm Kings called he arranged for her to accompany him. They had a brief but exciting adventure in the Canadian cities of London and Windsor, taking on the role of tourists and fitting in as much as they could. One of the highlights for Mike was seeing a show where he met two legendary players from the world of blues and boogie: pianist Johnnie Johnson, who played piano with Chuck Berry, and boogie-woogie maestro Bob Seeley from Detroit.

After two transatlantic flights in five days, with sell-out performances in Canada in between, they headed straight for the home of Mike's parents in Spain. They stayed for a week, after which Mike got his Rhythm & Blues Revue back on the road again at the *Great British R&B Festival* in Colne. Mike then travelled to Norway for a couple of shows in Kristiansund, and the next couple of weeks back at home proved to be the last time that he and Iren were together as a couple for a while.

Iren returned to Norway after a whirlwind summer with Mike, and a few days later she called him with the bad news that their relationship was over. It was a devastating blow to Mike – just minutes before he played a solo show at the Water Margin Chinese restaurant in Long Itchington. It was the first time that he had ever been affected badly so close to a gig, but he did his best to get through it, and there were no complaints.

His next engagements were in Norway, and it was a poignant trip coming so close after his split with Iren. He played two shows with Good Time Charlie, and the reserved Norwegians were amazed to hear him pour his heart out over Iren. By late October 2001, Imelda Clabby was becoming a regular as the band's seventh member. This included shows at the Robin Hood in Merry Hill and at Cecil Sharp House in London for promoter and deejay Tim Hardy, who had been a supporter and fan since the early days of Big Town Playboys.

Rowdy Yeats recalls the impact she had both on and off the stage: 'Imelda used to turn up with the band in the dressing room. She would go off to change, and then she would sweep back into the room, smelling divine and looking fantastic. The band would then have to smarten themselves up! She's a gorgeous woman and a very clever performer. When she was in the band, you knew where they were going to go.'

In mid-November Mike contacted Iren once again, and their relationship was rekindled. She missed him as much as he missed her, and they got back together in time for Mike's trip to Sweden to work on a new album. Andy Silvester had poured so many songs onto him in his early years with Big Town Playboys, a lot of which were never played live. Now he had the chance to record them with Knock-Out Greg & Blue Weather, as the Swedes were authentic in both sound and style. They went into the studio to create *Women & Cadillacs*, but with no funding they had to be resourceful. They planned to play a few gigs, and when the money came in, they would book more studio time. It meant that the project would take many months to complete, but that in itself gave them some satisfaction.

They used Real Music Studios in Bromma, Stockholm – a place that was already familiar to the band, who used it regularly for their own recordings. Mike was very impressed with the Swedes, who were perfection itself when their moment came. All that he had to worry about was playing his own part with equal perfection. The album included covers of Wynonie Harris, T-Bone Walker and many more of Mike's favourite artists, but one song in particular caused him a problem, as old friend Dave Clarke recalls: 'The Playboys used to play "Gamblin' Woman", originally by Big Walter Price, but it disappeared from their set. Many years later, Mike wanted to include it on this album, but he couldn't remember the words. He rang me at three o'clock in the morning from the studio in Sweden, as I was the only one he could think of that would know them, so I spent the next few minutes giving him the lyrics down the phone.'

Mike was very pleased with the end result, and he is particularly fond of their version of Percy Mayfield's 'The Voice Within'. The album remains one of the most authentic-sounding records that he has been involved with.

Mike spent several days with his Swedish friends, both in and out of the studio, and Anders Lewen remembers it as a happy time: 'Mike is very easy-going. Although he's one of the top performers in this genre, he's as far as can be from being a prima donna offstage. He always seems to accept the conditions around him: sleet and snow, or sun – he always makes the best of the situation. He can sometimes be a bit lazy. He likes to rest and take it slow, but being such a hard-working entertainer, he can be excused! I loved hanging with Mike and enjoying a good meal, having some beers and chatting about economic crises and the pollution that's going on all over the world. Mike was definitely concerned about the earth's health and how to deal with it!'

Knock-Out Greg And Blue Weather were already accomplished recording artists, and Mike was happy to contribute to their next album, *Telling It Like It Is*, which was released by Last Buzz in 2002. He played piano on 'Something True Became A Lie' and 'Do It If You Wanna' as they made full use of their studio time together.

Back in the UK, Mike still found time to play a few solo gigs, including Chiddingfold, where he opened the evening for King Pleasure & The Biscuit Boys, as well as others with his seven-piece band. Throughout a busy December he alternated between solos and the full band, but he still managed to relax with an unusual Christmas dinner.

Lynne Phillips, who had recently lost her husband, explains what happened: 'I wanted to be on my own, or have minimal company. I needed something to motivate me, so I suggested Christmas dinner. Mike thought it was a good idea, but I didn't think it was appropriate for us to be alone at his house or mine, so I made the dinner with all the trimmings and got a taxi to take it over to him. I did this a few more times, and once when I had visitors for Sunday lunch, I asked Mike if he wanted some. He said "Yes", so I got the visitors to drop it off on their way home. He was sat waiting patiently with a place set and knife and fork in hand!'

2002

The year 2002 promised to be a good one for Mike, with the prospect of two album releases, *Women & Cadillacs* and the Rhythm Kings' latest project, *Just For A Thrill*. After another holiday with his parents in Spain, Mike went into the Snake Ranch Studios in London for a somewhat relaxed session with Bill Wyman. Albert Lee recalls: 'We would just sit around and wait for Bill to tell us what to play. Mike could have done it all by himself: he was that one-man band.'

Mike particularly loved recording the Johnny Watson 1970s funk classic, 'Booty Ooty'. He had played it live several times with the Rhythm Kings, and had a tendency to get a bit too carried away with it. Andy Fairweather-Low loved it, although Beverley Skeete was not too keen on Mike jumping around like he was in a boy band. It even made him muse about what life might have been like if he had tried the funk and pop route, rather than the highway of blues and rock'n'roll, but he never let it distract him for too long!

Mike then flew to Stockholm for three days to do more recording on *Women & Cadillacs*. He returned to three consecutive shows alternating his seven- and four-piece line-ups, and after a couple of solo outings he was back in Stockholm again.

At the end of February 2002, Mike, Andy Silvester, Al Gare and Mark Morgan performed 'Sapphire', 'It'll Be Me' and 'Real Wild Child' in a short movie produced by BBC 1 Wales, *Class of '58*, which portrayed a Saturday night in Pontypridd in 1958. The film involved four bands and around one hundred teenagers, and Mike was particularly pleased with his own appearance, for which he wore his sharp red suit. Sadly, it seems to have been forever consigned to the archives.

In March there was a party for Jenny Wroe in Shropshire, followed by a rather poignant charity event. It was a benefit for the Kemp Hospice, who had looked after his assistant Lynne Phillips' husband in the final weeks of his life. Shortly afterwards, Lynne emigrated from the UK to New Zealand, but she still keeps in touch and will always be grateful to Mike: 'It was a fabulous night. They put on coaches from Kidderminster and the Robin let us have the venue. They put on a great show, and it doesn't matter how big the venue is or how much they are getting paid, they always give their best. We raised over £2,000 for the hospice that night.'

It seemed as though Mike was constantly on the road, but after another spell in Stockholm, he turned the tables on his Swedish friends. As they had never played in the UK before, he arranged a few gigs for Knock-Out Greg & Blue Weather and they drove from Stockholm all the way across Europe to Mike's front door in Kidderminster. They were exhausted, yet raring to go, as they would never have had the opportunity to play in the UK had Mike not encouraged and arranged it.

Greger Andersson remembers that Mike did whatever he could to make them feel at home: 'He was always really easy and laid-back. He is a funny guy, especially when he tries to speak Norwegian all the time. On the small tour of England, he really tried hard to make us feel comfortable whilst we stayed at his house in Kidderminster.'

Mike was becoming a regular at the *Burnley National Blues Festival*, and was pleased to be able to showcase Knock-Out Greg & Blue Weather at this well-established event. They drove together to a couple of shows in Belgium, and generally had a fun time on the road. At home, he hosted a paella party for them and several of his local friends, and with a 1949 Pontiac Chieftain parked outside and a house full of rock'n'roll enthusiasts, it was a memorable occasion.

After taking time out to do interviews for *Blueprint* and *Now Dig This* magazines, it was back on the road again. Having played their final show in Durham, his Swedish friends set off on the long drive back to Stockholm, whilst Mike went home via Cleethorpes, where he played the Blues Of The Month Club. Solo followed seven-piece followed solo, but he was really only filling in the time until his next outing with Bill Wyman.

At the end of April 2002, the Rhythm Kings spent almost a week in the Ritz Cottage Rehearsal Studio, Putney, then set off on a gruelling schedule of 27 shows in 29 days. One gig rolled into another, and all that Mike remembers about them is that, the closer they got to London, the more celebrities would turn up. There were just two days off, and on one of these Mike had to return home for a haircut. Eventually, the tour finished at Cliffs Pavilion in Southend, but there was no rest for Mike. The following night, he squeezed in a solo gig in Worcestershire before disappearing for a well-deserved holiday with Iren.

A very different venture opened up for Mike upon his return, where he found an unusual voice on his answering machine. The broad American accent came from movie soundtrack producer Budd Carr, and Mike still has no idea where he got his direct number from. Carr was well known for his work on *JFK*, *Natural Born Killers*, *Twister* and many other hit movies, and he wanted Mike to take the lead on the music for *I'll Be There*, an off-beat comedy starring Charlotte Church and Craig Ferguson. He was invited to be in charge of a band of hand-picked session musicians, including Jim Richardson on bass, Martin Drew on drums and Alan Darby on guitar. These quality players were put together to record some classic rocking tracks including 'Red Hot', 'Trouble', 'Jungle Rock', 'Ubangi Stomp' and 'Honky Tonk Train Blues'.

The intention was for the music to sound like an ageing Welsh rock'n'roll band to fit in with the plot, and Mike's voice was supposed to sound like a rocking grandfather. It was an interesting project, and Mike's first achievement was to get the recordings switched from the production company's UK offices in Ealing to Sweet Georgia Brown's studios, where he had worked so many times before. He was eventually credited as 'Musical Director', and coupled with his roles as researcher and performer, he was handsomely paid for his time.

There was a brief interlude as Mike took his seven-piece to another Gary Brooker charity event at Cowdray Ruins. Mike Sanchez & His Band opened the show, which was compered by Chris Tarrant. Ringo Starr's All Starr Band were the headliners, mainly performing Beatles' songs, and the bill also included Dave Gilmour, Mike Rutherford, Roger Taylor, Bob Geldof, Donovan, and of course Gary Brooker.

Over the next week, there were more rehearsals and four days at Sweet Georgia Brown's to complete the recordings for *I'll Be There*. In between, Mike somehow found time to play at the Shepherd's Bush Empire with the Rhythm Kings, who were still in the midst of their mammoth tour.

He had one day off at the start of July, then joined Bill and the band once more. The Rhythm Kings had an energetic set, and the vocals were generally shared. This was the case for the next six dates, but then Georgie Fame could not make the Aberystwyth Arts Centre, and so it was down to Mike to carry the load. With his natural exuberance, he easily assumed the mantle of frontman once more.

Mike had now become an integral part of the band, and Bill felt comfortable enough to gently poke fun at him: he would introduce him as the lunatic from Kidderminster who sweats a lot and leaves a trail across the stage like a snail. It was said with a good deal of affection, though when Mike's parents attended the Rhythm Kings' shows in Madrid, his father was protective of his son, urging him to stand up for himself and not let Mr Wyman talk about him like that.

The tour fell foul of the English summer at the *Henley-on-Thames Festival* in mid-July. It was a warm evening, and the huge stage was set up beside the River Thames. As night fell, the mosquitos and other insects started to hover around the stage lights, and then they scented the blood of the performers. Mike and Beverley Skeete were particularly targeted and every time they opened their mouths, the creatures would drop in. The keyboard playing was also affected, as the bugs landed on the keys of the piano and as Mike hit the notes that he had to hit, the insects were squashed, leaving blood everywhere. Despite all of this, Mike has fond memories of the gig. Perhaps the distraction of biting insects made them concentrate even harder on delivering another first-class show.

There was time for one more day at home before the Rhythm Kings set off on a troubled tour of Italy and Sicily. The tour manager,

Tony Panico, had had a few disagreements with the local Italian promoter and it came to a head after a gig in Palermo, Sicily.

Mike had a fascination with movie portrayals of the Sicilian Mafia, and this was in his mind as he heard raised voices backstage at the show, where the mood was dark. Tony was heard to shout, 'Where's our money?', only to be calmed down by representatives of the promoter. The area was populated by a number of well-dressed young men who appeared to be security guards. Strangely, there was also a group of older men sat around a dinner table, talking, and the whole scene looked as though it had been lifted straight out of *The Godfather*.

The rest of the band shared Mike's unease as they were taken to a restaurant next door to the large open-air venue. They sat down on the front patio, and with the road in front of them, Mike's paranoia told him that it looked like the ideal spot for a drive-by shooting. In hindsight, it seems irrational, but at the time his fear was very real. He went into the street to call his mum and dad to tell them that he loved them, and he also called Iren. He was almost shaking and, as he was on the phone, he looked across to the backstage area. It was perhaps a hundred yards away, but he saw two of the well-dressed guards staring in his direction and talking. One of them had a walkie-talkie and might have been communicating with other security staff closer to Mike and the band.

In time, they were ushered back to the venue, and finally it was time to go onstage. The fear temporarily subsided until Mike pictured in his mind just where he was: there were two towers at the top of the open-air auditorium, and if the band had been a target that night, a gunman would have had the opportunity to take them out before disappearing into the night. Mike sang like he'd never sung before. The adrenaline propelled him into one of the most powerful performances of his life.

The negative energy which had existed before the show dissipated and turned into a scene of ritual backslapping and congratulations, but Mike had no desire to go through anything like that again. It later transpired that the Italian sponsors lost a lot of money on the tour, due to a lack of ticket sales. There were also suggestions that Lionel Richie, who was selling out similar venues that same week, had benefitted from better promotion, which also detracted from the Rhythm Kings' audiences. Mike has never returned to Palermo since that night, and quite possibly never will.

The tour moved on to the *San Sebastián Jazz Festival* in northern Spain and another memorable night – this time for all of the right reasons. The festival was a very high-profile event with a huge stage and thousands of expectant music fans. The Rhythm Kings set the tone for the show, and Mike's performance was particularly spectacular as he jumped off the stage and into the crowd mid-song. They were followed by James Brown's legendary horn player, Maceo Parker, and his all-star funk band. The event was filmed and has been broadcast several times, and came as a huge relief after the traumas of Palermo.

Bill Wyman had once again recorded the Rhythm Kings' live performances and compiled a new 'official bootleg', *On The Road Again*, which was released in June 2003. Mike plays piano on all but one of the tracks and sings lead vocals on five of them.

After the last few Rhythm Kings dates in Spain, Mike stayed in the country for a short holiday into early August. It was a time to relax, and after a solo gig in Gloucester Mike and Iren decided to hold their own house party. He opened up his small back garden and cooked a huge paella for more than twenty people, temporarily transforming a small part of Kidderminster into a Spanish restaurant.

Soon after, Mike made another trip to Sweden, this time for a festival and some other shows, and then it was back to the UK and his seven-piece band. At the start of September 2002, he again travelled to Spain to visit his parents, but interrupted his stay for a one-off show with the Rhythm Kings. This was a private event for a Japanese company held at the Natural History Museum, where he had played before. This time, rather than being under the head of the diplodocus, they were told to 'turn right at the bird section and set up there'. Georgie Fame was unable to join the line-up, as he had a residency at Ronnie Scott's, and, although it was also inconvenient for Mike, the band were very well paid for their efforts. The gig itself was a disappointment, as hardly anybody watched them perform.

The Rhythm Kings had taken up a huge chunk of Mike's summer, but he quickly got back into the routine of arranging shows and performing with his own band. There was another event at Chiddingfold, followed by a wedding at Pinewood Studios. As he wandered through the corridors of the studios, Mike was fascinated by the framed vintage photographs and other memorabilia of the great British drama, comedy and horror films that had been produced there.

The following night, at the *Darlington Rhythm & Blues Festival*, the band stayed in a large dormitory. It produced real camaraderie as they stayed up late drinking from beer bottles. Inevitably, there was some singing, with Imelda returning to her roots as she ran through her repertoire of Irish folk songs.

In the 1960s, Mike's father had worked at the Grosvenor House Hotel in Mayfair, and now it was Mike's turn as he played with the Rhythm Kings at the Professional Cricketers' Association award night. The event had been arranged by entrepreneur and founder of the Bunbury charity cricket team, David English, whom Mike had met through Bill Wyman. David had many rock and pop stars and models as his friends, and Mike always considered him to be a very nice chap, who more than likely had a colourful past.

A week later, Mike took a break from recording to see Scotty Moore at the Glee Club in Birmingham. Scotty was Elvis Presley's legendary lead guitarist, and Mike's friend Paul Ansell was touring with him as vocalist. Paul was a real hardcore Elvis fan, always dressing and sounding like his hero. To tour with Scotty was a real thrill for him, and Mike thoroughly enjoyed his night off, meeting and chatting to them both.

October 2002 began with a trip to Norway, where he played two Irish bars as well as doing a radio interview. He also played the *Ørland Blues Festival*, where he again met up with Knock-Out Greg & Blue Weather, who were undergoing some changes, with less involvement from Greger.

Back in the UK, Mike went to the Pebble Mill Studios, where he recorded four tracks with his band for Paul Jones's radio show. A week later, there was another celebrity bash at the Café de Paris in London. This was for the launch of Bill Wyman's book, *Rolling with the Stones*, and it was a night filled with household names. Mike came offstage to be hugged by Bob Geldof, Annie Lennox and Bootsy Collins, and many more showed their appreciation. The band was a cut-down version of the Rhythm Kings without Albert Lee and Georgie Fame, so Mike did most of the singing helped out by Beverley Skeete. The star-studded crowd loved his dynamic performance, the archetypal frontman and natural entertainer.

His next job was to prepare for the launch of *Women & Cadillacs*, and many artists would have concentrated all of their efforts on that, but Mike already had plans for more. He went into Sweet Georgia Brown's with Imelda and the rest of the band to record tracks such as 'Let The Good Times Roll', 'Almost Grown' and 'Easy Easy'. This was the first session for what eventually became the *Almost*

Grown album. Mike's original intention was to release a box set or a double CD including artists like the Extraordinaires. The cover would be very much in the style of the Alan Freed recordings, with small pictures of every featured artist placed inside its own star. However, when the studio closed down in 2004, the project was shelved and the recordings were left to gather dust at Mike's house for ten years.

He flew to Stockholm, where Knock-Out Greg & Blue Weather were waiting to complete the mastering and running order for *Women & Cadillacs*, then returned with his Revue to play Colne, which hosts the UK's biggest blues festival every year. He spent the time between shows producing *Women & Cadillacs* and recording more tracks at Sweet Georgia Brown's.

At the start of December, Mike returned to the Snake Ranch Studios with Bill Wyman for more work on the Rhythm Kings' forthcoming *Just For A Thrill* album, then performed eleven full-on shows with various incarnations of his own band. These included taking the Revue to the Jazz & Roots Club at the Buttermarket, Shrewsbury on 19 December, where the performance was recorded by Chris Wroe and provided much additional footage for the following year's DVD reissue of *Red Hot...Live!* This had previously been released on VHS, but the addition of the Buttermarket show gave Mike the opportunity to release it in the new format.

2003

2002 had been an exciting and occasionally chaotic year, so at the start of 2003 Mike took a three-week break from touring. Towards the end of January, he travelled to Germany for a few shows organised by Steve Clayton and his wife. Steve was a good friend and a talented boogie-woogie pianist. He was originally from Birmingham, but had moved to Germany, where he made a living on the boogie-woogie and blues circuit. Mike and Steve played a series of double bills, complementing each other as their pianos rocked in harmony. Steve's other claim to fame was drinking beer out of his shoe – something that Mike never tried.

The Rhythm Kings' album was coming together after more studio sessions, and there was a feature on the band and an interview with Bill Wyman recorded for BBC Wales in Porth, Rhondda. The next three months were similar to the best days with the Big Town Playboys, as Mike played a few parties and a series of gigs at familiar venues which always welcomed him back. The main difference was that he was in control – and, of course, Imelda Clabby, who was getting rave reviews with the band.

Towards the end of April 2003, Bill Wyman started to put together the next tour, and there were still demands on Mike to make regular visits to the studio with the Rhythm Kings. He managed to fit in a few gigs that were close to his heart, including the *Lee Brilleaux Memorial Show* at the Oysterfleet Hotel, Canvey Island, where he guested with Dr Feelgood, and a duo with Andy Silvester for the Kemp Hospice charity at Kidderminster Harriers Social Club.

After many months of hard work, *Women & Cadillacs* featuring Mike with Knock-Out Greg & Blue Weather was finally released in May 2003. It was the first album to appear on Mike's own Doopin label – named after a guitar instrumental on *Now Appearing* which he'd co-written with Andy Silvester.

The CD was lavishly packaged in a six-page digipak format, designed by Mike's friend Chris Wroe. Chris admits that they had to be a bit creative: 'We could not get hold of a Cadillac, but there was a white Pontiac in a mate's garage. I took all of the photos, then I looked through my books and found a picture of a Cadillac, but it was facing the wrong way. I flipped it around and then placed it over the Pontiac photo, but the actual wheels on the picture are still those of the Pontiac. It was quite a challenge, and you would have to be eagle-eyed to spot it – which nobody has up to now.'

One unmistakable feature on the cover was Iren, whose stunning vintage look was ideal for the centrepiece.

Gothenburg-based Last Buzz Records had an impressive catalogue, and Mike gave them permission to release *Women & Cadillacs* in Sweden. They took the original artwork, simplified it, and sold the album using very cheap packaging. The band made very little money off the Swedish release, though fans at shows across Europe often brought copies for Mike to sign, which suggests that quite a few must have been sold– a pertinent reminder of one of the pitfalls of the business he was in!

Originally, Mike envisaged *Women & Cadillacs* as the first of an ongoing series of quality recordings for rhythm & blues fans everywhere, but for now the plan was shelved as other projects got in the way.

There was hardly any time to celebrate the release, or even promote the album, as at the start of June he had to fly to Sweden for several shows. There were three days of rehearsals with Bill Wyman's Rhythm Kings, and then a period where he spent more time in airport lounges than onstage. He often caught a flight for just one show before flying home, and the next day it would be repeated. The Rhythm Kings once again had an arduous schedule, but it meant that Mike finally got to play at the Olympia Theatre in Paris, where every great American jazz, blues and rock'n'roll artist had played before. Not wanting to tarnish the memory of his illustrious predecessors, he put in a wonderful performance.

The tour moved on to Spain, where Mike always had plenty of family amongst his fans. He would always arrange for tickets to be left on the door for his mum and dad, and then there were aunts, uncles and cousins. It gave him a warm feeling that so many of his family could be involved in what he loved to do, and these shows were always special. From Spain they moved on to Italy, France, and then back to the UK. Along the way, there was a brief stop-off in Monte Carlo, where they played at the Sporting Club. This was a prestigious show, with guests arriving in limousines and milling around the reception area looking regal and glamorous. Bill Wyman knew quite a few of them, and he chatted to some of his old friends.

One of these was Welsh singing superstar Shirley Bassey, and as the guests were seated at their dinner tables, Bill went backstage and explained to Mike that he had told Shirley to look out for him during the show. He also showed Mike just where she would be sitting – it was to the left of the stage, in the area in front of Mike's keyboard. Bill told Mike to 'do your thing' during the set, which entailed him leaving the piano, getting down onto his knees and rolling around the stage. He did this until he was within arm's reach of Shirley as she sat at her table below him. He reached out for her, and she extended her arm to him. He attempted to kiss her hand, but in doing so a river of sweat ran from his head and his mouth along the whole length of her outstretched arm. She smiled mischievously at him, and, although he was a little embarrassed by the incident, he still considers her to be such a beautiful woman.

This was followed by a welcome break at the beginning of August. Later on that month, Mike did something that he never wants to do again. He was due to play a solo gig for Steve Hadley, a fan from Warwick, when he completely lost his voice. He didn't want to let anyone down, so he played a lot of long boogies on the piano and mimed to a few album tracks. He hated himself for it and swore never to do it again.

Mike's preferred line-up was now an eight-piece, but the dream of his own touring blues caravan was no closer to reality. It was perhaps just a little too grand, as the shows would have been too costly for their regular venues and even for many festivals. It was a great idea, but he never quite got there.

He managed to fit in another holiday in El Tiemblo before it was time to hit the road again with the Rhythm Kings, including a date at the Royal Albert Hall. Shortly after this, he experienced one of the lows of his time with Bill: during the soundcheck at the Colston Hall in Bristol, he strained his back and was unable to do anything. He could not even sit at his piano, so he was taken to the local A&E, which fortunately was quite close to the venue. They gave him painkillers, but they only had a limited effect, and he was in pain for the rest of the evening. Things were no better the following day, and he was forced to pull out of the next four shows. He eventually re-joined the tour in Nottingham.

Towards the end of November, Mike went to see Fleetwood Mac at the NEC with Iren and Andy Silvester. Backstage, Mick asked him about his future plans, and suggested getting together for another project. Plans were made for Andy and Mike to meet Mick the following day, but Mike's punishing workload finally got the better of him. The last few months had been a constant rollercoaster of travelling, performing, more travelling, interviews and arranging more shows. Late nights were followed by early mornings, there were the sweating, jumping performances driven by adrenaline onstage, and the nerves.

Mike is the first to admit that he is not an accomplished session musician, and when he appears onstage with so many different superstars, he is often consumed with a fear of messing up. He always worries about hitting the wrong notes or jarring the chords, which could put off even the most professional singers such as Beverley Skeete or Georgie Fame. He still cannot read music, so if a song has more than six chords or a complicated melody, it causes him a problem. He generally overcomes this by running through songs many times in his head and many more on the piano, but all of this is forgotten when he steps out under the lights onto the stage.

The day after meeting Mick Fleetwood at the NEC, Mike woke up feeling exhausted. He had nothing left to give either physically or mentally, and decided that he just had to stay at home all day in

Kidderminster. The following day, he had arranged to meet Albert Lee in London and do a two-day session at Sweet Georgia Brown's, but he had trouble recalling the arrangements of what they were about to record. It was a worrying time, but he somehow got through it with help from Albert, Mark Morgan and Al Gare. The recordings were completed, but with no real plans, and the studio closed down shortly afterwards. Mike rescued the two-inch analogue tapes, and the recordings remained on a shelf at his Kidderminster home for many years. Every time he thought about doing something with them, his cash had already been set aside for other projects, and that has been a constant problem for the past ten years!

Mike managed a few days off at the beginning of December, although he did play at the Jazz & Roots Club in Shrewsbury, where some of the best photos of the Revue were taken by photographer Chris Nottingham. This show was also filmed by Chris Wroe with a view to a new DVD release, but it still remains 'in the can' awaiting production, as other projects have always taken priority.

The rest of the year was a much more relaxing affair for Mike. There was a Christmas radio show for Paul Jones at Pebble Mill Studios with his four-piece, as well as a few performances with the Revue and a couple of less stressful solo gigs.

2004

2004 was a busy year for the Rhythm Kings, and it began in January with vocal overdubs for the upcoming *Just For A Thrill* album. The tour that had started the previous November continued across the UK throughout January and into February, but Mike still found time to slot in three shows with his eight-piece band, including a great night at the 100 Club. He rejoined the Rhythm Kings for the French leg of their tour, after which he managed to spend a couple of days at home, relaxing with Iren as he celebrated his 40th birthday. There was no big event to commemorate this milestone; he just wanted to get back down to earth after the constant touring.

A few days later, Mike attended the *Irish World Awards* at the Galtymore Complex in London. Bill Wyman was receiving an award for his contribution to music, and the Rhythm Kings were the guests, but the highlight for Mike was Iren taking a picture of him in his tuxedo alongside Texan model and former Mrs Jagger, Jerry Hall.

The Rhythm Kings' schedule continued with studio visits and

shows, but the most memorable of these was undoubtedly the Lord's Taverners' charity event at the Royal Albert Hall. Mike was always nervous at these events, as there would usually be guests to run through new songs with – including some very big names, and some stars who Mike was a fan of. On this occasion, Chas & Dave opened the show, and the star names followed each other onto the stage throughout the night: Jools Holland, Sam Brown, the Zombies, jazz guitarist Martin Taylor, Bob Geldof, Mark Knopfler, Peter Frampton, Dave Gilmour, Peter Green, Eric Clapton and, of course, the Rhythm Kings as backing band for most of them. It was a real thrill to play with so many household names, and at a venue where he already had such an abundance of great memories. Eric Clapton joined them onstage for a few songs, and they also had Peter Green as a guest. Mike recalled that this was one of the most nerve-wracking moments of his life, as at the last minute he was asked to sing 'Black Magic Woman' unrehearsed because Peter decided he didn't want to do it!

After the Royal Albert Hall gig it was time for Mike to get his own band back on the road. He recognised Imelda's growing potential and went into the Fatback Rehearsal Studios in Birmingham to run through some new songs with her. She had been with the band for a couple of years, and he thought that it was time to freshen up the set.

At the end of May, it was back to the rehearsal studios with the Rhythm Kings in preparation for yet another tour. Before their summer schedule began, Bill released the DVD, *Let The Good Times Roll*, comprising two live concerts by the Rhythm Kings and a 30-minute documentary of the band on tour, and the album *Just For A Thrill*. Mike is a central figure on the DVD, but the album, which was released as a limited edition LP as well as on CD, is a more diverse collection of Bill's musician friends.

The shows kicked off in Germany and moved on to Luxembourg, Austria (where they performed with Steve Winwood at the *Vienna Jazz Festival* in the State Opera House), Denmark, Italy and Switzerland.

The highlight of the year came in early July, when they were involved in the 50th anniversary celebration of the official birth of rock'n'roll. This landmark commemorated the day that Elvis Presley recorded Arthur Crudup's 'That's All Right' on 5 July 1954. The Rhythm Kings performed a show from a huge marquee on the Albert Dock in Liverpool. On this occasion, the line-up included Georgie Fame, Roger Chapman, Andy Fairweather-Low and Martin Taylor.

Mike had a radio microphone, and, unencumbered by wires, he ran around the stage maniacally, occasionally venturing into the audience to huge cheers. The show was recorded, and over the next few years it was broadcast periodically on national television. Mike was very pleased with the exposure, as scores of people told him that they had seen him on television, and he believes that this probably led to an increase in private bookings.

The day after playing the Albert Dock, the Rhythm Kings moved on to another unusual venue in the shape of Chichester Cathedral. Mike thought that it was not quite right playing in such a grandiose and venerable place, and the sound was awful. It was so loud that every note echoed around the walls like an explosion, and with the volume turned up on the monitors, it was a horrible experience. Their next stop was the *Americana International Festival* in Newark-on-Trent, Nottinghamshire, then it was off to France, Ireland, England and Wales, and they finally ended the tour in Germany in late July.

For a month, Mike could forget about the Rhythm Kings, so he took the opportunity to visit his parents again, as well as fitting in a few of his own shows, but as September came around, Bill and his band came calling again. There was a show in Montpellier, and a week later a fondly remembered event at the Dorchester in Mayfair. This was for the 60th birthday party of BBC News world affairs editor John Simpson. Mike was very pleased with the photos that he had taken with John and his wife, Dee, and he enjoyed the novelty of seeing so many BBC News reporters relaxing, rather than risking their lives around the world.

Mike took his Rhythm & Blues Revue to *Blues On The Farm* at Pump Bottom Farm near Chichester. This was part of a popular annual beer festival arranged by promoter Julian Moores. He had first played there back in 1995 with the Big Town Playboys, and it was a welcome return to an unusual venue. Julian always loved Mike whatever band he was in and continues to book him today.

In October, the Rhythm Kings were about to set off on another UK tour, and after four days of rehearsals in London, there were 28 shows in a little over a month. The itinerary included a trip to Basel in Switzerland for one show at the Festival Hall, and this turned out to be Mike's last official gig with Bill Wyman's band.

He had spent a great deal of time on and off the stage with Bill, Beverley Skeete, Georgie Fame, Albert Lee, Eddie Floyd (the black American singer famous for 'Knock On Wood') and all of the other Rhythm Kings. He had listened to Bill's stories about life with the

Rolling Stones, had been enchanted by the sound of Beverley's exquisite singing voice, and enjoyed the experience of playing alongside Georgie Fame and Albert Lee, who were two of his musical heroes spanning four decades. He was touched by Eddie Floyd's reminiscences about life at the Lorraine Motel in Memphis, where Martin Luther King was assassinated and which is now a part of the National Civil Rights Museum, and he was thrilled during breaks in rehearsal when he played long-forgotten songs from Eddie's youth – rhythm & blues ballads such as the haunting 'Pledging My Love' by Johnny Ace – whilst Eddie sat and listened. Mike also loved the familiarity of the horn section, featuring former Big Town Playboys Frank Mead and Nick Payn, and he will always have the *Let The Good Times Roll* DVD to remind him of his time with them.

Bill Wyman reflects on the impact Mike had during his time with the Rhythm Kings: 'What other people were doing in the studio, he did on the stage, and he did it fantastically well. The more he played with the band, the more he took over – he was so used to running the Big Town Playboys and then his own band. By his third year, it had almost become "The Mike Sanchez Show". We all thought that he was a bit mad. He ate too much junk food, and he sweated too much, and no one wanted to stand next to him after the gig because of the sweat. I guess you'll know about the Shirley Bassey incident, but he was fun on the stage and fun on the tour bus. He left by mutual agreement, but it was tough replacing him, as he has a magic onstage and they were great, great gigs. He came back and played with us at the O2 for the Led Zep reunion and the after-show party, and when we were the house band at the Scotty Moore tribute. It was always good, and he always performed great.'

After almost four years touring with the Rhythm Kings, Mike decided it was time for a new direction. It was becoming increasingly difficult to juggle the Rhythm Kings' schedule with his own band's, as the call to go on tour would often come at quite short notice. He yearned for the freedom that he had tasted briefly at the end of his time with the Big Town Playboys, and to not have to cope with the pressure of having new songs that he did not particularly want to perform thrust onto him. He got far more recognition playing with the Rhythm Kings than he had with his own band, but for his own musical sanity he had to move on.

Albert Lee, in particular, was dismayed by his departure: 'Bill was undecided whether he wanted to continue with the band. He didn't give us a definite "Yes" or "No". Mike had his own band to concentrate on, but I really missed playing with him. The one song that always stood out for me was the Amos Milburn song, "Chicken Shack Boogie", but there were so many more. I love the guy, and I just loved playing with him. There are lots of guys who have the technique, but don't have the enthusiasm, and that is really important. Some people forget what it was like when you heard your first Chuck Berry or Jerry Lee Lewis record – but not him. He still had that boyish enthusiasm from his late teens or early twenties. People who see him never forget him.'

The Rhythm Kings had served Mike well, raising his profile and enhancing his reputation. He was now a headline act at festivals in many countries where he had only rarely appeared in the past, and it was time to venture out on his own once again.

CHAPTER 10

You Better Dig It!

Mike returned to managing his own line-ups and released several albums, including one of his best-selling CDs, You Better Dig It!

2004

On returning from his final show with the Rhythm Kings in Switzerland, Mike put the Revue together again for the Jazz & Roots Club at the Buttermarket in Shrewsbury. At times it was a struggle to remember who he was playing with, what he was recording, or where he was supposed to be tomorrow. His diary was already full and booking requests continued flooding in, but there were still occasions where he just could not say 'No'.

One such event was the *Water Rats Ball* at the Grosvenor House Hotel in Mayfair at the end of November 2004. It was an evening of New Orleans rhythm & blues organised and hosted by skiffle legend Chas McDevitt. Mike had always considered Chas to be a perfect gentleman, and Chas was a long-time fan of Mike and his music, and so his involvement was never in doubt. He put together a band with Mark Morgan on drums, Andy Silvester on guitar, Anders Janes on bass and Nick Payn and Frank Mead on horns. The audience was a good mixture of friends and fans, particularly Brian May who really enjoyed the show. Mike never really got to spend much time with Brian, but thought that they could be really good mates. He does remember Brian seeing him in the crowd at a gig once and calling out his name, so the potential was definitely there!

Mike's non-stop schedule continued, and he was suffering from exhaustion as he went into Abbey Road Studios in London on 2 December, but it was a date that he just could not miss. It was Scotty

Moore's tribute to Elvis, and the Rhythm Kings were the house band.

It was an incredible session, filmed in front of a small audience at the historic Abbey Road main studio. Many renowned musicians including Eric Clapton, Mark Knopfler, Dave Gilmour, Ron Wood, Steve Gibbons, Martin Taylor and Albert Lee had gathered to perform with Elvis's original lead guitarist, Scotty Moore. Mike gave it his all, despite his sore throat, belting out 'All Shook Up', 'My Baby Left Me' and 'Lawdy Miss Clawdy' dressed in a fabulous rockabilly suit, standing beside the incomparable Mr Moore. It was a memorable day, and Mike is proud to have his part in the proceedings recorded for posterity on the resulting DVD.

He was also grateful that he did not have to worry about the piano parts, as Joe Cocker's keyboard player, Chris Stainton, was there to do that. Mike had shared a stage with Chris many times with the Rhythm Kings whenever Georgie Fame was unable to tour, and they have a tremendous mutual respect. The production company released the DVD as *A Tribute To The King*, although originally it was supposed to have been a tribute to Scotty Moore, and it is generally considered that this is why so many great names performed for it.

Mike's work commitments meant that he saw less of Iren, though they did manage a short break in Rome before Christmas in 2004. However, she was missing her home life in Bergen, particularly her parents and younger brother, and there was no sign of Mike's schedule getting any easier. After returning from Rome, he played five consecutive nights at different venues across the country, as well as travelling to Somerset to play another gig at Westlands Leisure Complex in Yeovil before the New Year.

2005

With no Rhythm Kings engagements, Mike scheduled a variety of gigs for the start of 2005. He alternated his four-piece, seven-piece and the full Revue with plenty of solo appearances, as well as some duos with Al Gare. His travels took him to Switzerland, Belgium, France, Germany and Spain – where he played at the *Screamin' Festival* near Barcelona at the end of June. This was just one of many rock'n'roll and rockabilly events which had started to appear across Europe. Originally, these weekend events had been staged at English holiday camps such as Pontins and Butlins during the off season. When the first Europeans savoured the experience, they decided that they could host their own weekenders closer to home.

This occasion also witnessed Mike's first encounter with Dutch singer Sue Moreno, who treated him as though he were her prey. She was very enlightening and introduced Mike to the delights and possibilities of Myspace, encouraging him to keep in touch with her and many other friends through social networking. This was quite a revelation to Mike, as he discovered the thousands of rock'n'roll fans who were already using this means of communication, drawn together by one shared love. He also found that the social networks contained lots of bands, lots of hardcore fans of his kind of music – and lots of pretty girls!

A month later, he played an event that will always be high on his list of favourite gigs. It was the occasion of Jeff Beck's wedding to his girlfriend, Sandra Cush, and the evening was filled with one famous name after another. Mike fondly recalls many stories from the party, including guests such as Paul McCartney and Heather Mills arriving via the helipad. Jeff Beck and Peter Richardson still called the band 'the Big Town Playboys', as Ian Jennings, Andy Silvester and Mark Morgan joined Mike on the stage that was set up in Jeff and Sandra's garden surrounded by forest. In the middle of the set there was a power outage, and before the generators could be fixed, they managed to restore power to Mike's digital piano. It had small speakers built in, so he was able to carry on playing and singing without a microphone, and kept many of the guests enthralled as they gathered around this single source of entertainment.

When the power returned, most of the musicians were itching to get up on stage themselves. Jeff Beck joined in, and they started to run through familiar tunes by Gene Vincent and Johnny Burnette. Jimmy Page was next up, as Paul McCartney shared the vocals with Mike on 'Lucille' and several other Little Richard songs – although it was Paul who hit all of the high notes. Mark Lamarr joined in the fun on backing vocals, and they boogied well into the night. Mike also handed Vic Reeves' wife a CD, which seemed to upset Vic somewhat, had Cleo Rocos clinging to his arm for a large part of the evening, and gave Robbie Coltrane a big hug before the party ended.

Andy Silvester decided that he needed a rest from the band, but Mike had a ready-made replacement. Oliver Cheney used to open the evening at Mike's solo gigs at the George Hotel in Lower Brailes. He played bottleneck blues and added some vocals, but he was keen to progress. One evening he had asked Mike, 'How do I become like you?', and Mike grew fond of the young guitarist. He told him to carry on what he was doing, and advised him to just keep studying and enjoying the old rockin' blues music. When Andy left, Mike was more than happy to bring Oliver (who now called himself 'Oliver Darling') into the line-up, as by then he was playing great guitar. However, it was not the last involvement that Mike had with his mentor, and he has always considered it an honour that, whenever he calls, Andy is always willing to join him onstage.

At the end of July, Mike took his Revue to the *Gloucester Rhythm & Blues Festival*, which was promoted by Tim Porter. Tim still counts this event as one of his career highlights: 'We hired the run-down but characterful New Olympus Theatre on the east side of Gloucester city centre. Mike invited Andy Fairweather-Low to play. Imelda Clabby was in the line-up, as was new young guitarist Oliver Darling. Backing vocalists the Extraordinaires were there, and it was a big show – The Mike Sanchez Rhythm & Blues Revue plus guests – his dream project which probably never got enough outings. I also had American singer/guitarist Lisa Mills on the bill, who was accompanied by Big Town Playboy Ian Jennings on double bass. Towards the end of the evening, everybody was playing onstage. A brilliant occasion in an amazing, if slightly eccentric setting.'

Mike played a wonderful set with his seven-piece band at the *Maryport Blues Festival* in Cumbria, and he then took the Revue to Monaco for a show at the Sporting Club in front of the Monaco Royal Family. This was arranged by French promoter Maurice Suissa, who was a booking agent that Mike had met during previous French tours with Bill Wyman's Rhythm Kings. The band went down incredibly well, with Mike leading the way in his trademark red suit. The Revue was now as slick as it could be, with none of the nerves of the early performances, and the integration of the Extraordinaires and Imelda was seamless.

At the end of August, Mike and his band played a memorable engagement at the Keirby Park Hotel in Burnley. The occasion was *Blues & Rhythm* magazine's 20th anniversary party, which was attended by editor Tony Burke and many familiar contributors/fans including Brian Smith, Dave Clarke and Tony Watson.

A series of solo gigs followed, including a very special one in September for a rock'n'roll couple in Toulouse. Vanetia ran a fifties-style beauty parlour called Miss Betty, and her husband, William Seyssel, ran a rock'n'roll barber shop called Mutherkutter. It was an intimate event at which Mike made good friends with Vanetia and

William and their host of rock'n'roll clients and catwalk models. Eventually, they sold their businesses in Toulouse and set up a similar operation called It's Something Hell's in London's West End.

The logistical problems of putting together the Revue were highlighted at the *Goodwood Vintage Festival*. The Extraordinaires had not arrived by the time of the soundcheck, so Mike gave them a call. They were over 100 miles away in Essex, though they did turn up in time for the second set, but it confirmed just how difficult it was co-ordinating so many people.

Even the seven-piece was not without its traumas, as it proved just a week later at *Blues At The Fort*, held at Fort Purbrook near Portsmouth. New guitarist Oliver Darling crashed his car on the M40 as he drove to the show. Fortunately, his father ensured that he got there in time, but it was another near miss.

September also saw another Rhythm Kings release, this time the CD *Live*, recorded in Berlin on 15 June 2004. Mike plays piano throughout the recording, as well as providing vocals on 'I Got A Woman', 'If I Can't Have You', 'Jitterbug Boogie', 'Race With The Devil', 'Flatfoot Sam' and 'Roll 'Em Pete'.

Mike became something of a celebrity in Bewdley, especially when he played the *Bewdley Festival* in October 2005. Whenever he played in his hometown, his old guitar hero Tony Goodwin would try to attend, which made it even more special, and Mike would always try to give him a dedication from the stage.

Towards the end of 2005, Mike was averaging a show every two days, culminating with his seven-piece at Burnley Mechanics on New Year's Eve. Imelda Clabby – soon to become known as 'Imelda May' – had now been with the band for over four years, but it was clear that she was an exceptional talent who could become a superstar in her own right. It was during that night in Burnley that Mike realised he would have to do without her in the near future.

2006

In January 2006, Mike headed for Spain as usual to visit his parents, but the phone had stopped ringing, and in February he managed just one gig with his seven-piece at the 100 Club. This highlighted the fickle nature of the business he was in, with no guarantees as to when the next booking and the next pay cheque were going to come in.

Fortunately, things improved in March with a rock'n'roll festival in Riga. Pete Anderson, who had seen the BTPs at the 100 Club 14 years previously, explains how he got Mike to come to Latvia: 'I had established myself as a professional rock'n'roll singer and promoter in Latvia. Me and my wife, Anna, started to organise big international rock'n'roll festivals back in 2005, and then I thought that it's the right time to make my dreams come true. I strongly decided to find that guy, Michael Sanchez, and persuade him to play in my hometown, Riga, as the headliner at our festival.

'We thought that, as he's now a big star, it would definitely not be the easiest task to get him here. I was very grateful to Mike that he agreed and took the risk to come to our small country and to co-operate with people he was not too familiar with. I was grateful that he trusted me, and I found out that Mike was a very responsive, easy-going guy! The agreed fee was reasonable and we got the man in person with his eight-piece band featuring a special guest, the beautiful Imelda May, still on her way to stardom, whom Mike used to call the "cherry on the cake" for his show!

'This was for our second festival in a huge venue called "Dream Factory". The attendance was about 2,000 people. That same night, the fabulous Swedish rockabilly songstress Eva Eastwood also performed with her band, the Major Keys, as well as the best Estonian rock'n'roll band, Ivo Linna & Rock Hotel.

'Mike was definitely a blast and a true sensation! People had fun, they danced like crazy and everybody was absolutely mesmerised by Mike's show. The next day, there was a press conference with journalists and TV. This was the beginning of our long friendship with Mike. I got to know him as a great personality, always full of sparkling humour, extremely artistic, sincere and emotional, and at the same time very responsible.

'I discovered him also as a very loving son. I remember him calling his mum every day and being very proud and full of love towards his parents. While in Riga, he liked to sit at open-air street coffee shops watching people passing by. In the evenings back then, the Old City of Riga was a popular destination for a very different kind of tourist: drunk, rude, loud football fans, hooligans and crazy bachelor parties from the UK. Mike was very ashamed of these Brits. He was very concerned that the Latvians would think that all of the British people are like that.

'During his visit to Riga, Mike wanted to learn some Latvian

On tour with the Rhythm Kings: Mike poses with Bill Wyman at Montreux, July 2001.

Snake Ranch Studios, London, January 2002.
Left to right: Andy Fairweather-Low, Mike and Bill Wyman.

Mike in action at Cowdray Ruins, West Sussex on 21 June 2002
with Bill Wyman guesting on bass guitar.

Mike meets Ike, *Pistoia Blues Festival*, Italy, July 2003.
Left to right: Mike, Bill Wyman, Ike Turner and Albert Lee.

The Mike Sanchez Rhythm & Blues Revue.
Left to right: Dave Priseman, Pete Cook, Al Nicholls, Andy Silvester, Al Gare, Mike, Mark Morgan, Imelda Clabby and the Extraordinaires (Mark Hall, Gabriel Fofie and Roy Hall).

The Revue on stage at the Jazz & Roots Club, Shrewsbury, December 2003.
Back left to right: Al Gare, Mark Morgan, Andy Silvester, Al Nicholls, Dave Priseman and Pete Cook. *Front left to right:* Mike, Imelda Clabby and the Extraordinaires.

Mike in action with the Revue, Colne, December 2003.

Imelda Clabby and Andy Silvester at Jazz & Roots Club, Shrewsbury, 2003.

Al Gare and Mike at the *Burnley National Blues Festival*, 2003.

Ricky Cool guests on harmonica, Painswick Blues Club, April 2004...

...and Sir Paul McCartney joins in on vocals at Jeff Beck's wedding celebration, July 2005.

Rock'n'roll in Riga, Latvia with Pete Anderson, 2006.

Photo by Paul Harris

Rhythm Riot! November 2006.
The end of another great show with Little Willie Littlefield.

Mike with his beloved Antoria
semi-acoustic, Kidderminster
Town Hall, 2006.

Linton Festival, Ross-on-Wye, June 2010.
Mike played a solo set, and also guested with the Seatsniffers.

Mike and band at the Ziquodrome, Compiègne, France, February 2010.
Left to right: Mark Morgan, Big Boy Bloater,
Martin Winning, Nick Whitfield, Mike and Nick Lunt.

213

Burnley International Rock & Blues Festival, May 2013.
Left to right: Martin Winning and Nick Lunt.

Nick Whitfield at Burnley, May 2013.

Tom Bull at Burnley, May 2013.

Mike and Sarah on their
wedding day, 5 June 2013.

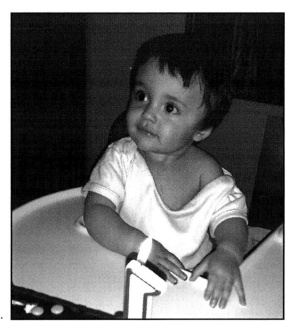

The next generation:
Louie Ray Sanchez, age 1.

Wedding celebration, 5 June 2013.
Left to right: Mike, Robert Plant, Sarah, Jeff Beck and Peter Richardson.

Wedding celebration, 5 June 2013.
Left to right: Nick Lunt, Nick Whitfield, Tom Bull, Mark Morgan, Martin Winning and Mike.

words and expressions – starting with the bad ones of course. We taught him a couple, so he was now very well-equipped to communicate in Latvia. One of the phrases was "Ej dirst!" which has many rude meanings, one of which is close to "Fuck off!". To everyone's amusement, Mike immediately started to use the phrase quite intensively and loudly. He also learned some nice words, for example, "Skaista meitene", a phrase that means "Beautiful girl". We gave him a ride around town, and he looked out of the car window and screamed at every beautiful girl, "Skaista meitene!!!"

'When he stayed at our apartment, we sang a lot of songs together and we still keep a video of those precious moments. I showed him my music collection and found that we had similar tastes in music and the same idols. I was impressed with Mike's deep knowledge of black American rhythm & blues culture.'

After a short tour of France, Mike played a date at Kidderminster Town Hall with his Revue. A month later, he attended a gig in Islington to check out Hazel Simms, a potential new female singer for the Revue. Hazel made her debut with the band at the Bristol Golf Club two weeks later, using her stage name of Sugar T. Ricky Cool also joined them on harmonica and saxophone. Mike was always happy to find a reason to include his old schoolteacher whenever he could.

As the year wore on, the bookings improved, with Cheltenham Racecourse and a rock'n'roll festival in Brussels on the agenda. The Revue was still a popular line-up with shows in Caen and Chiddingfold, and Mike covered a lot of miles on the road. This once led to a near-disaster when he was leaving Kidderminster on his way to a show in Sheffield.

He reached down in front of the passenger seat to retrieve a map, and the line of cars in front came to a sudden stop. Mike tried to brake, but it was too late and he hit the car in front. The driver was a mother who was taking her son to a birthday party, and although no one was hurt, the damage was most definitely done. The boy had a birthday cake on his lap, but the impact of the collision led to it falling in a heap onto the floor of the car. Mike apologised profusely, and offered some CDs as a goodwill gesture. This went down well, as it turned out that most of the other parents were Mike Sanchez fans, but he still got a bill for the damage, and also had to pay for repairs to his own vehicle.

Although Mike was well established on the rhythm & blues circuit, there was always something new coming along, and towards the end of May 2006 he was invited to guest on a variety show at the Café de Paris in London. At this event he got acquainted with a petite singer named Laura Nixon, who was also a fine Marilyn Monroe impersonator. Laura stirred some interest within Mike, but their liaison only lasted for a couple of weeks.

The festival in Riga the previous March had impressed a lot of people, so Pete Anderson decided to arrange more gigs for Mike in Latvia and neighbouring Lithuania. The first of these was at the Olympic Voodoo Casino in Riga. However, everything did not go quite according to plan, as Pete explains: 'The stage was unstable, and there was definitely a whole lotta shaking going on. Sometimes, Mike had to struggle with his piano and microphone sliding away from him, due to his energetic performance. It was not easy, but Mike even managed to make fun out of this as a part of the show. I was pleasantly surprised when Mike included in his repertoire a couple of beautiful lyrical ballads from the late '40s. At the end of the show, he invited me to join him on stage. We did "Red Hot" and "Hey Baby", and it was a real thrill and an honour for me.'

Mike's niece, Sarah Bastida, came to see the show in Riga. Sarah was now a successful international businesswoman, but she was happy to spend a few days with her rock'n'roll uncle. They had a lot in common, frequently flying to all corners of Europe, and Mike always welcomed the opportunity to catch up with her in person, rather than via occasional text messages telling each other where they were flying to next.

Upon Mike's return to the UK, Dutch singer Sue Moreno came over to appear as guest vocalist with the Revue at *Blues On The Farm* near Chichester and a festival in France. She then returned to the Netherlands as Mike set off for Germany, where he played in Stuttgart before heading off to the Black Forest for the wedding of his friend, Bert Boll, who is also a singer and pianist. Mike took the opportunity to renew his acquaintance with singer Britta Medeiros, and then proceeded to drink far too much. It was one of the few occasions that he actually allowed himself to get drunk in public, and he regretted it as soon as he saw the photographs afterwards. Unfortunately, these photographs are not available for inclusion in this book.

By the middle of 2006, Mike began fitting in more solo appearances as it became increasingly difficult to get gigs that paid well enough to justify more than four musicians. An exception was a return to Cowdray Ruins with his seven-piece arranged by Mike Rutherford.

At the end of July, the Revue played in Pau, France, which Mike remembers mostly for a guy in the crowd who kept pestering Imelda. Mike and Imelda posed for photos after the gig, and said guy could be seen in the background of the pictures with glowing red eyes, like something out of a horror movie! A few days later, there was another trip to Monaco to play at the Sporting Club for the Royal Family.

Mike also played a one-off solo gig at the George Hotel in Shipston-on-Stour, where Sarah Wynne worked. Sarah sat at the front watching him play, and, unlike seven years previously, this time he noticed her immediately. She was a natural, lovely, sexy, rather young-looking girl who seemed to smile throughout the entire evening, and she returned the attention he gave to her. 'We were giving each other the eye all night,' she recalls. 'Halfway through one of the songs, I got up to go to the loo, and he called to me from the stage whilst I was in there! He signed a poster for me afterwards, and he was definitely flirting.' It could have been the start of a relationship, but at the time Mike was concentrating on his career.

He was planning another album, and decided that it would be good to collaborate with his old friends Knock-Out Greg & Blue Weather, although they had meanwhile undergone some personnel changes and were now known as The Beat From Palookaville.

Women & Cadillacs had been a great success, and the Swedes had ready access to their regular inexpensive studio complete with Per Angkvist, an excellent engineer. Angkvist was also the owner, so it was an obvious choice. In addition, the knackered old piano at the studio gave the recording authenticity, which is something that Mike craved. He travelled to Sweden, where he played a few gigs, and in between started recording what would eventually be released as *Babes And Buicks*. He was fascinated by all of the huge American cars he saw, particularly out in the small towns and villages across Sweden, and that provided the inspiration for one of the signature tracks on the album, 'Everybody's Got A Buick'. Mike discovered that many Americans who are in search of a vintage Buick or Cadillac actually find them in Sweden and have them shipped back home.

In September 2006, Mike travelled to the *High Rock-a-Billy* rock'n'roll festival in Calafell, Spain. He was not on the bill, but he just decided to go along as a rare treat for himself, experiencing life as a punter rather than as someone that people had come to see. Unfortunately, he did not really enjoy the experience. By the end of the festival he had spent a lot of money and was glad to leave the small

Catalan seaside town and head inland to stay with his parents in El Tiemblo.

After a week or so, he returned to the UK, where he was joined by Iren. At this stage, they could only be together for around a month every year, as she did not want to spend any more time than that in England, and Mike was always either on the road or trying to catch some much-needed relaxation back at home. Initially, it did not really cause any stress in their relationship, as it was something that they both accepted and never really talked about. However, it led to Mike starting to look elsewhere, and eventually he and Iren drifted apart.

France, the Netherlands and Latvia came in quick succession during the autumn, after which promoter Pete Anderson and his wife, Anna, arranged a couple of shows in Lithuania. Mike flew to Riga, from where Pete and Anna took him to the Baltic Sea resort of Jurmala, as well as showing him the Riga Motor Museum. That night, he again played at the Olympic Voodoo Casino, whilst his band flew directly to the Lithuanian capital, Vilnius. The next morning, his hosts drove him to Lithuania, and it was an eye-opening trip, as Pete explains: 'Mike was definitely shocked and scared by the horrible condition of the biggest part of our roads: dark and narrow, and full of holes. I offered him the chance to drive, but he refused – he was scared to death.

'On our way to Lithuania, we talked a lot about a musician's life on the road. Mike explained about the lack of a manager, and he told me that he has to organise everything by himself. All the time, the phone rang and he was discussing the details and conditions of the upcoming gigs with different promoters from all over Europe. Then, he called musicians to check their availability for particular dates. We also talked about the vintage and classic cars, and I found out that his dream car was a 1950 Buick 8 or Buick Special, or even a Buick Roadmaster.'

As they continued on through the Latvian countryside, Pete and Anna proudly showed off the beaches, seaside resorts and museums. They explained that the houses in the best spots are heavily secured with electric fences, remote control gates, no windows, and cameras throughout. These are generally owned by local gangsters!

Across the border in Lithuania, they took time out to visit Grūtas Park, a vast area of open woodland intersected by streams and containing a number of huge statues of Lenin and other symbols of the Soviet Union. They followed pathways where they heard the haunting sound of tannoy speakers playing vintage 78 rpm records from the age of Communism. They also came across large cabins containing memorabilia and artefacts that were a reminder of the horrors and misery that had taken place in that part of the world.

Mike started to read books about the history of the Latvians, Lithuanians and Estonians, and was horrified at the torture and atrocities that they suffered at the hands of first the Soviets and then the Nazis. He got deeper into their tragic story, and felt despair when the Soviets returned, sending trainloads of people to Siberia to work until their bodies gave up. It was a thought-provoking time, and it gave him a new respect for the Baltic peoples and their will to survive.

The brief sightseeing tour ended at the Forum Palace in Vilnius, where Mike met up with Imelda and the rest of his band. He had all of the emotions of his Baltic history lesson still swimming around his head, and that possibly led to one of his band's greatest-ever performances in front of a tremendously enthusiastic crowd. Pete Anderson was delighted at the way it went: 'All of the musicians were at the top of their craft. At the end of the night, Mike again called me up on stage to perform "Great Balls Of Fire" with him. He sold a lot of CDs after the gig: people were standing in a long line to get the signed album and to get photos with him.

'He then played a show at the spa resort of Druskininkai, where Mike showed his skills on guitar as well as piano. He again performed very emotionally, and even went to the audience and sang lying on the floor and standing on his knees. Ladies were almost melting!

'Me and Anna are very proud and happy to have Mike Sanchez among our friends. We will never forget the days we spent together!'

Mike was extremely grateful to Pete and Anna for making this happen, and for promoting American rock'n'roll in a land once run by the Soviet Union. Back then, they lived in fear of a knock on the door by the KGB, and this came to fruition on more than one occasion. Pete received threats against his newly born child, Joanna, if he continued with his obsession, and he was constantly questioned by the KGB about his subversive musical activities.

After a couple of days back home, Mike returned to Spain with his band to play as the support act to Ike Turner's Rhythm & Blues Show at a festival in Barcelona, where the crowd showed him as much appreciation as they did the headliner.

It was a busy time again, and the next stop was Ronnie Scott's in London for Bill Wyman's 70th birthday party. Cleo Rocos was delighted when Mike asked her to accompany him as his guest, and they met up in Soho before the party for a drink. Mike thought that he could impress her by introducing her to all of his friends, but as it turned out, she had more friends there than he did. He saw Roger Moore, Nicholas Parsons, Richard and Judy, Donovan and many more across the room. He tried to squeeze past two people who were a little the worse for wear, and they turned out to be Jack Bruce and Donald 'Duck' Dunn, two of the greatest bass players of all time. Mike once again became a Rhythm King for the evening, and the party was interrupted as a giant screen was brought out on which the Rolling Stones broadcast their live birthday wishes to Bill.

At the beginning of November 2006, Mike found a female singer named Natalia Farran, who he hoped might become a replacement for Imelda. He met her via the Internet, although at first he could find no photographs of her. When he did find some pictures, he was excited about the prospect of working with her. Natalia was long-legged and intelligent, with a famous grandfather in writer and poet Robert Graves. Her father was Spanish and a jazz drummer, bandleader and arranger in the style of Buddy Rich, and Mike saw many similarities between himself and Natalia. They became good friends, and although it never really happened onstage, Mike was thrilled when he managed to hook her up with his own dad on the phone, so that she could recite Spanish poems from his childhood to him.

He started to surf the Internet more frequently, and he stumbled across Tayva Martinez from Winslow, Arizona, who lived directly on Route 66. She sent him a friend request on Myspace, as she had become a big fan and she had recently been divorced from her Dutch husband. She was a heavily tattooed retro-fetish and pin-up model, often designing her own tattoos, and they started a long-distance relationship that would become a physical reality the following year.

Meanwhile, Mike's *Babes And Buicks* project was coming along slowly, helped by three more cold days in the studio in Stockholm.

Upon his return, he played a solo gig at the George Hotel in Lower Brailes, where Sarah Wynne was once again in the audience. They chatted after the gig, but it was not quite everything that she had hoped for: 'He was very attentive, but then he was basically staring at me, which was a bit creepy. He gave me a photo and put his email address on the back, then we started emailing each other with light-hearted notes.'

The following day, Mike was at the *Rhythm Riot!* weekender at Camber Sands, Rye, where he backed Little Willie Littlefield. He was coping much better with the exhaustion that had floored him twelve months earlier, and he interrupted the *Rhythm Riot!* to play at the *Rocking Gone Party* in France. He had found a new energy, and was living the archetypal rock'n'roll lifestyle: he had several girlfriends all over Europe, and he dressed his slim frame in tight leathers.

He reached Lyons tired but ready for action, and after a solo show and a short break, he joined Imelda's husband, Darrel Higham, and his band, the Enforcers, for a great rocking set. This featured bass player Michael Wigfall, who had been the sound engineer on the Sweet Georgia Brown's sessions. The songs were familiar, but they were delivered off the cuff and uptempo. The adrenaline flowed, and the audience responded. The show ended, but there was no time for rest. The following day, Mike was back at the *Rhythm Riot!* for its full-on closing night, after which he retired to Natalia's house in Shepherd's Bush for eighteen hours of much-needed sleep.

Feeling refreshed, Mike then played host when Natalia invited her sisters and a few friends for dinner. It was the last chance he got to relax for a while, as his diary was completely full for the next month. The Revue played at Carmel College in Darlington on 16 December in what proved to be its last outing. The Extraordinaires failed to show, and Mike believes that they only realised how far north Darlington was when they prepared to set off that morning, as they were not great travellers. It was also apparent that he was no nearer to finding a permanent replacement for Imelda.

For this final show, Louise Boyer featured on baritone saxophone. Mike had had some encounters with Louise previously, but Natalia was becoming his girlfriend at the time and she was also the singer with the Revue. Mike was relaxed about the situation, and they had some nice group photos taken backstage, but then things started to get out of hand. That night at the hotel, Louise lured Mike to her room, but he said that he could not take things further because of Natalia. When he finally left Louise's room, Natalia saw him in the corridor with his shirt and trousers undone, and she quite understandably suspected the worst. She was in tears for most of the long journey home the following day, and Mike realised that he had upset a new but valued friend and he was going to need to find another singer.

In mid-December, Mike played a party in Leamington Spa for Jane Shakespeare, a loyal and dear fan who was leaving for Australia with her family, and then the annual Christmas party at Brailes Village Hall that he liked to do. Sarah went along once more, but she had to go home before she got the chance to speak to him. Fortunately, she knew guitarist Oliver Darling quite well, and he gave her Mike's number. She sent him a text message telling him how good it was to see him and apologising for not saying goodnight. Texts between the two of them began to flow regularly after that.

Mike appeared at a few more festive events including one at Huntingdon Hall, after which the *Birmingham Post* suggested that Mike Sanchez is what you would get if Jerry Lee Lewis and Little Richard ever got married. There was also a show at Kidderminster Town Hall, which he played with his full seven-piece band at the request of Robert Plant. It was for the Proton Effect charity organised by Jo Hill, and, as Jo explains, it had far-reaching implications: 'Mike was certainly around the scene for as long as I remember since I moved to Kidderminster in the mid-'80s, but I knew him just to say hello to until the show at the Town Hall. It was then that he asked me if I might have time to help him "sort out his working life"! He had left Bill Wyman's Rhythm Kings and was trying to organise his own gigs, as well as performing them too! Well, I absolutely loved what he and his band did – so exciting, such an entertainer – and so I accepted.'

With an assistant in place, Mike felt a lot more comfortable with his professional life. He had a rough idea of how many CDs he had sold by deducting what he had left from what he originally had pressed, and he diligently noted his mileage. Car parking, meals and other expenses were also recorded to send to the tax man.

His accounts were in order, now he just had to sort out his personal life as he flew to Nice for a memorable New Year's Eve. This was at the Sporting Club, Monaco, and Natalia had agreed to sing on condition that she could have her own room. Unfortunately, the booking was flawed, and they ended up with six rooms rather than seven. Mike took Natalia outside, and they discussed the awkward situation on a balcony with a spectacular view of Monaco in front of them. He was very persuasive, and enjoyed another night of passion with the lovely Natalia.

2007

At the start of 2007, Mike went to Shipston-on-Stour to take Sarah out on their first official date. They went to the White Bear and then to the Cherington Arms, where Mike was playing solo.

Their relationship started to get more serious as Mike dropped her off one Sunday evening. Sarah still worked in various pubs, and

Sunday and Monday were her days off, so the following day she drove to Kidderminster to see him. Eventually, this was how she came to spend most Mondays, and Mike's assistant, Jo Hill, gave her the affectionate nickname of 'Monday Girl'.

The Mike Sanchez Rhythm & Blues Revue was fading into oblivion as promoters shied away from booking such a large-scale act, and he realised that he could never do it all on his own. A significant cash outlay was required to cover backstage staff like roadies and sound engineers, as well as the cost of a tour bus. To further emphasise the potential issues, at that time Mike did not even have a booking agent. It was like trying to keep a football team in order, and he no longer wanted that responsibility.

In addition, Imelda May was now becoming a big name and she had her own commitments away from Mike, but he will always be proud of the part he played in launching her career. She recognises this, and took time out to contribute to the cover notes for his 2012 album, *Almost Grown*: 'I have been very privileged to work with the fabulous Mike Sanchez. He is one of the best, and a great man to learn from. When I first came to England from Ireland, I had only ever gigged in pubs and clubs, and so was delighted to be offered my first permanent singing job touring with Mike. He gave me a chance. I was confident singing, but less so performing to bigger audiences – which is where I learnt a lot from him, because other than being a great singer, musician and songwriter, he's also a brilliant entertainer and has a great rapport with his audience. Touring with Mike helped me hone my craft. He's a born performer.

'Thanks to Mike, *Almost Grown* was a lot of fun to make, and I think it captures the sound of a great bunch of people having a ball and making music that they're passionate about. I'll be an eternal fan of the infectious, charismatic, wild fireball, aka Mr Mike Sanchez!'

While pondering his future, Mike went to see a Chris Isaak show in Wolverhampton. His drummer, Mark Morgan, brought along Nick Whitfield, and they shared a drink before the gig. Nick remembers the meeting well: 'I thought that Mike was a little shy and out of his comfort zone as he walked through the beer-guzzling crowd of gig-goers to join us at our table. We talked in depth about music, and I gave him my credentials from people whom I'd worked with on double bass. One of these people was Paul Ansell – somebody who Mike had admired from an early age – so we kind of hit it off. I offered my services, as I'd heard he was using deputy bass players in Al Gare's absence at this time. We thoroughly enjoyed the concert, said we'd keep in touch, and Mike said that he would send his set list to me to learn.'

Reluctantly, Mike decided that he must concentrate on other things away from the Revue, and in 2007 he branched out into the US, firstly at the *Viva Las Vegas* rockabilly weekender in April, and then at the *Rockin' 50s Fest III* in Green Bay, Wisconsin, a month later.

Sarah knew that Mike had met Tayva Martinez through Myspace, and that he would meet up with her in Las Vegas, but it seemed that there was little she could do about it: 'I fell madly in love with him, but I knew about Tayva. I knew it was happening, as Mike was always honest, but I felt hurt by it all. I decided that I was going to go off with my friend, travelling around England. It was a cry for attention, but I'm not sure who from.'

Mike did indeed meet Tayva, who travelled from Arizona to Las Vegas to see him. He had become involved with a fan named Dave Harvey, who, together with a London tailor named Carlo Aldo, set up the vintage outfitters Riviera Clothing, and Dave supplied him with a new suit for the trip. He appeared at the renowned *Viva Las Vegas* festival in April with his four-piece, with Ian Jennings temporarily standing in for bassist Al Gare.

With a brand new suit and the super-cool Tayva on his arm, life was good. Mike took the opportunity to stay with her for a few days before heading back to the UK, and they made plans to meet up every few weeks. Tayva was intense, angry and exciting, but she came with a past history in the shape of three children by two different fathers.

Their next meeting was at the Green Bay festival, where Mike was constantly amazed at the legends that he bumped in to. It seemed that everyone who was anyone in the world of rock'n'roll was there, and every morning at breakfast there would be dozens of iconic rockabilly and rhythm & blues players. There were also a select few contemporary performers such as Darrel Higham, and Mike got on particularly well with Lemmy from Motörhead. Tayva was thrilled with this, as she had previously worked for a Motörhead fanzine, and one of the first tattoos that she ever got was the Motörhead logo on her arm.

Back at home, bookings were becoming increasingly erratic, so Mike took the opportunity to visit his parents in Spain for a week in July. In August, he returned to the US for *Elvis Week*, commemorating the 30th anniversary of the King's death. This was at the invitation of Dave Harvey, who paid for the flights and accommodation, in return for which Mike agreed to become a model for Riviera's catalogue of quality fifties-style threads.

Whilst in Memphis, he met up with Tayva again, who was by now administering his website. They managed to cram a whistle-stop tour of the tourist spots into three days, but it was often uncomfortable in the baking heat of a Tennessee summer.

Mike loved his time with Tayva. He made several trips to see her and there was always something different on the agenda. He enjoyed the incongruous sight of Navajo people shopping in Walmart, and the breathtaking scenery of the Arizona desert. He visited the Hoover Dam and the Grand Canyon, and he marvelled at being able to buy knives from a shop in the middle of the desert called Knife City. Life with Tayva was amazing, if a little expensive for a weekend away.

A date at the 100 Club in September could have been a problem, as Al Gare was unavailable, but Mike remembered Nick Whitfield from earlier in the year. This was Nick's debut with the band, but his involvement was to last much longer than just one gig, as he explains: 'After I did my first show, Mike seemed more than happy with it, and I continued filling in for a year or so whilst Al Gare was touring with up-and-coming star Imelda May. My first impression of Mike as a shy person proved to be correct, and I can't imagine him ever frequenting the local pub. He is a very private person. That said, in the natural habitat of one of his concerts, he can always be found loitering around after the show, meeting the folks, kissing the girls and making time for photos with his fans.'

Mike's popularity in Europe remained constant, and he played shows in Switzerland, France and Italy, where he met up with the Goodfellas. The Italian outfit welcomed the opportunity to play with a big rock'n'roll star such as Mike, whilst promoters were always happier to use local bands, as it saved on airfare.

As 2007 turned to autumn, Mike's UK bookings picked up, helped by regular shows at the Pigalle Club in London and guest spots at Flash Monkey in the Café de Paris, likewise in London. This was a burlesque show with a comedian, glamorous girls and a live band. These events were becoming popular, and bass player Al Gare and his wife, Saffron, had also put together their own version – the Candy Box – at the Glee Club in Birmingham. Mike also played at the *Bewdley Festival* with his seven-piece band and a number of guests. It was a return to a favourite venue, and he was joined by other local heroes Ricky Cool and Ian Jennings.

At the end of October, he flew to the US again to see Tayva, and, after a heady week of passion, returned for a busy November. A month later, he found himself drawn once again to the hot Arizona sun and Tayva's love nest. This time, they drove through the night from Winslow to LA, where they visited El Pachuco, a shop that sold affordable forties-style zoot suits – including the chains, hats with feathers and shoes. He bought two suits, one black and one red, and he made good use of them very quickly. Later that afternoon, he wore the black one for a photo shoot that he did with photographer Marco Patino, together with Tayva, two other models named Catherine Garcia and Frenchy La Femme, some make-up girls and a Buick.

The long-distance relationship was intriguing, with a thrill of anticipation as to what was waiting for him at the end of the long flight, but Mike had to put it to one side for one last outing with the Rhythm Kings, for which he wore his new red suit.

Throughout 2007 there had been talk of a Led Zeppelin reunion, and the occasion was to be a tribute concert to Ahmet Ertegun, one of the co-founders of Atlantic Records. Ertegun had a major influence on the early career of Led Zeppelin, as well as those of Eric Clapton, the Rolling Stones, Aretha Franklin and Ray Charles. At the start of November, Mike received an invitation from Bill Wyman to appear as guest vocalist and pianist with the Rhythm Kings at the event, along with Albert Lee and Beverley Skeete.

The show, at the O2 Arena in London, was originally scheduled for the end of November, but was hastily rearranged due to Jimmy Page sustaining a finger injury. The Rhythm Kings rehearsed in Putney and then put the final touches to their set at the O2 the night before the show. The 18,000 tickets sold out in minutes, and the concert was opened by an elaborate version of 'Fanfare For The Common Man'. Then it was the Rhythm Kings' turn.

Mike has always been justifiably proud of his part in the show, as so many great artists followed, but he was the first vocalist to perform that night. The Rhythm Kings were joined by rock vocalist Maggie Bell and guitarist and singer Alvin Lee, whilst other great stars who performed included Paul Rodgers, Paolo Nutini and Foreigner duo Mick Jones and Brian Tichy. Led Zeppelin played together for the first time in 19 years, with John Bonham's son Jason guesting on drums. The show has inevitably gained legendary status, with Mike taking his place amongst the legends, and was certainly the largest arena audience that he has ever played to.

That same evening there was an after-show party at the indigO2 Club, a smaller venue inside the O2 itself, and many believe that this was the *real* Ahmet Ertegun tribute. The Rhythm Kings started the show at around 1 a.m., then Geraint Watkins took over from Mike for a few songs. He was followed by Sam Moore, Percy Sledge, Ben E. King and finally Solomon Burke. They all sang their many hits, and the show finished around 6 a.m., when the exhausted performers retired to their nearby hotel.

Profits from the show, said to be in the region of £26 million, went to the Ahmet Ertegun Education Fund.

Unlike the lull after the first concerts Mike did with Eric Clapton at the Royal Albert Hall, the phone continued to ring with bookings, but despite this his career did not quite get the impetus that he might have expected. Three days later, he was back to his regular shows, with solo and four-piece gigs carrying him through to the end of the year.

Meanwhile, Mike was showing no signs of dropping his infatuation with Tayva, and so Sarah started a new relationship of her own. She carried on sending him occasional messages, and she would still go to see him if he was playing nearby, but she felt that she had really moved on.

When sax man Martin Winning finished his stint with Van Morrison, Mike took the opportunity to add him to his six-piece line-up. For Martin, it was a dream come true: 'I joined one of the greatest rhythm & blues bands on the planet. I had been into rhythm & blues and roots music for many years, and of all of the performers that I have come across, there are only a handful of contenders in the UK. Obviously Van Morrison, who I worked extensively with, James Hunter, Geraint Watkins and Mike Sanchez are the real thing. They don't just like the music, they have *eaten* it!'

2008

Mike spent a large part of January 2008 in Spain, this time accompanied by Tayva. It looked like the relationship was starting to get serious, but Mike still had a living to earn. He played shows in the Netherlands, Germany, Belgium – including a live radio broadcast – and the UK, and also started work on his next project, the album *You Better Dig It!* This was inspired by a lot of black rock'n'roll music that Tayva had in her collection, and Tayva also contributed to it by designing the cover. He decided to sing everything in the same key as the originals –which was quite a gamble, as some of the vocalists had great ranges.

The recording of *You Better Dig It!* was, as ever, a lengthy process involving constant trips to the studio. As Sweet Georgia Brown's in London had closed down, Mike opted for the Green Eye Recording Studio in Birmingham with producer Danny McCormack. The musicians involved were Mark Morgan, Oliver Darling, Nick Lunt and Al Gare. Al's schedule with Imelda May was growing at such a pace that these were some of the last recordings he did for Mike. Martin Winning was unavailable, so Danny recommended Paul Corry, who came in on tenor saxophone. The sessions were *very* productive, and the whole band contributed to make *You Better Dig It!* the exciting, high-energy album that it is.

Tayva came over for two weeks in March 2008, returning to the US just before Mike attended an unusual private event in Hull. This was a solo appearance at Northcott School, and the hall was full of children with special needs. Mike told them to jump up and down in time to the music, and for a while the place rocked as the teachers and carers sat on the sidelines keeping a watchful eye on their charges. It wasn't too long before the whole thing got hysterically out of hand, but at the end of it everyone concerned was laughing and smiling at the fabulous show. Two days later, it was back to more traditional gigs, as Mike and his band again supported Little Willie Littlefield at the *Burnley National Blues Festival.*

At the beginning of April, Van Morrison re-released his 1999 album, *Back On Top*, with several bonus tracks. One of these, an alternative version of 'Philosopher's Stone', features Mike on piano and dates from the sessions he did with him at the Wool Hall Studios near Bath back in March 1997.

Mike's involvement with Tayva blossomed as he flew out to see her at the end of April, and within a month she came back to visit him in England. He continued to play solo, as well as with his four- and six-piece line-ups, and with Tayva's help he was able to keep his fans updated via his website. The webmistress returned to Arizona in early June. This was a turning point, as they both began to endure the complications of a long-distance courtship. There were Tayva's three children from previous relationships to consider, as well as issues with citizenship if they were to go through with plans for marriage. It all became too much for Mike, as he had to stay focused on keeping busy, touring and performing. He played festivals in Germany, Suffolk and France, and then a solo gig at the Cherington Arms near Shipston-on-Stour. On this occasion, Sarah Wynne came along to watch with her friend Charlotte, and she noticed that Mike was not his usual self, appearing somewhat distant and distracted. She suspected that all was not well in his relationship with Tayva, and after the show they got together and discussed things. He realised that he preferred to be with Sarah, and she felt the same about him.

By this time, Mike was getting quite adept at using Myspace, and through it he met Peter Wynne, a long-forgotten singer from the early 1960s. Peter had a classical voice, and Mike thinks he could have had a lot more success if the sounds of the Beatles had not taken over the British popular music scene. Through Myspace they discovered that they lived just three miles apart, so Mike cycled across to the Queen's Head in Wolverley, where they spent a pleasant evening together, reminiscing about the era of the 1960s. They got on well, and the following month Mike invited Pete over with his daughter Dani for an evening of paella.

Mike then received an invitation to perform live on Mark Lamarr's *God's Jukebox* show on BBC Radio 2 on 9 August 2008. Mark was already a fan, and the appearance coincided with Mike releasing *You Better Dig It!* Sales went well, helped by another BBC Radio 2 live session for Paul Jones on 14 August, and re-runs of the album had to be ordered. Robert Plant commended Mike on the quality of the vocals he had recorded, and it seemed that the decision to stick to the original keys had paid off.

Despite the never-ending demands on his time, the new Mike Sanchez stayed relaxed, as Nick Lunt recalls: 'I did a couple of CDs with the Big Town Playboys, and then this one. Mike made everyone feel at ease. There was no stress, even when it went wrong.'

In August 2008, Mike found himself back at the Queen's Head in Wolverley, this time to celebrate Robert Plant's 60th birthday. Robert had invited Mike, Ian Jennings and Andy Silvester, as well a host of his long-term friends from the world of music. Halfway through the evening, with the rain lashing down outside, a huge coach pulled up in front of the pub. Rumours spread that it was a busload of fans who had come all the way from Germany for the party, but when the door opened it was Lenny Kravitz and his band. They were in the middle of a UK tour and had decided to help Robert celebrate his birthday on one of their nights off.

A few days later, Tayva arrived again, and she and Mike headed for Spain to see Mike's parents. Tayva was also keen to discover her Spanish roots, as she had gone as far as she could on the Internet. She knew that she had a distant relative from Toledo who was one of the original conquistadores, so they went to the registry office at the cathedral. There they were told that all of the records had, unfortunately, been destroyed in the Spanish Civil War, and so she could go no further with tracing her ancestry.

Mike was now getting regular return appearances at festivals, including Ørland in Norway and Cerdanyola in Spain, but he still enjoyed the private events. One of these was the wedding of personal trainer Dean Hart, and when Mike asked the groom why he wanted him to be the entertainer at this particular celebration, he replied, 'Because, Mike, you give me energy!'

At the start of November 2008 there was a nostalgic return to the Robin 2 at Bilston. Ricky Cool hosted an evening of music featuring the original Big Town Playboys line-up, as well as the Rialtos and the Hoola Boola Boys, who were his current band. Ian Jennings, Andy Silvester and John Spinetto all got together with Ricky and Mike, and the BTPs once again ruled the stage.

Robert Plant visited Mike on a couple of occasions that month, accompanied by his son Logan. They ran through some rhythm & blues songs, with Logan singing on a few of them. This was in the run-up to Robert's ex-wife Maureen's 60th birthday celebration which took place at the Kingsford Caravan Park, and Robert was keen for Logan to sing at the event. Maureen always loved Mike, and often said that he was like a son to her.

Mike did another session at the BBC studios in Maida Vale, this time for the *Paul Jones Christmas Special*, where he was on the same bill as Elkie Brooks, as well as Paul's own Blues Band, that was eventually broadcast on 29 December on BBC Radio 2. As Christmas approached, Mike took up a five-night residency with his four-piece at the Moods club in Monaco. This was frequented by some of the wealthiest people in the world, and the band were housed in very large and plush hotel rooms. In the daytime there was very little to do, as they were nervous about venturing out. The cost of drinks was prohibitive, so they spent most of their time in their rooms. Mike remembers Al Gare telling him that it was the cleanest he'd ever been, as he had several baths a day just to pass the time.

After playing Monaco, Mike moved on to Belgium for a show

with top Belgian roots rock outfit the Seatsniffers, then returned to the UK in time to hear the Paul Jones session broadcast just after Christmas.

2009

At the beginning of 2009, Mike headed to Sweden for some intensive studio work on his next album, *Babes And Buicks*. Once again, he turned out another impressive collection of obscure and original tracks featuring Anders Lewen and the rest of The Beat From Palookaville.

In January, he played a great set with his six-piece at the *Rockers' Reunion* in Reading, followed by a brief holiday with his parents. After a gig in Lille, Tayva returned to the UK and arranged a professional photo shoot in his cellar. This had a S&M theme, but, although Mike has quite a liberal outlook, it was not something that he wanted to explore further.

Tayva returned to the US at the beginning of March while Mike continued to put shows together. He did a couple of gigs at Bewdley Rowing Club arranged by his niece, Sarah, who was also a member of the local rowing team. Ricky Cool, who had gone back to teaching in a Birmingham school many years earlier, arranged for Mike and a few other musicians to join his students in recording some reggae and ska tracks. Mike really enjoyed it, and still jokes about changing genres one day, though he is concerned about how many purist rock'n'roll fans he would lose!

Nick Whitfield became a permanent fixture as he replaced Al Gare on bass, and Mike looked forward to a stable line-up for the months ahead.

Mike's next door neighbour, Doug Wagstaffe, had bought his house from Mike's parents. His original intention was to rent out the rooms, but eventually he moved in himself. Doug had worked for most of his life in explosives, but gave that up to become a painter and decorator. They became occasional friends, and three or four times a year they would get together for an evening of chess. This was a welcome distraction which helped Mike to relax – particularly at the end of March as he prepared to head back to Stockholm to finish off *Babes And Buicks*.

After the recording session, he headed to Cologne, Germany, where his friend Andreas Kollenbroich ran a band called Ray Collins'

Hot-Club. Andreas aka Ray wanted him to record a session of original songs for his next album, *Ray Collins' Hot-Club Goes Intercontinental*, with Mike on vocals rather than himself. Mike considered this to be a great honour, as Ray is a wonderful singer in his own right. The CD version of the album includes three tracks with Mike on vocals, 'Rocking And Rolling Tonite', 'Half Blind' and 'Right Here In My Arms', while the LP also contains a fourth, 'No More'. The album also includes two tracks featuring 'King of the Honkers', sax legend Big Jay McNeely. In particular, Mike feels that 'Half Blind' is one of his best-ever recordings, and remembers that his father numbered it amongst his favourites too.

Mike returned home for a week before visiting his parents again, and this time his brother, Juanjo, came along too. This was an unusual coincidence, as Juanjo rarely visited Spain, whereas Mike went there at every opportunity.

There was a seven-date tour of Germany scheduled for the middle of May, and Mike asked Will Wakefield to help out. They hired a minibus, and embarked on an old-fashioned rock'n'roll road trip, with Mark Morgan, Nick Whitfield and Oliver Darling making up the band. The itinerary was particularly demanding, with a show in Berlin followed the next day by one on the far side of Bavaria, then back to the other side of Germany again.

Oliver had been with the band for around four years, but during this German trip Mike started to get increasingly frustrated with his attitude. He seemed to have become complacent, turning up late for shows and not quite hitting it onstage. As they were walking offstage after one particular show, Mike noticed that, rather than showing his appreciation to the audience, Oliver was busy texting on his phone.

Mike was getting increasing support around Europe, with The Beat From Palookaville in Sweden, the Goodfellas in Italy and the Seatsniffers in Belgium all happy to play with him. In June 2009, the Drew Davies Rhythm Combo became his latest European partners when he played in Limoges, France.

Drew, a singer and tenor saxophonist, has a band consisting of Parisians, even though he is actually English. He found a lot of work in France, so he decided to stay. His Rhythm Combo is relatively successful across France, but the collaboration with Mike has given him exposure to more festivals under Mike's name. The arrangement has benefitted Mike too, as Drew provides a ready-made backing band whenever he ventures across to France, and they have become good friends. However, Mike strongly feels that he needs to give his own band the opportunity to perform overseas with him whenever possible. His line-up for most performances, especially with drummer and close friend of twenty years Mark Morgan, has always knitted together like a well-oiled machine.

Onstage, there was a trend away from the UK towards Europe, and in July Mike performed in France, Belgium, Italy and Spain. He then went to Sweden for more gigs and studio time with The Beat From Palookaville, before returning to Winslow and Tayva for one final trip.

With doubts about Oliver Darling growing, Mike started to keep an eye out for a potential replacement. Guitarist Tom Bull recalls how he became involved with the band: 'I first encountered the band around two years earlier at a blues festival in my hometown of Leicester. The line-up consisted of Mark Morgan on drums, Oliver Darling on guitar and Al Gare on bass. I was blown away by Mike's stage presence and energy. I hadn't really seen a performer as powerful as him before. When he was looking for a deputy guitarist, I got involved by our mutual friends Mark Morgan and Nick Whitfield. I went to a rehearsal in Birmingham, as there were a few upcoming shows in the diary, and the gigs went really well. I remember the first few being a bit daunting, as Mike has a huge repertoire and didn't mind throwing a few unknown songs on me. I guess he must have felt comfortable enough with my abilities to do that. He often throws songs on us all mid-set, whether we know them or not – he is always good fun to work with in that respect. No set lists are usually followed, and Mike often drifts from tune to tune without notice, which keeps the music flowing and keeps us all on our toes. Mike seemed very happy with my performances and kept me as a deputy for Oliver.'

In October 2009, Mike's fears regarding Oliver Darling became a reality. The band were due to play at the *Speyer Festival* in Germany, a show that had been in the diary for several months. Flights had long since been booked and paid for, but some months later Oliver got a booking for his own band, the Dirty Robbers, for the same date, and announced that he could not make the trip to Germany. There were still a few weeks to go until the festival, but it was virtually impossible to find a replacement at such short notice. Eventually, Mike's friend Walter Broes, previously of Belgian outfit the Seatsniffers, agreed to help out, but his flight from Brussels to Stuttgart was an additional expense.

Mike had an idea how he could recoup this unforeseen outlay.

When he recorded *You Better Dig It!*, he had verbally agreed with his band that he would pay them their regular fee for the sessions. This was his standard arrangement, as, although it was over the top in terms of the normal level of pay for session musicians, they were his band and his mates, and he wanted to treat them properly. Earlier in the year, he had paid everyone the first half of the fee, with the remainder to be paid when sales generated sufficient cash.

At around the time of the *Speyer Festival*, Mike had paid Mark Morgan, Nick Whitfield and Al Gare the balance of their fees, but sent Oliver an email indicating that he would be deducting the cost of his replacement at the German show. He offered him the remaining balance, and awaited confirmation from Oliver that he agreed, but it never came.

Mike kept himself busy finishing off *Babes And Buicks*, as well as playing plenty of shows, but then unexpectedly received a letter from the Musicians' Union stating that he owed Oliver the balance of the studio fee and threatening court action if he did not pay. Mike was furious, and felt very let down after having spent four years encouraging the young Oliver into the right styles of vintage music. He had given him experience and good exposure, and had been threatened with legal proceedings in return.

Fortunately, he quickly managed to recruit a renowned guitarist into the band. Big Boy Bloater had known of Mike since the early days of the Big Town Playboys, and attended many of his gigs. He was an accomplished guitarist and singer, and Mike believes that Andy Silvester's playing was a major inspiration for him. When Bloater joined the band, it was the first major change in the line-up in over four years.

CHAPTER 11

Almost Grown

Approaching the age of 50, Mike lost both of his parents, got married, and became a father. Now that he has passed that milestone, he is starting to make plans for the next phase of his life.

2010

In January 2010, Mike was playing an afternoon gig with his band at a tattoo and rock'n'roll festival in Ostend. When the show finished, he returned to the dressing room to get changed and saw that his brother, Juanjo, had called his mobile. He realised that Juanjo would not ring unless it was very urgent, so he returned the call and his instincts were correct. 'Michael, your father has just died,' Juanjo's voice brought the dreadful news.

Mike was devastated. He felt as though everyone at the concert had heard the same news and that it had spread like wildfire, but he was alone. Stuck in Belgium and unable to return to the UK until the following day, his despair worsened as he realised that he would normally have been with his family at this time of year, but had for a change decided to stay in the UK and do some shows. It had also been a few weeks since he had last heard from his father, and so did not even know that he had been ill.

Mike usually telephoned his parents every couple of days. It was rare for his father to be the one to pick up the phone, as he was often out in the garden tending to things, sometimes just sitting amongst the fruit trees with his dogs, or simply having a nap in his bed. Manuela would frequently do all of the talking during the call, and even if there was no news to chat about, they would spend at least ten minutes on the telephone. She always rose early and usually stayed up until midnight, so if Mike was at a loose end and had his parents on his mind, he knew that he could always call to chat with his mother. On the most recent occasions that he had spoken with his father, Jesús had discreetly mentioned Manuela's growing issue with the onset of Alzheimer's disease – which accounts for why Mike did not find out that his father had been sick and bedridden for several days until after he had passed away.

The journey back home would have been unbearable and possibly dangerous without Mike's drummer, Mark Morgan, who drove his car back from Belgium to Kidderminster through the heavy snowstorms that afflicted Britain at the time. Mike will never forget the actions of his true friend, getting him home in one piece whilst he sat in the passenger seat in floods of tears and with a bottle of bourbon by his side.

By the time Mike returned to Kidderminster, his father had been cremated, in accordance with his wishes: he did not want any hanging around whilst people gathered – no ceremony, no religion, no church service and no flowers. He wanted his ashes to be brought back to the house and to be scattered in the garden, close to the graves that they had created for their pet dogs Rusty, Blackie and Pancho. Another dog, Curro, passed away just a month after Jesús.

Mike wanted to tell people how he felt, so he posted the following passage on his Facebook page:

My dear friends

This message is just to thank all the many of you dear people who have sent me messages of condolences over the death of my dad, Jesus Sanchez Diaz.

It was indeed awkward to have to receive such a phone call from my brother, Juanjo, directly after having played a show in Belgium early last Saturday evening, telling me the dreadful news that my father had passed away an hour before in his bed at home in Spain.

I believe he had been ill with what seemed to be a case of pneumonia for just a few days and had confined himself to his bed, where last Friday he had a doctor visit him and give him medication. I am aware that he also had constant medication for high blood pressure and other issues to do with blood circulation in his feet, though that had been a problem that seemed to have been curing itself over the last year or so. In general, he had been reasonably well in health and so this sudden tragedy was a great shock to my mum and everyone else who knew him.

Around 5 p.m. on Saturday, my mum had called up her sister and my cousins in Madrid, who called for an emergency. By the time everyone turned up, my father had quietly passed away. I am told by my cousin Manolo, as he closed my dad's eyelids, that he looked like he had died very peacefully.

By the time I returned home the following day, my dad had already been cremated in El Escorial, where my mother, her close sister my auntie Maria and Maria's three sons and their families attended the reception. At home in Kidderminster, I called my cousin Manolo, who had just arrived home from a two-and-a-half-hour ordeal after the cremation, through the heavy snow that was falling over the Madrid area that evening.

I could not believe how quickly a living person dies and is turned into a box of ashes, within twenty-six hours of his heart stopping.

My mother is safe and sound, currently with her sister Maria in Maria's flat in central Madrid. Maria's three wonderful sons – my dear cousins Manolo, Jose Francisco and Miguel – are all just a few kilometres apart from each other in the same part of the world.

Maria and especially her sons have been absolutely superb at taking care of everything possible to help my mum through this awful time.

I can rest at home for a couple of days and try and save up as much of my energy as possible, so I can be strong for my mum when I am with her next week. She will need for me to be brave, and that I will be.

I travel to Spain on Monday, 18 January, where I will stay until I return to perform at La Pigalle, London, on Saturday, 23 January.

I believe the rest of the family will be waiting for me to arrive, and then Tuesday we will drive over to the house, where we will spread my dad's ashes over a part of the garden where his beloved dogs are buried and where my mum will also join him when she is ready.

After Tuesday I will be staying at the house with my mum and Maria, so I can have time to begin going through the world that my dad had been living in.

I feel there will be many more visits to Spain that I will have to fit into my schedule over the coming months when I am not working. Much has to be done with regards to my mum, as now it's impossible for her to be alone in the house in Avila. Yes, there's much to sort out!

For my experience in Belgium last Saturday I wish to send a special thanks to Bloat, Lisa, Nick, Mark and all the event staff backstage who felt as they did for me and greatly helped in getting me through the initial shock that I received that night. By chance the show took place early and was finished by 7 p.m.. Lord knows there would not have been a show if I had received the news before we went onstage.

To Mark, especially, I wanna thank for taking care of me and driving me and my car home at a time in my life that would have been difficult for me to even see straight, never mind control a car safely on seven hours of snow-covered roads.

There will be many people that don't actually know about my dad's passing and who I have no idea how to contact. With some of these people, my dad would not have wanted them to know about him anyway.

A lot are people in the West Midlands who he worked alongside in the catering/restaurant business since the mid-'70s, at a Lex garage in Stourbridge, Minster Garage in Bewdley, the Swan Hotel in Stourport, the Stone Manor in Kidderminster and the Mill Hotel at Alveley. Most of my dad's best friends that I remember from those years have already passed on.

There's only so much crying that any of us can do in such situations. If we spend our lives crying, then what is the point in being alive?

Thanks to my dad, I live a wonderful life. A life filled with gratitude for being able to make a career for myself by giving pleasure to thousands of people and by doing something that I love. Thanks to my dad.

Thanks to my dad, I never had the worries of being homeless, for he set up the home that I still live in to this day. I paid him back bit by bit at a time where I would never have been able to get a mortgage on my own. I thank my dad.

I thank my dad for having kept true to his marriage vows and for remaining a faithful, reliable, sober-headed and hard-working husband for his wife, my dear mother, Manola. They spent exactly fifty years together. Fifty whole years!

They met and fell in love in 1960 in London, were married in Paddington in 1962; I was born in Hackney in 1964; they moved from renting a flat to getting a mortgage on a home in Kingsbury, North London, just as I started junior and middle school. In 1975. they moved to Bewdley in Worcestershire, where I did my high school years and enjoyed the freedom in life to somehow become the person that I am today.

During this whole time my dear parents worked so very hard every day and saved every possible penny to make a better life for all of us.

If only I had the awareness, control and discipline that my dad tried to teach me, I'm sure I would have moved a lot further in this life than where I am at now! But that's OK. I will not fill my mind with any kind of deep regret, though I'll always remain aware of the choices that we make, what directions we decide to take, at what cost and at what pleasure.

The years seem to fly by. What a crying shame for the people that spend their lives suffering, working and living such unhappy lives, hoping to retire, just so they can die. At least my dad enjoyed fourteen years back in his homeland of Spain, living in a beautiful paradise with long summers, the smell of pine trees, birds and wildlife all around, the healthy air, the thousand stars on a clear night, the 200 fruit trees to water, the dogs to keep company, the smell of mama's good cooking from the kitchen, his books and Sky television, where he would enjoy listening to German and French shows, his awareness of the world from a distance. My dad was a walking encyclopaedia of history, thoughts, poems.

I know my dad wished many obvious things for me: success, money, etc., and to different degrees I have succeeded in many of these materialistic things. As we continue through this life, so too will our improvements.

This is the first time in my life that someone so close and dear to me has passed away. I know there will be many more times like this and there's nothing any of us can do. Each day we live is another day in our lives that brings us closer to our own deaths. Most people usually take it all for granted until someone close to them is no longer with them. Hopefully then, they can open their eyes and realise just how simple this mortal life truly is and how important it is that we enjoy this life we have.

I'm glad that while I live I have such a great purpose in life, I am much loved by many, I have my freedom, I have my dignity and I think my dad should be very proud of me. I love my papa.

To love and be loved. Nothing is greater.

Mike Sanchez

After the death of his father, Mike was in turmoil. As he did not want to let anyone down, he was juggling his obligations to play shows with taking care of his mother, who had been diagnosed with Alzheimer's disease. Away from home for long periods, he failed to notice the letters and notifications of court hearings that were stacking up. By the time he got around to dealing with them, his debt to Oliver Darling had increased, swelled by fines and legal costs. He was astounded that Oliver could do something like this, and his bitterness over the matter still shows no sign of mellowing.

His relationship with Tayva had virtually finished before the end of 2009, and, as fate would have it, Sarah had recently split up with her boyfriend. Mike had grown very fond of Sarah, though she was very different to the other girls that he knew. He felt completely at ease with her, as she was a down-to-earth, hard-working and very unpretentious soul. She was a fighter who knew how to look after herself, and quite mature for her age. She was also very attractive, and with no ties they naturally started to contact each other more often. Soon afterwards, Mike arranged for Sarah to visit him in Spain, as that's where he now spent most of his time, looking after his mum. After a week, their relationship blossomed again, but Mike had already made plans to move to Spain permanently – which did not bode well for their future.

Sarah explains what happened: 'Mike thought that the prospect of a long-term relationship would be difficult, and so he broke up with me. He could not see how it would work. I said that I would move over to Spain with him, if that is what it would take to be with him, but he said that it was over.'

Sarah was devastated and Mike felt horrible about himself for having to do it, but with her friends and family still back in England, he genuinely thought that he was doing it for the best.

Babes And Buicks was finally released in April 2010, with a cover design once again done by Tayva, but Mike was not really in a position to push it, as he had too many other things to worry about. However, Anders Lewen is particularly proud of the collaboration: 'We recorded both *Babes And Buicks* and the earlier *Women & Cadillacs* at Real Music Studios in Bromma, Stockholm. They were recorded in the same way, with as few mics and overdubs as possible. Working with Mike in the studio was very easy. He's always in a good mood, and although he's not always well prepared, he's so talented that if there wasn't any material to record when the day started, it always ended with some great takes anyway! He sometimes wrote the lyrics in the studio, or the night before the session, but he always had some ideas hanging in the air. I remember when he explained "Everybody's Got A Buick" to us, and at first we thought he was kidding. He was talking about punk-mambo-swing and humming the riff while he was gesturing the breaks, but I think that turned out to be one of his greatest songs on the album: a true Mike Sanchez original that no one else could have created!

'I mixed the whole *Babes And Buicks* album, and then Big Boy Bloater mastered it. It was a big success. I remember being on the road with Mike's seven-piece band for gigs in Switzerland and France, and Mike put it on the stereo of the tour van. I hadn't heard the mastered result yet, and I actually was a bit shocked hearing it! It kicked off with "Hip Boots", and it sounded like an old-fashioned rhythm & blues orchestra that had been transformed into a punk band! Back then, I thought it was too compressed, but now I'm really proud of those two albums!'

The *Babes And Buicks* album was another solid achievement, and Mike envisaged that there could be many more in the pipeline for himself and his Swedish friends, all titled along the lines of chicks and cars, but that project has been put on hold, at least for a while.

He went back on the road in Britain and around Europe, including several shows with Ray Collins' Hot-Club. He played with old friends like the Seatsniffers, the Drew Davies Rhythm Combo and the Goodfellas, and he went to northern Poland for a boogie-woogie festival.

Martin Winning joined him for many of the UK shows, and explains the difference that constant playing makes: 'I've never rehearsed with Mike – sometimes we each have our parts and we go away and learn them. When we meet up, it all fits together so easily. Mark Morgan is the best rhythm & blues drummer in the world, and Mike's got him, which is a big help. When we have a few consecutive gigs, it all comes together quickly. The first show might be a bit off, but by the third or fourth the band is really cooking. With Mike, I've never played a duff gig.'

In June 2010, Mike introduced female singer Laura B. from Laura B. & The Moonlighters into the line-up, and, although she was busy with her own shows, she performed at a number of successful gigs with Mike and his band.

In the meantime, Mike had met a Spanish girl from Malaga named Priscilla Gavino on Facebook. She had sent a simple friend request, and he had accepted, intrigued by the photographs of this beautiful woman who was into his style and his music.

Priscilla had recently had a baby boy from a marriage to a Swedish musician. She came with tales of terrible violent times with her recent husband, but she seemed like a stable, reliable young woman in need of a break. Soon afterwards, she left her job working in a shop at Malaga Airport and moved up to El Tiemblo, where she could help out with looking after Mike's mother whilst he was away on trips. Mike felt he had no choice but to find someone to live in at home, as his mum was staunchly against going into a residential home. Priscilla could ensure that she was safe and had someone to talk to, and Mike could continue playing across Europe, happy in the knowledge that things were all right at home.

As his mother's illness grew worse, Mike struggled to cope, and Priscilla was invaluable in helping him get through the ordeal. She knew so much about the way of life in Spain and how to get things done, which was all new to Mike. It was almost idyllic, until her jealousy started to surface. She started to accuse him of staring at girls across the road, in the bank – anywhere. Her eyes held a dark fury whenever he mentioned another girl, or when she accused him of infidelity. It got worse when he smiled at some boys and girls walking along the road and she accused him of being a pervert. He started to feel as though he had lost control. The desperation she induced was something he had rarely encountered with anybody else. He was trapped by a covetous woman who was looking after his very sick mother, and there was no way out. In his frustration, he smashed his fist into a large mirror, making a mess of his hand.

Although Mike had called time on their relationship, Sarah still kept in touch with him via email, and came to the rescue when she unearthed Priscilla's devious side: 'I sent him an email one night and ended it with the words "Love You". I received a reply saying that he was starting a family in Spain and that I shouldn't contact him any more. He even said that he felt sorry for me. I knew that these were not Mike's words, so I contacted him directly, and he confirmed that it was Priscilla who had sent the message. She had gone through his emails and my mobile text messages whilst he was asleep. At first, he did nothing about it, as Priscilla was still looking after his mum, but the damage was done.'

Whilst all of this was happening, Mike continued to perform. His own band line-up at the time still contained Big Boy Bloater on guitar, and Mike intended to one day release an album with Bloat, but it was not to be. He travelled to Germany, Spain, France and Belgium, and also played two shows on a ship off the Swedish coast. *Rock At Sea*, as it was known, was a raucous affair which essentially involved Scandinavian rockabillies getting incredibly drunk.

He still played in the UK as well, including the *Rhythm Riot!* in November, which Sarah went to, as she knew that Mike would be there. She was disappointed to discover that Priscilla was still at his mother's house in El Tiemblo, even though there was no longer any affection between them. They agreed that Priscilla would only be there when Mike was away, so that she could attend to his mother's needs for a few days at a time until he returned, at which point she would leave. Priscilla needed the money, and Mike was happy to pay her for the care she provided, as he did not want to have to put his trust in a complete stranger, particularly where his mother was concerned.

December was as busy as ever, and on New Year's Eve Mike was booked to play with the Mad Tubes at Senigallia Pier in Italy. The promoter had also arranged for Priscilla and her baby boy to join them for a pleasant four-day break in the picturesque seaside town, but by then the relationship had broken down completely and he travelled alone.

2011

2011 began with the release of *Numero Uno!*, an album by Mike's Swedish friends, The Beat From Palookaville. He recorded a ten-second introduction as well as taking the lead vocal on 'Knocking On The Backside'.

Meanwhile, Sarah was getting increasingly frustrated with her on-off relationship with Mike, and at the start of 2011 she started an online relationship with a guy from Wales whom she got on really well with. She cancelled plans to go to El Tiemblo in favour of Wales, but had doubts about her decision: 'I was crying all of the way to Wales, and even when I was there I was texting Mike. I missed him so much.'

Over in Spain, Mike was in the process of removing Priscilla from his life. Eventually he came to his senses, knowing that there was only one thing that he really wanted: to be at home, peaceful and happy with the lovely Sarah. He went over to Shipston-on-Stour to see her, and she gave him an ultimatum. He immediately asked her to be his steady girlfriend, and she was delighted to accept.

Mike woke up one day at Sarah's flat in Shipston after she had gone out to work. He had a strong, emotional feeling that felt very natural whenever he thought about her. After many years of hoping for a stable love, finding something and losing it, sharing his innermost feelings and then realising it was all a mistake, he had finally found what he was looking for. All of the good memories, all of the sad and dark memories could now be put into context. Mike had always been able to blur the rough edges of his memory, so that even the most negative things could be smoothed over, but now they could all fade into the distance. He knew that he could stop searching. He had finally found the girl that he wanted to spend the rest of his life with.

He could look back on his past with a smile, when he thought of all of the experiences he had been through since he first kissed a girl. He knew that he would no longer have any of his past 'curiosities' that would put his relationship at risk – curiosities from a time when he admits that, if there had been girls in outer space, he would probably have dated a Martian!

From this point on, Mike and Sarah knew that they would get married. There was no proposal and no official engagement. They just agreed that marriage was what they both wanted.

Mike didn't return to playing until mid-January, when he performed solo at a boogie-woogie festival on the outskirts of Paris. Then, it was the usual merry-go-round of European shows, often playing with his friends from Belgium, Sweden and Italy, as well as familiar venues around the UK.

Big Boy Bloater had his own band, the Southside Stompers, with his wife Lisa on saxophone, before joining Mike, and he wanted to put his own project together once more. He formed Big Boy Bloater & The Limits and continues to do well with shows and album releases. Tom Bull became Mike's new permanent guitarist in April 2011.

By this time, Mike's mother was becoming more and more difficult to take care of at home, and he began looking at the possibility of getting her moved into Las Cuatro Palmeras, a modern and spacious residential home just five minutes away from her home in El Tiemblo. He eventually persuaded her to stay there on a couple of occasions for a few days at a time whilst he was away performing, and she had begun to familiarise herself with the friendly nurses and this new environment. However, Manuela would sometimes get angry and demand that she be taken back home, and life started to become harder for everyone involved. Mike and Sarah both realised that she needed round-the-clock care, and so in the summer of 2011 they took the painful decision to move her into the residential home permanently. It was such a difficult time for Mike, particularly coming so close after his father's passing. Sarah made things easier by quitting her job and moving out to Spain a month later, and Mike could take comfort in the knowledge that his mum always knew who he was when she saw him, and that she had all of the love in the world for him.

He now also embraced the European boogie-woogie circuit, and played with Swiss pianist Silvan Zingg in Lugano, Germany's Jo Bohnsack in Sylte, Renaud Patigny in Brussels, Axel Zwingenberger in Hamburg and Martijn Schok in Ermelo, the Netherlands, amongst others. These were quite different occasions, played in huge concert halls on grand pianos, with the leading exponents of boogie-woogie looking resplendent in their formal concert attire.

Although they opened up a whole new audience for Mike, before these events he would feel nervous about, and intimidated by the prospect of sharing a stage with such fluent and often classically-trained pianists. Onstage, he would release the wild animal within him, exuding sweat and charisma, and singing his heart out whilst trying to keep his hands from collapsing on a real piano. For years, he had been pumping digital pianos, which have a lighter action that finger and arm muscles become accustomed to. After three or four songs on the harder action of a grand piano, the strain could be clearly felt. This was exacerbated by the much quieter monitors than he was used to at rock'n'roll shows, which in turn encouraged a tendency to hit the keys even harder. However, the audience loved his voice, which he projected as his main instrument – unlike the other performers, who were purely instrumentalists – and the appreciative crowds were always keen to buy whatever CDs he had with him.

At the end of September, Mike played with his six-piece band at *Rockabilly Bombardment* in Austria, as well as backing Big Jay McNeely on the same stage, which he regarded as a great honour. There was a brief rehearsal, followed by a fast-paced show during which even the high-energy Mike Sanchez found it a challenge to keep up with the extraordinary horn player.

November saw the release of the Blues Band album, *A Few Short Lines*, which featured Mike on 'My Brother Was A Sailor', 'Sway With Me' (with Linda Lewis) and 'Statesboro Blues'.

In December, Mike played a solo gig at the Greystones in Sheffield – an intimate venue that he loved, as it gave him the chance to really connect with the audience. It was there that I spoke to him about writing his biography, and it did not take long for his ideas to come flooding out, though it was another twelve months before he actually did anything about it.

2012

Throughout 2012 Mike began to bring some order to his life. He would leave his mother's home in El Tiemblo on a Thursday or Friday, play a couple of festivals or smaller gigs over the weekend, and then return on Monday to spend the rest of the week close to her.

At the start of February, the boiler broke down and the house was absolutely freezing. A new boiler arrived, but could not be installed for almost two weeks. Mike and Sarah had to wrap up warm and do their best to survive without heating or hot water. The nearest they got was filling the sink from a kettle. When their new boiler was eventually fitted, they cranked the dial up to the maximum and revelled in their new-found warmth. They celebrated with baths and pampering, cheap champagne, and each other's love. It is no surprise that during this week their first child was conceived.

In March, Mike put his house in Kidderminster up for auction, and the sale was completed the following month. Sarah still had a second-floor flat in Shipston-on-Stour, which now became his UK base.

While packing up his belongings ready for the move to Spain, Mike came across the old 2002 session tapes from Sweet Georgia Brown's and decided to polish them up and release them.

First of all, he had to get in touch with Imelda May, who featured heavily on many of the cuts. Hugh Phillimore, Imelda's manager, confirmed that she was fine about it, but he then had to check with her record company, Decca, who would have been keen to avoid anything being released that would harm Imelda's own sales.

Eventually, all of the permissions were obtained, and in May 2012 Mike went back into the studio to add the final touches. He chose Lazy Moon Recording Studios in Upper Brailes owned by American producer/songwriter Kenny Young, who is probably most famous for co-writing the Drifters' 1964 hit, 'Under The Boardwalk'. The converted barn was virtually on Mike's doorstep, and the studio had the added advantage of not charging London prices.

All of the tracks had been recorded back in 2002, except for some of Mike's vocals, and backing vocals on the title track. His current line-up – Mark Morgan, Nick Whitfield and Tom Bull – as well as Sarah Wynne all contributed to the backing vocals, whilst former BTP guitarist Tony Coni provided the cover artwork. After lying dormant for a decade, *Almost Grown* was finally released in 2012 to great critical acclaim.

In June, Mike played at the wedding of Peter Richardson's daughter Alice in Devon. Mike had an idea that Sarah would be a great addition to his band, and the wedding was the first time that he invited her to sing live onstage. There had been no rehearsals, and she was very shy and nervous, but she drew great applause. A week later, she was well and truly thrown in at the deep end at a festival in the Belgian city of Charleroi, where she was partnered with another female singer, Yvette Hillebrandt, who had been one of the pretty faces around the English rock'n'roll scene for some time. It was almost like the old days of the Revue, and Mike was thrilled with this new development.

Now in her late eighties, Mike's mother was growing increasingly frail and suffered a stroke in the summer of 2012. She spent a week recovering at Avila Hospital before returning to the home in El Tiemblo. It was a tough time, but Mike and Sarah relied on each other's strength to get through it. It was now obvious that Sarah was pregnant, and it meant a lot to Mike for her to show her bulge to his mother.

Mike was now hardly ever in the UK, but he made an exception to appear as an extra in the Peter Richardson *Comic Strip* production, *Five Go To Rehab*. He flew into Heathrow and drove across to Exeter, arriving at an old, run-down building. The crew were a few miles away on a hill outside Totnes, so they sent a runner to pick him up. They drove to a train station, then transferred to a jeep to go up a muddy track. Eventually, they arrived at a hedge beyond which was a picturesque valley, where the action was taking place.

Nigel Planer was dressed as a policeman, whilst Dawn French and Ade Edmondson were also waiting to act out their parts. There were two small tents that were being used as makeshift dressing rooms, and, as the crew had assumed that Mike would arrive ready for action, he had to hurriedly change. Peter had asked him to look like a gangster, and so his costume was a grey suit with a pair of fancy shoes. Unfortunately, Mike had had the suit for several years, and it no longer fitted as it once had. His part involved running down a very steep field chased by police, but the field was full of cow pats and it was wet and slippery. It was a lot of fun, but conditions were challenging for such a novice actor. However, Mike thoroughly enjoyed it and says he would do it all again, particularly if asked to do so by his good friend, Peter. After the filming, it was back to the stage for Mike, and shows in

France, Spain, Switzerland and Germany.

Despite his impending fatherhood, Mike maintained a full schedule throughout September 2012. This even included two days at sea on a *Rockin' Cruise* between Norway and Denmark. Shortly afterwards, Sarah returned to the UK for the final stage of her pregnancy, and Mike allowed himself a break from all but the most essential bookings.

On Sunday, 4 November 2012, Sarah gave birth to Louie Ray Sanchez at Warwick Hospital. There was no real wetting of the baby's head, although she did manage a glass of wine on the day she left hospital – her first taste of alcohol for many months. Mike was so proud, and looked forward to the Christmas holidays, when he would be able to take Louie to see his grandma. Sadly, this was destined never to happen.

Mike permitted himself some well-deserved paternity leave, interrupted only by a festival in Belgium two weeks later. He started to perform regularly again in December, with another appearance at the Greystones, where he finally began to produce material for these pages, and later in the month he was reunited with Imelda May and Paul Jones for a charity event at Cranleigh in Surrey.

Everything was going well until Christmas Eve, when he was woken in Shipston-on-Stour by a phone call from the residency in El Tiemblo. Antonio, the director, told him that his mother had suffered a massive stroke and had been taken to the hospital in Avila. He told Mike that it was important to get himself to the hospital as soon as possible, as it appeared that she would not make it through more than a few days. Later that day, Juanjo travelled down from Bewdley, and he and Mike booked early-morning flights from Gatwick to Madrid.

After a three-day vigil, surrounded by her loving family, Manuela Bastida Gil quietly passed away on 28 December 2012. Mike felt he had to tell the world how he felt and sent this email to his close friends:

My dear mama has passed away.

Manuela Bastida Gil
3 December 1923 – 28 December 2012

Dear friends

As a lot of you will know, I had spent most of December 2012 in England performing several shows, solo and with my band line-ups.

My last show was Friday, 21 December, in Shipston-on-Stour, Warwickshire, where I also have a flat with my fiancée Sarah and our eleven-week-old son, Louie. The month had gone rather smoothly, and I was soon happy to return to our lovely home in central Spain on Christmas week, only this time with my brand new little family.

My biggest desire was that my dear mum would finally get to be handed our little Louie the next time I would be at the residency where she now resided.

That never happened.

Since the summer of 2011, we had arranged for mum to be living in this wonderful residency just five minutes away from our home on the mountain. There, in this well-managed, clean and spacious home with great staff and a restaurant overlooking several palm trees in the gardens, I knew my mum was safe, well fed and taken care of by the lovely nurses.

Twice she had been rushed from the home in El Tiemblo to Avila hospital; the first time was due to breathing difficulties, though two days later she was back at the home, totally recovered. The second time was at the start of August 2012, when she suffered a serious stroke. Myself and some of my cousins, as well as my auntie Maria, had spent most days that week by mum's side worried sick, but also watching her slowly recovering. By the end of the week, she had returned once again to the home but looking and feeling more frail than ever, her voice was now fragile, her words came out very slowly, often she would now also need a wheelchair to be moved around the home, so, things were gradually getting worse, though she would at times still come out with humour in her thoughts and words; mum was still there, all right.

I took a few trips back and forth during November 2012 from the UK to be with my Sarah and Louie, then a week to be at the house in Spain and visiting mum. Every time I visited her, I would bring some rough prints of photos we had taken of Louie back in Shipston. The nurses would gather around mum and cheer her up by saying how beautiful her new grandson was and how everyone was looking forward to finally meeting him when we returned around Christmas/New Year to Spain.

Whilst we were still in Shipston, early in the morning of Christmas Eve I received a call from the director of the home telling me that mum had suffered another serious stroke and had been rushed to hospital once again. This time it was very serious. I called up my family in Madrid, who straight away headed to the hospital two hours away in Avila. I then spoke to my cousin Manolo, who, upon arriving at the ward, had been told by a doctor that mum had maybe only hours left to live.

Christmas Day morning, my brother Juanjo and I took an early flight to Madrid, hired a car and headed straight to mum to find her in a coma with an oxygen mask, gently breathing. Mum remained this way until 13.10 on Friday, 28 December, when she peacefully passed away.

Mum was cremated the following afternoon in Avila, and on 2 January 2013 my brother and I picked up the ashes and brought the urn back to El Tiemblo to join my dad's ashes in the same plot of land next door to where they had both originally buried their four dogs, Blackie, Curro, Rusty and Pancho, which they had loved so much.

Since my father passed away in January 2010, I had been spending every day I could with mum at the house in central Spain. I had become very aware of the illness of Alzheimer's that mum had already been suffering with for the last few years. It was something that would take her memory either slowly or suddenly, and there would never be any improvements.

I've had countless friends tell me of the sad times they have experienced watching their parents' or grandparents' mental health declining with each passing month and year. Eventually, the person suffering this disease doesn't remember most of the basic things they've always done either in the kitchen, the bathroom, the garden, recognising family members or neighbours, always forgetting who has been to visit her that very day. It is impossible to single-handedly care for someone with dementia or Alzheimer's and the worse it gets, the more that person can behave frustrated and angry as they realise they are losing the use of something so vital.

As work came in for me where I had to leave mum in the house for a day or two, I would arrange for some good neighbours to 'baby sit' and give mum companionship, to keep an eye on her, make sure that she didn't burn the kitchen down or have an accident in the house or garden and to make sure she took her medicines, but mum refused to be taken care of and used her anger in irrational ways because she really believed she was fine and needed no help at all from anyone. Why, she would be so adamant as she told you she can walk down the mountain to the main road, catch the bus for the one-hour trip to central Madrid, then get a cab and find her sister's flat, all this when she hasn't even seen the door keys or handbag in several weeks because she lost them somewhere.

There were also the days when she would regularly open up dad's wardrobe and carefully stack all his jackets and shoes on the bed and then ask me to see what I wanted to take back to England with me. I would then ask her to put those clothes back in the wardrobe, that I did not want to try anything on and that I had not lived in England for over two years, but that I had been living downstairs in the same house as her. At times she would not believe a word that I told her.

Mum would get angry at almost everything, but sometimes I felt that her anger was a good thing, because it gave her fire in her soul and a sureness in her that was so reminiscent of when she was a strong-headed, fierce and clear-minded woman, before the illness had begun.

I often wonder what has been the worse feeling for me, to be told that my father has died when I didn't even know he was ill, or to spend three years watching my mum slowly passing away at first from memory loss and eventually from strokes.

A big part of me is glad, very glad, that she died peacefully, but even more glad that she had lived a very healthy life for most of her eighty-nine years. I then think of the people I know who had parents pass away on them when they were still only children or in their teens while they were still so young, and it makes me feel fortunate that I never had to experience such a life without knowing my dear parents the way I do.

Needless to say, mama passed away at the worst time of year possible, when the world is celebrating Christmas and the coming year ahead, when families are all together in the warmth of their loving homes, the smell of good cooking, the glow of candles and decorations, the excuse for a pleasant few days of holiday, whether religious or not, and most of all a time for all generations to enjoy the smiles in children's faces as they open up their presents.

I had a large number of friends who emailed and texted me over Christmas and New Year, and who I have not yet replied back to, as it would have been difficult for anyone to hear about how my holiday time was going (I don't think I was capable of talking much anyway!). I hope all of you get to read this message and for you to know that everything is as fine as can be now.

You can never recover from that feeling of loss towards close family and loved ones. I just needed a while to be able to get back into my old life, back on my feet again.

Mama left me just as a new life came into this world, my beautiful little son, Louie, who's gonna have the best loving daddy in the world.

This was such a sad time, as Mike's parents had always been there for him, but now they were both gone. They had always been very supportive of their son – particularly his mother, who was never judgemental, even when she disapproved of Mike's actions. Chris Wroe recalls one such occasion at Kidderminster Town Hall: 'Mike was performing as usual, and his mother was at the front, resting on her elbows. When his gyrations got a bit too raunchy, she simply looked away, expressionless, before turning back a short time later to watch the end of the show.'

2013

After the death of his mother, Mike took a break from performing for three weeks, then embarked upon tours of France and Germany.

Towards the end of April 2013, he played a gig at Wolverley Social Club for the Proton Effect charity. It was billed as a solo appearance, with his old school friend Beefy providing the PA as well as performing with his current band, the Hayriders. Beefy had a feeling that it could be a special night: 'We walked in as the soundcheck was going on, and I heard this voice heckling us, telling us that we were not as good as Mike Sanchez. Out of the darkness Robert Plant appeared, but even he did not know the full line-up that evening. Neil Wright had persuaded Andy Silvester to turn up, and Ian Jennings flew in from Switzerland. We were a bit apprehensive about the relationship between Ian and Mike after the Playboys split, but everything was fine, and I suppose after over thirteen years there should not have been any doubt. Neil also contacted Ricky Cool, and he was really up for it. Ex-Hoola Boola Boy Ted Bunting completed the line-up on sax, and it was almost the original Big Town Playboys. Andy was reluctant to get up on stage at first, but when everyone was there, he just had to join in. It was a fantastic night, and I really hope they get back together again.'

Ian Jennings thought it sounded as though they had never stopped, but Mike was less impressed. The perfectionist in him noted that they had not rehearsed together for many years, though there is no doubt that as a band they still had a spark.

Mark Morgan had by this time been with Mike for twenty years. Although there was no momentous occasion to mark this milestone, Mark will always be grateful for the time he has spent with the band: 'Mike was always really patient. I had problems with my hands and was told to give up the drums. I can no longer do what I see in my mind, but he stuck with me. When he and Ian split up, it almost broke my heart, as they were like parents, musically. Now, with Nick and Tom, we have another great band. After all this time I feel I can now be quite open with Mike, and question what we do when I see fit.'

In the summer, Mike's schedule grew once again, including another visit to Burnley for what had become the *International Rock & Blues Festival*, now celebrating its 25th anniversary. It was a fitting return, as he had played at the inaugural event with the Big Town Playboys. He subsequently played several shows with the Drew Davies Rhythm Combo in Belgium and France.

5 June 2013 witnessed another momentous event in Mike's life. He married Sarah Wynne in Stratford-upon-Avon, and their guests at the Shakespeare Hotel included Robert Plant, Jeff and Sandra Beck, Peter Richardson, and many of Mike's band members both past and present. Peter later noted that, 'There were sixty or so guests, of which fifty were musicians, and none of them got up to play!'

The honeymoon was an unusual affair, as Mike was booked to do three shows. The first was in Barcelona with the Barcelona Big Blues Band; the second was at the international boogie-woogie festival in Laroquebrou, a picturesque town in South-Central France; and the third was a festival at Mougins, close to Cannes. Mike, Sarah and Louie enjoyed a few days off in both Barcelona and Mougins, though in the process they drove a total of around 2,000 miles through scenic landscapes across Spain and southern France.

At the beginning of September, Mike was interviewed at his home in Spain by internationally renowned food and wine critic Victor de la Serna. De la Serna was amazed that such a prominent rhythm & blues performer could live in Spain without most of the population being aware of it, and his interview was published in leading Spanish newspaper *El Mundo*.

As the end of 2013 approached, Sweden, France and Denmark were all on the agenda – as well as Louie Ray's first birthday.

2014

Robert Plant has known Mike since his early days practising upstairs at the George Hotel with the Rockets. He once saw him play an upright piano unaccompanied, and said that Mike showed more power and charisma than he himself could ever muster at Madison Square Garden. He was also asked for career advice by a young up-and-coming band. He told them: 'Look at Mike Sanchez, copy him, retain your integrity, and play what you love to play.'

Mark Morgan explains that his own success with the band is not just a musical partnership, but more to do with the man himself:

'With the Big Town Playboys, both Mike and Ian were influential in different ways. Mike is, of course, a performer – but he is much more than that. He is a mentor without even knowing it. His knowledge of the music he plays and how it should be done is unsurpassed. Sometimes I take this for granted, until I see him do a solo performance or play with another band, and then I am reminded of his force.

'In the early days of my tenure with the band, we occasionally socialised together, but Mike is more comfortable doing this in his own home. He cooks a mean paella too. He is private at times and prefers to be surrounded with people he knows, mostly the guys he works with. Mike wouldn't be too bothered about going to the pub unless he's in his comfort zone with friends and musicians he's already acquainted with. Of course, a major part of his social life really is performing and meeting his fans. He's got family now, and we don't get much time to rehearse with him living in Spain. We all give him a gentle poke about his weight and his health, and I am really pleased that he was given a clean bill of health recently [after a routine check-up]. Sometimes I think that Mike should write more of his own stuff, as he is a good writer, and often our set list is similar to ten years ago. He's got the potential to get a whole new set together, and that would put even more life into the stage show.'

Nick Whitfield has been Mike's bass player of choice since 2009 and is comfortable with their working relationship: 'I feel very fortunate to have shared the stage with Mike over the years. We've played some wonderful gigs and festivals, and we're always treated well. Mike's an easy-going guy, though not a soft touch. There's freedom onstage, but he knows what he wants. We often joke that if you haven't received a "fish eye" – a sideways look of disapproval – from him onstage, then you haven't lived!

'Mike is a serious musician, at the top of his game, but he doesn't take himself too seriously. Sober as a judge before going onstage, but always up for a serious after-show-vino nightcap back at the hotel. He told me recently, "I've had the best summer of my life," and I believe him. His marriage to his sweetheart and soulmate, Sarah, the birth of his son, Louie, and relocation to his recently departed parents' house in Spain has Mike in a good place.

'When I first went to Mike's townhouse overlooking the train station in Kidderminster, he had two caged lovebirds in his kitchen. He likes the birds, does Mike – no pun intended! I imagined him putting on a Nat 'King' Cole record, opening a bottle of red, watching them, and turning to mush whilst winding down after a long drive back from a gig. We also have a mutual love for the heron too, and often joke about writing it into a song. Maybe we have too much time to think sat around airports. Anyway, he's out in the Spanish mountains now with the woodpeckers: "Rock woodpecker, let's rock!"'

Guitarist Tom Bull is another who just relishes his involvement with Mike: 'I joined the band because I loved the style of music. Mike and, indeed, the rest of the guys were great to work with and hang around with. The gigs were well paid, and I like to travel, so it was good that many of the shows were in Europe. My favourite Mike Sanchez track is "Everybody's Got A Buick", one of his originals from the *Babes And Buicks* album, as it shows his aggressive and powerful side, with a pumping left hand, energetic pace and some madness about it with the screaming sax at the end. It's also from the heart too, as he would love to own an old Buick, and gets quite jealous when picked up by promoters in old American cars. Mike can be a little out of touch with reality sometimes, but that's understandable since he has never had a *normal* job: he has always performed for a living. He is one of the most sensitive and caring people I've ever known, and would never purposely upset anyone.'

Mike certainly builds relationships within his working environment, and they often go way beyond that, as assistant Jo Hill can testify: 'Seven years after meeting him, I'm still trying to sort his working – and sometimes private – life out! He is a genuine, sensitive, honest and thoughtful guy who's now become a very dear friend and confidant. We've been through a lot together regarding his life, girlfriends and music. He is so passionate about his music, and I'm constantly amazed at the knowledge he has. He's pushed so many CDs my way from artists I'd never heard of from the '40s, '50s and '60s, and this roots, rock'n'roll, boogie-woogie and rhythm & blues has become a genre I love. However, on a recent visit to his home in Spain, I was pleased, and a little amused, to hear him play some modern heavy rock and pop CDs!

'His fans know Mike the entertainer, the guy who's always happy to chat and sign a CD at the end of a frenetic show, still dripping with sweat! They have a photo taken and they keep coming back for more, and after all this time he's still humble and thankful that they do. He admits to me that he's still nervous before going onstage, won't/can't eat, but you'd never guess that when he hits those keys! Pure professional.

'Over the years, I've been along to many shows including some abroad. It's evident that he is very respected by all promoters, whether they be old rock'n'rollers, Teddy boys or suited-and-booted gentlemen. They all love his music and the man himself. He has a superb band, many of whom have been with him for a long time, and I know they love and respect him too.

'He's a comedian, a storyteller who can wax lyrically better than most, and someone who can pour his heart out when he needs to. He's also someone who needs to lose some weight!'

It has been a successful partnership, but Mike is wary about what might happen after seven years. Andy Silvester looked after the affairs of the Big Town Playboys for around that period of time, and Ian Jennings' tenure was also seven years. When Mike went solo, he looked after his own affairs for seven years, before Jo took over the arduous task. He is wary that, having reached the magical number, she doesn't decide to call it a day.

Mike Sanchez continues to headline across Europe, as well as selling out many well-known venues in the UK such as the 100 Club and the Robin 2 in Bilston. He is one of the first names to be considered when the ever-popular rock'n'roll festivals are being put together, and as Mark Lamarr said, 'Mike Sanchez would have invented rock'n'roll if no one else had bothered.' As a musician, his authentic sound makes him a popular choice for studio sessions, and he has the ability to make great musicians sound even better. He has played in front of thousands, and he has played in front of just two or three. He has played to royalty, celebrities and, of course, his fans, and he treats them all the same. On one occasion, he even played at a fan's funeral – in front of the coffin – where his set was just two Irving Berlin songs. Mike did not know the deceased man, but his daughter Sheila was a fan who followed him wherever he played in the West Midlands. It meant so much to Mike that he simply could not refuse. It was a nervous experience as he sat at his piano beside the altar and the coffin, and the ambience was heightened by the emotional tears of the bereaved as he delivered the powerful Berlin songs, including 'When I Leave This World Behind' and 'When I Lost You'.

His fans will always be at the forefront of his mind, as promoter, friend and follower Ian Hartley testifies: 'Over the years, I met Mike a few times and worked with him at some private and public events. At one private party in the Midlands, I mentioned to Mike that we were hoping to come and see him at *Burnley National Blues*

Festival in three or four months' time. He offered to put me on the guest list, and I was naturally pleased to accept. The weeks and months went by and I didn't hear from him. Nevertheless, I wanted to see the man in action and went to the event, and as I had not heard from him I went to the box office early to buy our tickets. I was told that the whole event was sold out with no chance of a ticket. I was just walking away from the booking office when my phone rang and Jo – Mike's agent/secretary and all round good egg – spoke to me, telling me that Mike had phoned her on his way to the event, as he didn't have my number with him. He asked her to call and tell me that I must ask at the box office for the two guest tickets he had arranged to put aside for us. I was amazed that, after about four months, Mike had not only remembered about the tickets, but also organised a call to make sure I remembered. I'm not sure how many other artists would have done that. Needless to say, the great man was sensational on stage. Since then, I have got to know Mike and Sarah a lot better and am always impressed by his offstage modesty, kindness and sincerity.'

At the start of 2014, Mike had just one show in January. After that, the year was busier, with two weeks of touring in Germany and a whole month in the UK. His base in El Tiemblo, just outside Madrid, is ideal for gigs throughout Europe, and of course he no longer has to cope with the British weather, the traffic jams and the speed cameras. His energetic playing means that he now has to get a new Roland or Yamaha piano every couple of years. Long gone are the times when one would last for a couple of decades, though many of his venues know what he wants and so will have an instrument ready for him when he gets there.

His recordings are now available across the Internet through ReverbNation and other music download sites. He has embraced the power of Facebook, which has replaced Myspace as his social medium of choice, and he sent his first tweet in 2013, but admits that, when there are no gigs in the diary, he can sit in front of his PC screen for days at a time. He enjoys the power of the Internet that can bring his music to new fans on a daily basis.

Now that he has turned 50, he is ready to open the next chapter in the colourful book of his life, and there are plenty of opinions as to what that chapter should contain.

Guitar legend Jeff Beck has some unfinished business: 'We should redo *Crazy Legs*. It sounds like the original, but I want to remix it because we didn't get the voice distortion quite right. You have to use ribbon mics for that authentic Gene Vincent sound. I used to be against re-releasing stuff, but it would get to another audience that never knew about it.'

Will Wakefield believes that Mike's future lies within: 'He may not have always made the right decisions, but he is lucky to have made a living at something that he really wanted to do. The Big Town Playboys on their form were the best live band *ever*. Mike wrote loads of his own stuff, but he is his own biggest critic and so much of it never saw the light of day. He should go back and have a look at all of those songs.'

Tim Porter has been promoting Mike for over ten years, including his last two Christmas shows at Shipston-on-Stour, and he also produced a feature on Mike for *Blues in Britain* magazine in April 2013. He loves to work with Mike, but supports Will's view about his future direction: 'I can always guarantee a good crowd when I book him, whether solo or with a band. He's one of the few artists who have a wide appeal, both to hardcore rock'n'rollers or people who have never seen him before but appreciate his showmanship. Mike has never disappointed. I'd like to see him moving onto some new material, and getting the credit and work he deserves. I don't see him play guitar much any more, which is a shame. He did a good version of "Shake Your Hips".'

Martin Winning agrees that originals are the way forward: 'Mike has a great talent for original material. I'm surprised he hasn't done more of his own stuff in his shows. He should record an album of original material and put more of them in his own set.'

Rowdy Yeats is another who would like to hear more of Mike's own stuff, but he has some additional advice based on his many years of working in the music industry, and with Mike: 'He should release an album of his own songs, and he should try some publicity. He has had several deals on the table over the years that he walked away from. This would have got him CDs in record shops, recording deals, DVDs, but he has always been in it for the long haul. Now it is time to capitalise on what he has already got. When he was with the Playboys, you could remove any member of the band and you would still have the Big Town Playboys if you still had Mike Sanchez.'

It is one of Mike's great regrets that he has not written more original material, and he intends to put that right. He finds that, once he is in a creative mood, he can have three verses and a chorus put together in about twenty minutes, and that has led to some of his best compositions.

Swedish guitarist Anders Lewen believes that Mike still has a lot to offer: 'Every now and then we still play together, and I think it always will be like that, because we're both devoted to this music. Onstage, Mike is just as explosive as in his younger days, and his vocals are just getting better and more powerful every year. Now, when we perform it's like having fun onstage with a good friend.'

Andy Fairweather-Low has a few regrets: 'It's a shame that the original Big Town Playboys with Andy Silvester didn't stay together that long. They were the best, with Ian and Mark Morgan. But it baffles me why Mike has not done better than he has. We had a residency at the 100 Club every Sunday night, and it would be packed. Everyone had a great time, and I would drive home to Wales every Monday thinking that doors would open, but they never did. Nothing changed. I don't think he should do anything differently. He should just keep doing what he does.'

Peter Richardson offers an opinion as to what has held him back: 'Mike's recording career is sometimes too much like the original guys. With Mike, the music must come from that era, and it's not easy to get that music appreciated by a new audience.'

Albert Lee sees the road ahead: 'Mike should continue to do what he has always done. There are always challenges, and we are all getting older, and over time our audiences change. It's hard to get the younger kids interested in what we do, but I really do hope that he can find that wider audience as he deserves to be heard by the whole world.'

Rick Vito sums him up: 'Mike Sanchez possesses truly great onstage charisma, and I never tire of hearing his vocal and instrumental take on his many original compositions, as well as his faithful yet unique versions of classic rhythm & blues and vintage rock'n'roll. He is a very special talent, a great guy, and someone that I'm proud to know and call a friend. Mike Sanchez deserves the best because he *is* the best.'

Sound engineer Roy Williams remains convinced that Mike still has a big future: 'He is a great performer, and a lot more people should see him. He should be a bit more picky about his gigs and not burn himself out so much, and he could definitely benefit from someone helping him out. Now and then even the great artists could benefit from saying "No", or taking some advice. Maybe if he had the right manager with him that big break could happen.'

However, Nick Lunt adds a note of caution: 'We played a gig a couple of years ago at which there were a lot of young ladies. Mike and sax player Martin Winning decided to roll around on the floor to impress these girls, but then they couldn't get up. It was hilarious, and just a reminder that we are all getting a bit older! At the end of the day, though, what Mike does best is thumping the piano and knocking out great rhythm & blues. For that style of music there is no one that can do it better. He is the man – and he's not got a bad voice either! When we are playing and the six-piece goes down to a four-piece without the horns, Martin and myself stand at the side of the stage and enjoy every minute of it.'

Chris Wroe believes that *Women & Cadillacs* holds the key: 'On that album is my all-time favourite track, "The Voice Within". It stood out because there was a shift in the vibe. The band added a lot of subtlety, and Mike was able to go in a new direction. It was more Nat 'King' Cole style and less rock'n'roll. He could have been the first Michael Bublé. Back then there was nobody to advise him to go in that direction. Now he is his own man, and he can try all sorts of different styles to let his personality come out. He has already appealed to all levels of society without even knowing it.'

Guitarist Tony Coni would just like to be involved: 'If he changed anything, he wouldn't be Mike Sanchez, but he should give me a ring and release a single with me. It would be something dirty – his stuff is a bit too nice – and on vinyl, so that we could give it to all the deejays. After that, we could talk about an album. Seriously though, he taught me a lot, about grooves and stuff. Sometimes you have to wait in the background until it is your chance to shine.'

Friend and fellow musician Jim Merris believes that Mike was born too late: 'When I listen to him play, he is the real deal. A natural-born musician, whose voice and onstage persona puts him amongst the greats of rock'n'roll. I truly believe that if he had been performing in the late '40s and '50s he could have been as big as household names such as Jerry Lee Lewis, Little Richard, Fats Domino, etc. He could have been the British Elvis. His voice is a perfect instrument that can re-create the hard-edged rasp of '50s rockabilly or emulate the soft tones of Nat 'King' Cole, with everything in between. Now that the wild man has been tamed with a lovely wife and child – with the greatest rock'n'roll name ever – he needs to pass on his expertise and immerse his young son in classic rhythm & blues music, so that the name can be continued.'

Paul Ansell has perhaps got the best advice of all: 'He should grow old gracefully, and just do what makes him happy. He's always given everyone else so much pleasure, and I've never heard a bad word said about him.'

Old friend and musician Julian Benjamin believes that Mike should appreciate the success that he has had: 'It's nice to think that we were both singing into hair brushes in the '70s, and are both making a good living now doing exactly what we dreamed of then. I have always – and will always – feel blessed to be able to do something that I love so much. This is what unites us fortunate ones that, throughout whatever means, we are lucky enough to have this strange ability to make music and entertain so many thousands of people.'

Julian's words certainly ring true for Mike, and he has always considered himself privileged to be able to perform his music around the world.

Mike Sanchez has always surrounded himself with great musicians. Technically, he rates Jeff Beck as one of the best, with a couldn't-care-less attitude mixed with a level of something really exciting, though he admits that he would have loved to have seen Peter Green in his younger days. Emotionally, Aaron Neville made him cry when he heard him singing at the *International Jazz Festival* in Molde, as did the Buena Vista Social Club at the same festival some years later. He shed more tears sharing an evening with Solomon Burke at the indigO2 club and on a Spanish tour with the Rhythm Kings, though perhaps the occasion that got to him most was at the Catfish Club in Brighton. The crowd were a mixture of rock'n'roll and soul fans, but when the Five Blind Boys of Alabama delivered their gospel set, it was a truly moving experience. Mike has been touched by many musical styles, and there is still more to discover.

He is keen that his legacy should remain long after he has gone, in the shape of many great albums of great music. His voice has now mellowed, and so he is considering an easy listening compilation which he would dedicate to his parents, but he would also like to record a wild, high-energy Little Richard-style album. A tribute to Texas singer-pianist Amos Milburn is high on his list of priorities. He wants to experiment with a string section, and he wants to take Sarah into the studio so that she can record some of her own work.

Importantly, Mike does not want anyone but himself to have control over his life and his career – particularly managers and other music industry people. If he can live comfortably just doing his thing and being with his family, then that is everything he needs.

Whatever he decides to do, you can be sure he will still be putting his heart and soul into it, as he remains one of the best rhythm & blues performers around. His legacy will always say that he left high school at the age of 17 and has never had a full-time day job, so he must be doing something right!

CHAPTER 12

Mike on Music

Mike's encyclopaedic knowledge of roots music spans many decades. Here, Mike describes in his own words the major influences on his rock'n'roll style.

My first memories of music come from my years in London. Growing up and listening to the radio during the late 1960s and early 1970s, I was exposed to all of the current mainstream pop and rock, which did very little for me. Quite often, the deejay would play what have always been called 'golden oldies', and I could usually hear the obvious differences in sound between what had been recorded in, say, 1958 and something new coming out in 1972. I instantly preferred the older music. In general, the older records sounded so much more exciting, especially if the music was rock'n'roll or simply had a good beat to it. The biggest thing I always noticed about the old music was that I could usually hear and understand the words that were being sung, and that the vocalist often had a distinctive style that he had maybe copied from somewhere else, but that he had ultimately made his own. For example, a Billy Fury or Cliff Richard record sounded like they were doing their best Elvis Presley impression, Adam Faith often sounded like Buddy Holly, and early Beatles sounded so much in the style of the Everly Brothers.

My brother, Juanjo, had also left me with some old singles that he'd picked up when he was growing up. Mum and dad had an old Dansette record player and, together with this little bunch of singles, I was at times very busy playing one single after another: records by Johnny Burnette, Brenda Lee, Cliff Richard, Adam Faith, Buddy Holly, Little Richard, Pat Boone, Chubby Checker, Johnny & The Hurricanes, Elvis Presley, the Everly Brothers and Winifred Atwell.

I guess this is where I realised that I had a lot more interest in music from that period than the current music on the hit parade of the time. From British beat music into late 1960s rock, I recall a preference for early Beatles tunes such as 'She Loves You' and their versions of songs such as Arthur Alexander's 'Anna', rather than anything from the *Sgt. Pepper* album, where the lyrics and sounds made no sense to me at all. I found the early sounds of the Rolling Stones, the Who, Small Faces, etc., quite exciting, but they still never made me wanna go crazy in the way Little Richard or Gene Vincent & His Blue Caps' first hit records made me feel. I guess I was hooked on classic rock'n'roll from the start.

The sound of real vintage instruments playing raw, exciting rock'n'roll music with a heavy beat that makes you want to start hitting things – now, that's where I was! I completely agreed with the energy of punk rock, but I never wanted to get political, militant, or preach anarchy in any way. The messages in the songs were straightforward, and I loved them.

Every time I heard Eddie Cochran's 'Summertime Blues' or 'Somethin' Else', I knew and understood, just like I did when I heard Gene Vincent's 1956 Blue Caps records such as 'Hold Me, Hug Me, Rock Me' or Larry Williams' 'Slow Down', and I realised that there was a whole world of great music out there just waiting for me to discover it.

Once I had soaked up the classic rockabilly and popular rock'n'roll artists of the 1950s, it wasn't long before I started to discover where the music came from, and then I was gone! If today I could create the greatest cocktail of energy from back then, it would include Little Richard, Johnny Burnette's Rock'n'Roll Trio, Ike Turner's Kings of Rhythm, Wynonie Harris, Big Maybelle, Little Walter, Bo Diddley, James Brown, Otis Redding, Howlin' Wolf, the Five Blind Boys of Alabama, Little Willie John, Big Jay McNeely and way too many others to mention. The recordings of all of these artists have kept millions of us buzzing for several decades!

This was real rock'n'roll, and much of it was recorded many years before it was coined as rock'n'roll for the white people, and I loved it!

I set myself a goal to learn every song that Elvis ever recorded for Sun Records. Listening to this music, I discovered that Elvis Presley's 'That's All Right', 'My Baby Left Me' and 'So Glad You're Mine' were written and recorded a few years before by Arthur 'Big

Boy' Crudup; 'Tomorrow Night' was a big hit for Lonnie Johnson long before Elvis; 'Reconsider Baby' was by Lowell Fulson; and 'Good Rockin' Tonight' was written and recorded by Roy Brown, and then covered by Wynonie Harris. There was a whole new world out there, like a magical musical swimming pool, and I was ready to dive straight in.

So if, for example, I start by discovering Elvis, then I discover all the many great artists who also recorded at Sam Phillips' Sun Studio in Memphis, and there then opens up the world of country and folk music, country blues, rockabilly and urban rhythm & blues. With all of these connections, I begin to unearth what was going on around the rest of North America, from the east to west, north to south: New York, Chicago, Texas, St Louis, Kansas, Mississippi, Louisiana, Los Angeles and the West Coast; singers, crooners and blues shouters, guitarists, harmonica players, saxophonists, boogie-woogie and blues pianists, small bands and big orchestras.

When I read studio session details, I began to recognise the same session musicians playing on many of those tracks that were recorded in particular cities, as well as thousands of one-off wonders who recorded two successful tracks and then disappeared, and I began to realise there's a whole world of beautiful music out there, most of which is long forgotten by the world due to the fast-changing trends and styles of music and culture. But I keep delving into it and going back in time with the music I found, back into the earlier parts of the twentieth century before Elvis was even born, when Louis Jordan was still an unheard-of pioneer and Duke Ellington had just started at the Cotton Club. The history of popular music is so amazing!

I have a strong love for the music that came from New Orleans that brought about some of the greatest rhythm & blues music ever recorded, as well as being the birthplace of funk. That music also had such a huge influence on the developing music of Jamaica, thanks to the sounds of artists such as Fats Domino on New Orleans radio stations being picked up in the West Indies. All of these connections made me pick up on Jamaican rhythm & blues, ska, bluebeat and reggae, as well as gaining a clearer understanding on how rhythm & blues developed through the 1960s and 1970s with soul and funk. I also became a fan of the Memphis sound, Booker T. & The MGs, Stax, Motown, etc..

From another angle, I have always had a love for Latin/Hispanic music from the 1940s and 1950s, especially South American and

Afro-Caribbean music: artists such as Mexico's Trio Los Panchos, Chilean bolero singer Lucho Gatica and the orchestras of Cuba and Puerto Rico.

Above everything, my love for music stems from the rawness of recordings being as live and exciting as possible, whatever the style of music may be, and whatever flaws were in the recording or the skills of the artists being recorded. Most of my favourite records have got mistakes and imperfections in the recordings, because for me what matters is the soul and the feeling that was captured at that moment. I chose the simplistic twelve-bar-based music of blues and rock'n'roll because it allows the freedom for the music to be loose and raw. Forget about chord progressions and just groove or rock!

Fifties rock'n'roll was epitomised by Richard Penniman, better known as Little Richard, who had a manic stage presence all of his own; St Louis blues shouter Screamin' Joe Neal, who took this persona a step further; and Johnny Burnette, who died less than six months after I was born. Johnny Burnette's Rock'n'Roll Trio, who recorded a classic version of Tiny Bradshaw's 'The Train Kept A-Rollin'', released on the Coral label, became a huge influence on many of the British beat and rock bands of the sixties' era. Ike Turner's Kings of Rhythm laid down grooves in the early 1950s, long before Ike met Tina, featuring Billy Gayles' powerful vocals on tracks such as 'No Coming Back'. Nappy Brown was another influential rhythm & blues singer that I loved, as his vocals on tracks such as 'Night Time Is The Right Time' were raw enough to send shivers down my spine. James Brown crossed the decades with his mix of jump blues and gospel, and then soul and funk. Johnny 'Guitar' Watson is another perfect example of a great artist who naturally moved with the times, from the piano rhythm & blues of the early 1950s to the funk guitar styles of the mid-1970s.

Otis Redding, best known for 'Dock Of The Bay', had a much wider appeal, moving through rhythm & blues to soul, thanks to the undoubted influence of Little Richard during the time Otis spent in his backing band in the 1950s. Little Willie John sang sensational rhythm & blues, including some of the most classic, soulful blues ballads of the 1950s and early 1960s. The same goes for Jackie Wilson and Sam Cooke: unbelievable voices.

Digging still deeper, I discovered the female rhythm & blues voices of Big Maybelle, Ruth Brown, Wynona Carr and LaVern Baker, all of whose gospel roots were evident in their music, as well as blues shouters such as Wynonie Harris and Roy 'Good Rockin'' Brown who were forerunners of rock'n'roll, long before the term was ever invented by deejay Alan Freed.

There was the Chicago blues of Muddy Waters, Bo Diddley, Otis Spann, Willie Dixon and Otis Rush. From the moment I heard the track 'My Babe', I was crazy about the voice and innovative harmonica of Little Walter, as he simply sounded unlike anyone else. Bo Diddley also created a unique sound, but with guitar instead of harmonica, where his chugging rhythms transcended blues into rock using the power of electricity, a heavy drum beat and a bunch of maracas, whilst in contrast there was no one who could match the distinctive voice of the legendary bluesman Howlin' Wolf.

When I picked up a copy of *Chuck Berry's Greatest Hits*, I was completely hooked. Every song was an original masterpiece of rock'n'roll that told the best stories about girls, big cars and frustrated teenage life in the late fifties. All of this was played out to the backdrop of the finest Chicago session musicians, led by Willie Dixon, and featuring the piano of Berry's bandleader, Johnnie Johnson. It was the sound of that piano in the background that, to this day, I enjoy trying to emulate.

I also grew a love for the sound of the saxophone in rhythm & blues, particularly the combination of tenor and baritone saxophones that are often heard together on the New Orleans recordings of Little Richard and Fats Domino. I discovered Plas Johnson, who played the tenor saxophone on the famous 'Pink Panther Theme', but there were so many others that I found as my thirst for musical knowledge took me deeper into the subject matter. Lionel Hampton's Orchestra had a huge wartime hit with 'Flying Home', which featured a fabulous tenor solo by Illinois Jacquet. This became a cornerstone for all of the many big band saxophonists, who were now finding themselves in smaller combos due to the financial crisis that the war imposed on orchestras during the 1940s. Swing music was very quickly gaining a rougher edge, and so, as well as Louis Jordan's wild jump blues, it was also moments like Illinois' solo that prompted younger and angrier saxophonists to emerge – players such as 'King of the Honkers' Big Jay McNeely, who developed a 'honking' style all of his own and who still plays that way today. It was all sexy, dangerous, and I was hooked and thirsty for more.

I consumed the great singer-pianists such as Jerry Lee Lewis, Little Richard and Fats Domino, and then discovered lesser-known artists such as Clarence 'Frogman' Henry and Jimmy Beasley, both of whom sang and played in that same catchy Fats Domino style. Some of the great New Orleans pianists performed in styles much harder for me to understand, but much more accessible were the singer-pianists Amos Milburn, Charles Brown, Floyd Dixon and Little Willie Littlefield. I am proud to say that I shared a special friendship and performed numerous times over the years with Texas pianist Little Willie, who moved from the US to the Netherlands in the early 1980s, and where he stayed until he passed away in 2013. Watching Little Willie perform onstage from the mid-1980s until recent times was a huge and constant influence on me throughout my career. It has been an epic voyage of discovery, and such is the heritage and history of rock'n'roll and blues music, it is a journey that will continue, enhanced by the power of the Internet.

This magical tool has now given us all the ability to communicate with people everywhere, and to read up on news from around the world that has not or may not have been manipulated by the global media machine. I am very interested in what scientists are discovering about our little planet and what's out there in the vastness of space, and also the speed at which humans have created a world that's being pushed to the brink of disaster through mass population growth, pollution, war, race and religion, the entrapment of the monetary system, the nuclear age and the complex madness that surrounds us all. As well as observing world news and affairs, I also watch a lot of interviews on YouTube with people such as George Carlin, Ricky Gervais, Henry Rollins, Christopher Hitchens, Russell Brand, Stephen Fry, Ian Dury and Richard Dawkins, and documentaries such as the *Zeitgeist* series.

For unimportant celebrity bullshit to make the headlines much more than the war and famine that envelops billions of sufferers should make anyone with a heart and soul question the system we all live in.

So, yeah, with my PC I watch from a distance and see what people have to say around the world.

There's certainly a lot more than happy feel-good music going on, and the fact that I am often on a stage doing my thing and helping people to feel good, if just for a day, a week or a month, then I feel like my 'job' is a beautiful one indeed.

How on earth can playing this simple, happy roots music that gives me so much pleasure and that every year helps to bring so much pleasure to thousands of others be wrong in any way? I mean, what a wonderful way to live your life!

With this in mind, then, why are not schools everywhere encouraging children and students to get more involved in the arts and in music and theatre, etc.? Why, throughout decades or even centuries, have the educational systems put creativity such as the arts and music down at the bottom of any system, when it is these very subjects that, if studied and learnt, could help everyone to express themselves more with love and freedom than with the greed for money and power? I guess that this is the main struggle for today's performing artists, as most governments in this world gradually try and stop our freedom of expression by quietly suffocating our cultures until we have no more civil liberties.

Thirty years ago in England, it seemed that every town had several places – pubs, clubs, theatres and venues – where you could set up as a band and perform a show. Our cities were filled with live music scenes for fans of all kinds of rock, punk, reggae, pop, etc.. Since the late '50s, all sorts of halls and clubs feasted weekly on new talents who wanted to make something of themselves, become stars, become the new Elvis, and throughout the '60s until the '80s new and old music cultures flourished in a rainbow of styles and fashions, aided by improvements in sound technology onstage and in recording studios, and with managers and record companies who used the media to make the music business huge in terms of record sales and stadium concerts. Then punk and alternative scenes hit the streets and made the music reachable to kids once again, and we all had identities; we belonged to something.

Now it seems that most kids and adults are sat at home in front of their PCs whilst the live music venues that were once buzzing with love, gossip, anger and frustration are no longer there. Thousands of pubs everywhere are now boarded up as people remain at home and share their thoughts with others via social media... for online we can now do all our shopping, find our future partners, do our banking and arrange our own funerals... and now we *also* have to welcome Big Brother, as we are being watched... and all in the name of 'the war against terror'.

If this is not enough reason for me to wanna let out steam on a stage with rock'n'roll, then nothing is!

If today a kid decides to form a roots rock band with a spirit cocktail made up of Ray Charles, Joe Strummer, Little Richard, James Brown, John Lennon, Bob Marley, Jimi Hendrix and Otis Redding, then that kid should deserve the best that the world can offer!

Often over the years I have met youngsters who were knocked out by what I had done onstage, and they've come up to me after the show wanting to know more about where this music came from. Years later, I have met them again, and they were now on a stage performing their version of the music that I had originally introduced to them.

For me to be able to spark an interest and potentially change a person's life in this way, the way I felt that spark when I first saw live bands myself, then that's another part of my work done in this world!

The great Nat 'King' Cole sang in 'Nature Boy': *'The greatest thing you'll ever learn, is just to love and be loved in return.'*

For now, I have put together the fifty songs that I consider to have had the biggest influence on my life and on my career. I hope that you enjoy all of the classics, and if there are some on there that you have never heard before, I hope that you will take the time to check them out and enjoy them as much as I did. The list below is in no order whatsoever.

'Good Golly Miss Molly' – Little Richard
'Down The Road Apiece' – Amos Milburn
'The Train Kept A-Rollin'' – Johnny Burnette Trio
'Rudy's Rock' – Bill Haley & His Comets
'(Every Time I Hear) That Mellow Saxophone' – Roy Montrell
'Rooming House Boogie' – Cab Calloway & His Orchestra
'Surfin' Bird' – Trashmen
'Oh Marie' – Louis Prima
'Brand New Cadillac' – Vince Taylor & His Playboys
'My Heart Is Mended' – Charles Brown
'Pledging My Love' – Johnny Ace
'Real Wild Child' – Jerry Lee Lewis
'The Wobble' – Jimmy McCracklin
'Hip Boots' – Boots Brown & His Blockbusters
'Goodnight My Love' – Jesse Belvin
'Chicken Shack Boogie' – Amos Milburn
'Yeh, Yeh' – Georgie Fame & The Blue Flames
'No Coming Back' – Billy Gayles with Ike Turner's
                              Kings of Rhythm
'Shake Your Hips' – Slim Harpo
'My Babe' – Little Walter
'The Glory Of Love' – Five Keys
'Peggy Sue' – Buddy Holly

'Ooh Little Girl' – Floyd Dixon
'Heeby-Jeebies' – Little Richard
'Tallahassee Lassie' – Freddy Cannon
'Lovin' Machine' – Wynonie Harris
'It'll Be Me' – Cliff Richard & The Shadows
'Buckeye' –Johnny & The Hurricanes
'Coal Miner' – Nappy Brown
'One Night Of Sin' – Smiley Lewis
'Hold Me, Hug Me, Rock Me' – Gene Vincent & His Blue Caps
'Long Blond Hair' – Johnny Powers
'Jungle Rock' – Hank Mizell
'Heartbreak Hotel' – Elvis Presley
'I'm Ready' – Fats Domino
'River, Stay Away From My Door' – Charlie Rich
'Cat Man' – Gene Vincent & His Blue Caps
'Shakin' All Over' – Johnny Kidd & The Pirates
'Bony Moronie' – Larry Williams
'K.C. Loving' – Little Willie Littlefield
'Money (That's What I Want)' – Sonics
'Ain't Got No Home' – Clarence 'Frogman' Henry
'Please Send Me Someone To Love' – Percy Mayfield
'Batman Theme' – Link Wray
'Teen Flip (Texas Twister)' – Ernie Fields Orchestra
'(Get Your Kicks On) Route 66' – King Cole Trio
'Green Onions' – Booker T. & The MGs
'Mumblin' Guitar' – Bo Diddley
'Feelin' Good' – Little Junior's Blue Flames
'Sleep Walk' – Santo & Johnny

Discography

This discography contains details of all of Mike's key releases as a solo performer, as a member of the Big Town Playboys and Bill Wyman's Rhythm Kings, and as a guest on other artists' recordings. Reissues have only been included where they are of special interest. Compilation albums have been ignored, except where the material is otherwise unavailable. To complete the picture, additional sections covering Mike's VHS, DVD and film soundtrack recordings appear at the end.

45 rpm Singles

Big Town Playboys

Making Waves DRIFT-103	Down The Road Apiece / I Like It / Gotta Do More For My Baby[1]	1985

LPs

Big Town Playboys

Making Waves SPIN-203	**PLAYBOY BOOGIE!** Hurry, Baby / Chicken Shack Boogie / Happy Pay Day / Walkin' / She Walks Right In / What More Do You Want Me To Do? / Playboy Boogie / Come On / Down The Road Apiece / I Done Done It / Shake Your Hips / Roomin' House Boogie / Driftin' **Recorded live at the Dublin Castle, Camden Town, London in May 1985. Reissued on a bootleg CD in 1997 with three extra tracks.**	1985

---

[1] This is actually 'I Want To Do More'.

Various Artists

BBC Records
REN-610

BLUES ON 2   1986
Lowdown Dog *(Big Town Playboys)*

The Blues Band

Ariola 210 095

BACK FOR MORE   1989
Mike plays piano on 'Can't Get My Ass In Gear'
(with Big Joe Duskin and Plas Johnson) and
'Normal Service' *(with the Memphis Horns and
Plas Johnson).*
Also released on CD.

Big Town Playboys

Blue Horizon
BLUH-010

NOW APPEARING   1990
Hungry Man / Who Showed My Baby How To
Love / Baby Please / Drinking Beer / You Must
Be Foolin' / In The Middle Of The Night / I'm So
Satisfied / The Wobble / The Blues Come Rollin'
In / Doopin' / Everytime I Hear That Mellow
Saxophone / What A Shame
Studio recordings. Also released on CD.

Jeff Beck and the Big Town Playboys

Epic EPC-473597-1

CRAZY LEGS   1993
Race With The Devil / Cruisin' / Crazy Legs /
Double Talkin Baby / Woman Love / Lotta
Lovin' / Catman / Pink Thunderbird / Baby Blue /
You Better Believe / Who Slapped John / Say
Mama / Red Blue Jeans And A Pony Tail / Five
Feet Of Lovin' / B-I-Bickey-Bi-Bo-Bo-Go /
Blues Stay Away From Me / Pretty Pretty Baby /
Hold Me, Hug Me, Rock Me
Also released on CD.

The Big 6

Vinyl Japan JRLP-18

READY TO ROCK   1995
Lets Hang Out Tonight / All Of Me / Sombrero /
Out Tonight / At Last / Jump Al Jump / Mama
Weer All Crazee Now / Lady Of Nagoya / Happy
Baby / Sincerely / Tiger Feet / 20th Century Boy /

Stop It I Like It / Groovey Geezer / She Walks
Right In / Fire / New Orleans / Long Tall Sally /
Are You Ready To Rock / All Night Long
Also released on CD.

Bill Wyman's Rhythm Kings

RandM RAMLP-007   **JUST FOR A THRILL**   2004
Limited edition

Mike sings vocals on 'Roll 'Em Pete', 'Booty
Ooty' and 'You Don't Know', and plays piano
and sings backing vocals on 'Taxman'.
**The UK CD version has extra tracks, but no
additional tracks featuring Mike. The US CD
contains one more track by Mike.**

Ray Collins' Hot-Club

Brisk BRLP-001   **GOES INTERCONTINENTAL**   Germany, 2009

Mike plays piano and sings on 'No More',
'Rocking And Rolling Tonite', 'Half Blind'
and 'Right Here In My Arms'.
**The CD version has two extra tracks, but does
not include 'No More'.**

CD-EP

Knock-Out Greg & Blue Weather

Last Buzz BUZZ-7008   **FROM THE CD ALBUM**   Sweden, 2002
Promo   **BUZZ-8035, TELLING IT LIKE IT IS!**

Mike plays piano on 'Something True Became
A Lie' and 'Do It If You Wanna'.
**Both tracks also appeared on the CD album
Last Buzz BUZZ-8025.**

CD Albums

Various Artists

JSP Records   **THE FIRST BURNLEY NATIONAL**   1989
JSPCD-228   **BLUES FESTIVAL (23rd-27th MARCH 1989)**

Baby Please / Red Hot Mama *(Big Town Playboys)*
Recorded live on 23 March 1989.

The Blues Band
Ariola 260 095   **BACK FOR MORE**   1989
Same as LP Ariola 210 095.

Big Town Playboys
Blue Horizon   **NOW APPEARING**   1990
CDBLUH-010   Same as LP Blue Horizon BLUH-010.

Various Artists
Valve 9301   **THE BLUES ACCORDING TO...**   Germany, 1993
Hallelujah I Love Her So / Sit Right Down And
Cry Over You / Little Fine & Healthy Thing /
No Particular Place To Go *(Mike Sanchez)*

Jeff Beck and the Big Town Playboys
Epic EPC-473597-2   **CRAZY LEGS**   1994
Same as LP Epic EPC-473597-1.

The Big 6
Vinyl Japan JRCD-18   **READY TO ROCK**   1995
Same as LP Vinyl Japan JRLP-18.

Various Artists
Indigo IGOCD-2051   **ALEXIS KORNER MEMORIAL**   1995
CONCERT (VOLUME 2)
Mike plays piano on 'Route 66' *(Dave Berry)*.
Recorded live at Buxton Opera House, Buxton,
Derbyshire on 21 May 1995.

Various Artists
Indigo IGOCD-2052   **ALEXIS KORNER MEMORIAL**   1996
CONCERT (VOLUME 3)
Be Careful / Reconsider Baby / Down The Road
A Piece *(Mike Sanchez)*. Mike also plays piano
on 'Just A Little Bit' *(Dave Berry)*.
Recorded live at Buxton Opera House, Buxton,
Derbyshire on 21 May 1995.

Big Town Playboys

Blue Horizon **HIP JOINT** 1996
CDBLUH-017 Ain't No Big Deal On You / When It Rains It
Pours / Shake Your Hips / Glamour Girl / I Don't
Care Who Knows / Kiddio / Forever True /
Rock Me Again / Girls All Over The World /
My Heart Is Mended / No Place To Go

Mike Sanchez

Mike Sanchez MS-001 **JUST A GAME** 1997
M.S. Boogie / Found What I'm Looking For /
Three Months, Three Weeks, Three Days /
Forever True / El Boogie Con Carne / Just A
Game / I Don't Stand A Chance / I Need A
Woman / Let This Lovin' Begin / Undecided
Fool / Bugg Bugg Boogie / I Can't Stop

Big Town Playboys

Making Waves **PLAYBOY BOOGIE!** 1997
SPINCD-203 **See *Bootleg CDs* section.**

Big Town Playboys

Eagle EDGCD-007 **OFF THE CLOCK...LIVE** [2-CD] 1997
❶ Deep In The Heart Of Texas / Lights Out /
Roomin' House Boogie / Don't Lie To Me / It'll
Be Me / Found What I'm Looking For / King Bee /
Bop Sit-In Blues / Rock Me Again / Something
You Got / Glamour Girl / In The Middle Of The
Night
❷ Hey Mama, Keep Your Big Mouth Shut /
Companion Blues / Poor Boy / My Girl Josephine /
Gin House / You Better Believe It / Red Hot
Mama / She's Tough / Girls All Over The World /
I'm Mad / Jam Up
**Recorded live at the Robin Hood Inn, Merry Hill,
Dudley on 4 April 1997.**

Peter Golding

Indigo IGOCD-2063   **STRETCHING THE BLUES**   1997

Good Rockin' Tonight / Stretching The Blues / Thanks To The Blues / Fashion Designer Blues / Burglar Jump / Treasure Of The Blues / The Stumble / Crucify Me / Living In A Memory / Chattanoogie Shoe Shine Boy / Pete's Bop / Blues In The Night/Train / Good Rockin' Tonight *(Finale)*
(Mike plays piano throughout, and also sings vocals on 'Living In A Memory')

Rhythm Kings[2]

BMG Classics / RCA   **STRUTTIN' OUR STUFF**   1997
Victor 74321 51441 2   Mike sings vocals on 'Jitterbug Boogie'.

Original Soundtrack

Milan 74321 60822 2   **THE TRUMAN SHOW**   1998
Mike plays piano and duets on vocals with Pat Reyford on '20th Century Boy' *(Big Six)*.
Live version recorded at the Big Six's first gig at Ealing Town Hall on 7 January 1995.

Bill Wyman's Rhythm Kings[3]

BMG Classics / RCA   **ANYWAY THE WIND BLOWS**   1998
Victor 74321 59523 2   Mike sings vocals on 'Struttin' Our Stuff'.

Big Town Playboys

BTP 005   **6 PACK – A LIMITED EDITION SPECIAL**   1998
Mini-album   **BREW BY THE BIG TOWN PLAYBOYS**
Ooh Little Girl / You're Gonna Win / Every Day Of The Week / It Always Rains / Driftin' / Undecided Fool / *Bonus track:* Hole In My Pocket

---

[2] The US release (Velvel, 1998) and German reissue (Repertoire, 2009) of this album were credited to Bill Wyman & The Rhythm Kings.

[3] The US release (Velvel, 1999) was credited to Bill Wyman & The Rhythm Kings.

Mike Sanchez
Mike Sanchez MS-002 **JUST CAN'T AFFORD IT**   2000
Just Can't Afford It / Vamos A Bailar / Three
Months, Three Weeks, Three Days / Cuttin' In /
Messed With An Angel / Goodnight My Love /
Sombras / Adam Come And Get Your Rib /
Brown-Eyed Handsome Man / Ramblin' Boogie /
Coalminer / Wakin' Up Baby / Wow I Feel So
Good / Red Light Shack

Mike Sanchez
Mike Sanchez MS-003 **BLUE BOY**   2001
Someday / Hurtin' Inside / Tell Me Who / Blue
Boy / Come Back Baby / Sapphire / Fast Train /
Strange Love / Shame, Shame, Shame / Everyday,
Everynight / Love My Baby / I Want To Do More /
Wildcat Tamer / Well Baby / I Miss You So

The Bootleg Kings[4]
Ripple RIPCD-003 **TRAVLIN' BAND**   2002
Chicken Shack Boogie* / Walking / One & Only /
Love Letters / Jitterbug Boogie* / Cats Eyes /
This Little Girl's Gone Rocking / Hit The Road
Jack / I Put A Spell On You / Tell You A Secret* /
Makin' Whoopie / *Bonus track:* Makin' Whoopie
(Mike plays piano throughout, and also sings
vocals on tracks marked *)
**Recorded live at various UK locations during June
and July 2001.**

Knock-Out Greg & Blue Weather
Last Buzz BUZZ-8025 **TELLING IT LIKE IT IS!**   Sweden, 2002
Mike plays piano on 'Something True Became
A Lie' and 'Do It If You Wanna'.
**Both tracks also appeared on a 5-track promo
CD-EP, Last Buzz BUZZ-7008.**

---

[4] This is the name used by Bill Wyman's Rhythm Kings on their 'official bootlegs'.

	Mike Sanchez with	
	Knock-Out Greg & Blue Weather	
Doopin 01	**WOMEN & CADILLACS**	2003
(also released in	Cadillac Baby / All She Wants To Do Is Rock /	
Sweden on Last Buzz	The Voice Within / Hot Dog / You Gonna Win /	
BUZZ-8031)	Strollin' With Bones / Let This Lovin' Begin /	

Women And Cadillacs / You Got Money / If
Lovin' Is Believing / Gambling Woman Blues /
Poor Boy / Easy Boogie / Drunk / King Kong /
I Need A Woman / *Unlisted bonus tracks:* Just
Because / Please Believe Me / Yama Yama
Pretty Mama *(2 versions)*

The Bootleg Kings[5]

Ripple RIPCD-004 **ON THE ROAD AGAIN** 2003
Down In The Bottom* / SOS / Too Late / Trust
In Me / Jump, Jive & Wail* / Days Like This /
He's A Real Gone Guy / Kiddio* / Midnight
Special / Lights Out* / Chantilly Lace* / Melody
(Mike plays piano on all the above tracks, and
also sings vocals on tracks marked *)
**Recorded live at various UK locations during May,
June and July 2002.**

The Blues Band

BGO BGOCD-600 **BE MY GUEST** 2004
Contains reissues of both of Mike's tracks on
the 1989 Blues Band LP/CD *Back For More*.

Bill Wyman's Rhythm Kings

RandM RAMCD-007 **JUST FOR A THRILL** 2004
Same as LP RandM RAMLP-007.

Bill Wyman's Rhythm Kings

Fuel 2000 **JUST FOR A THRILL** USA, 2005
30206 14592-2 Same as above, except Mike also plays piano and
sings on the live bonus track, 'Hit The Road Jack'.

---

[5] This is the name used by Bill Wyman's Rhythm Kings on their 'official bootlegs'.

Bill Wyman's Rhythm Kings

RandM RAMCD-0016   **LIVE**   2005

I Got A Woman* / Jump, Jive And Wail / Baby Workout / If I Can't Have You* / Jitterbug Boogie* / Bright Lights, Big City / Muleskinner Blues / You Never Can Tell / Taxman / Race With The Devil* / I Shall Not Be Moved / Disappearing Nightly / Flatfoot Sam* / I'll Be Satisfied / Let's Talk It Over / Wild One (Real Wild Child) / Roll 'Em Pete*
(Mike plays piano throughout, and also sings vocals on tracks marked *)
Recorded in Berlin, Germany on 15 June 2004.

Van Morrison

Polydor 5305 453-2   **BACK ON TOP** *(reissue)*   2008

Mike plays piano and guitar on bonus track 'Philosophers Stone' *(alternative version)*.

Mike Sanchez

Doopin 02   **YOU BETTER DIG IT!**   2008

You Better Dig It / She Can Rock / I'm Shakin' / One More Kiss / Boss Chick / Make Me Feel A Little Good / Lipstick Traces / The Kangaroo / I'm A Fool To Care / You Can't Hide / Heebie Jeebies / There Is Something On Your Mind / Bom Bom Lulu / Sick & Tired / Bottle It Up And Go / Highway 60 / No Good Lover / Baby Shame / That's All I Need

Ray Collins' Hot-Club

Brisk BRCD-001   **GOES INTERCONTINENTAL**   Germany, 2009

Mike plays piano and sings on 'Rocking And Rolling Tonite', 'Half Blind' and 'Right Here In My Arms'.
The LP version (Brisk BRLP-001) is two tracks shorter than the CD, but includes an additional song featuring Mike, 'No More'.

Mike Sanchez with
The Beat From Palookaville[6]

Doopin 03   **BABES AND BUICKS**   2010

Hip Boots / The Question (Whatcha Gonna Do) / Babes & Buicks / Let's Be Friends / Driftwood / Isabella / Found What I'm Looking For / It's Time To Rock / Everybody's Got A Buick / I'm Wise (Slippin' and Slidin') / Got You On My Mind / Crawfish / Shiver and Shake / Pretty Legs / Scream & Howl / Party Time / *Unlisted bonus tracks:* I'm Looped / Hi-Fi Baby / She Felt Too Good / Let The Four Winds Blow / It T'Ain't What You Say / Babes & Buicks *(alt. version)*

The Beat From Palookaville

Enviken   **NUMERO UNO!**   Sweden, 2011
ENRECCD-155

Introduction by Mike Sanchez. Mike also sings vocals on 'Knocking On The Backside'.

The Blues Band

Repertoire   **A FEW SHORT LINES**   2011
REPUK-1149

Mike plays piano on 'My Brother Was A Sailor', 'Sway With Me' and 'Statesboro Blues'

Mike Sanchez and his band
*featuring Imelda May**

Doopin 04   **ALMOST GROWN**   2012

Let The Good Times Roll* / Voodoo Voodoo* / Almost Grown / I'll Go Crazy* / Shirley / If I Can't Have You* / Every Night In The Week / Driftin' / Matchbox* / Vacation's Over / Easy Easy* / Let's Have A Party / My Man* / Wear Your Black Dress / *Unlisted bonus tracks:* Honky Tonk Train Blues / Happy Pay Day **Studio recordings from 2002 (not 2004 as stated on the album cover).**

---

[6] Former members of Knock-Out Greg & Blue Weather and Trickbag.

Bootleg CDs

Masterport 226

Jeff Beck and the Big Town Playboys
LIVE REHEARSALS [2-CD]   1993
❶ Your True Love / The Train Kept A-Rollin' /
Lonesome Train (On A Lonesome Track) /
Going Down /
❷ 'Cause We've Ended As Lovers / B-I-Bickey-
Bi-Bo-Bo-Go / Blues Stray Away From Me /
Race With The Devil / Pink Thunderbird / You
Better Believe / Red Blue Jeans And A Pony
Tail / Cat Man / Who Slapped John / Pretty
Pretty Baby / Hold Me, Hug Me, Rock Me
Live studio rehearsals, 1993.

Klondyke KR-017

Jeff Beck and the Big Town Playboys
A TRIBUTE TO CLIFF AND GENE   1993
Crazy Legs / Double Talkin' Baby / Cruisin' /
Woman Love / My Little Mama / B-I-Bickey-
Bi-Bo-Bo-Go / Blues Stay Away From Me /
A Race With The Devil [*sic*] / I Got It /
Maybelline / Cat Man / Red Blue Jeans And
Pony Tail [*sic*] / Who Slapped John / Lonely
Street / Pretty Baby [*sic*] / I Found Your Love /
Baby Blue / Say Mama / The Stumble / Lonesome
Train / True Love / Train Kept A-Rollin' / Going
Down / Rock Me Baby
Recorded live at La Cigale, Paris on 23 April 1993.

Making Waves
SPINCD-203

Big Town Playboys
PLAYBOY BOOGIE!   1997
Reissue of 1985 LP Making Waves SPIN-203
with three unlisted bonus tracks: 'I Like It',
'I Want To Do More' and 'Well Oh Well'.
**The Making Waves label went out of business
around 1991.**

VHS Videotape

Mike Sanchez

Ents Network
ENTS-002

RED HOT...LIVE!   2001

Mess With Me / Driftin' / Hurtin' Inside / Girls All Over The World / I'm Mad / 3 Months, 3 Weeks, 3 Days / Rock 'Em N Roll 'Em *(with the Extraordinaires)* / Let The Good Times Roll *(with Imelda Clabby)* / I'll Go Crazy *(with Paul Ansell)* / Blue Boy / In The Middle Of The Night / Baby Please / Wildcat Tamer / Till The Well Runs Dry *(with Imelda Clabby and the Extraordinaires)* / Undecided Fool / Jump Children *(with the Extraordinaires)* / Wild One (Real Wild Child) / Almost Grown *(with Imelda Clabby and the Extraordinaires)* / Red Hot Mama / Fast Train / Shake Your Hips / Sapphire / Jam Up

Recorded live at the *13th Burnley National Blues Festival* on 16 April 2001, with additional footage from the George Hotel, Lower Brailes and the 100 Club, London. Reissued on DVD in 2003 with additional material.

DVDs

	Mike Sanchez	
Ents Network	**RED HOT...LIVE!**	2003
ENTSDVD-001	Same tracks as VHS videotape above + extra	

footage from an appearance at the Jazz & Roots
Club, Shrewsbury in December 2002: Companion
Blues / Breathless / I Miss You So / Coalminer /
Boogie Con Carne / Ramblin' Boogie

	Bill Wyman's Rhythm Kings	
DTS DVD-7084X	**LET THE GOOD TIMES ROLL**	2004

Rockin' The Roots: I Got A Woman / Jitterbug
Boogie / Jump, Jive And Wail / Baby Workout /
Kiddio / Down In The Bottom / Comin' Home,
Baby / Flatfoot Sam / Real Wild Child / Lights
Out / Tear It Up
Let The Good Times Roll: You Never Can Tell /
Mule Skinner Blues / Days Like This / Jump
Back / I'll Be Satisfied / Race With The Devil /
Hit The Road Jack / Pink Champagne / I Put A
Spell On You / Tell You A Secret / Chicken
Shack Boogie
On The Road *(30-minute film of the band on tour)*

	Bill Wyman's Rhythm Kings	
Universal Music	**A TRIBUTE TO THE KING**	2005
9872949	My Baby Left Me / All Shook Up / Lawdy Miss	

Clawdy *(Mike on vocals only)*

Film soundtracks

Touchstone   **THE COLOR OF MONEY**   1986
It's My Life, Baby *(Eric Clapton and the Big Town Playboys)*
Soundtrack LP released by MCA, but above track was not included.

Palace Pictures/   **THE POPE MUST DIE**   1991
Channel 4 Films   Baby Please / Hungry Man / In The Middle Of The Night *(Mike Sanchez with the Big Town Playboys)*
No soundtrack album.

Paramount   **THE TRUMAN SHOW**   1998
Mike plays piano and duets on vocals with Pat Reyford on '20th Century Boy' *(Big Six)*
Live version recorded at the Big Six's first gig at Ealing Town Hall on 7 January 1995.
Soundtrack CD released by Milan (see CDs).

Warner Bros.   **I'LL BE THERE**   2003
Honky Tonk Train Blues / Jungle Rock / Red Hot / Trouble / Ubangi Stomp *(Mike Sanchez Band)*
'Rock'n'Roll Ruby' was also recorded, but was not used.
No soundtrack album.

INDEX OF PEOPLE'S NAMES

Spanish names: In Spain, a person's forename(s) are customarily followed by two surnames, the first of which is usually the father's first surname, and the second the mother's first surname. In most situations other than legal or formal settings, the first forename and first surname tend to be used, and this convention has also been followed in this index. Accordingly, Mike's mother, who was born Manuela Bastida Gil, may be found listed under Bastida, and so on.

Bold page numbers refer to illustrations.

ABBA 118
Ace, Johnny 197, 274
Adkins, Hasil 78
Alarm 74, 155
Aldo, Carlo 226
Alexander, Arthur 268
Alexander, Honey 92
Allen, Lee 159
Allsop, Nick 44, 79
Allsop's Jazz Band, Stanley 79
Amen Corner 117
Anderson, Anna 204, 220-1
Anderson, Pete (& The Archives)
  116, 204, **211**, 218, 220-1
Andersson, Greger
  149, 179, 180, 184
  See also Knock-Out Greg
Angelatos, John 173
Angkvist, Per 219
Ansell, Paul 78, 168, 174, 189, 225, 265
Armstrong, Louis 22
Art Of Noise 109
Atwell, Winifred 35, 267
Ayres, Gordon 161
B-52's 104
B, Laura (& The Moonlighters) 244
Badau, Lee 158, 163
Badland, Adrian 121
Baker, LaVern 270
Baker, Mickey 'Guitar' 148
Baker, Ralph 120
Balham Alligators 85
Bananarama 98
Barcelona Big Blues Band 257
Barker, Geoff 31
Barrett, Paul 77

Bartholomew, Dave 30
Basie, Count 22
Bassey, Shirley 192
Bastida, Isabel *(Mike's mother's sister)*
  15, 16, 17, **61**
Bastida, José *(Mike's maternal grandfather)*
  15, 16, **61**
Bastida, Josefa 'Fifi' *(Mike's mother's sister)*
  15, 16, 17
Bastida, Juan José 'Juanjo' *(Mike's brother)*
  17, 23, 24, 25, 50, **64**, **66**, 163, 234, 237,
  251, 267
Bastida, Manuela *(Mike's mother)*
  15, 16, 19, 21, 24-6, 33, 38, 54, 56, **61**,
  63, **64**, **66**, 132, **133**, 156-7, 166, 237-8,
  242, 243, 245, 247-8, 249, 250, 251-6
Bastida, María *(Mike's mother's sister)*
  15, 16, 17, **61**
Bastida, Miguel *(Mike's mother's brother)*
  15, 16, 17
Bastida, Rosemary *(Mike's brother's wife)*
  24, 25
Bastida, Sarah *(Mike's niece)*
  120, 218, 233
Bastida, Tomasa *(Mike's mother's sister)*
  15, 16, 17, **61**
Bastida, Vincenta *(Mike's mother's sister)*
  15, 16, 17
Baylis, Barbara 97, 102
Baynton-Power, Dave 101, 105
Beaker, Norman 130
Bearne, Tim
  48, 52, 54, 56, **67**, **68**, **69**, 80
Beasley, Jimmy 271
Beat From Palookaville, The
  219, 233, 234, 235, 246

Beatles 22, 26, 35, 39, 103, 170, 186, 231, 267, 268
Beaujolais, Roger 85
Beck, Jeff
  31, 102, 106, 108, 109, 111, 112, 115, 116, 117, 118, 119, 120, 121, 126, 127, **138**, 148, 156, 201, **216**, 257, 261, 265
Beckham, David 164
Beggs, Steve 79, 83, 106
Bell, Carey 101
Bell, Lurrie 101
Bell, Maggie 228
Belson, Geoff 48-9, 53
Belvin, Jesse 274
Benjamin, Huw 'Bunny' 35, 39, 40, 161
Benjamin, Julian 39, 40, 265
Berlin, Irving 260
Bernholm, Jonas 83
Berry, Chuck 23, 45, 181, 198
Big Bad Voodoo Daddy 169
Big Boy Bloater **213**, 236, 244, 245, 247
Big Maybelle 268, 270
Big Six
  60, 127, 128, 129, **141**, 145, 168, 170
Big Town Playboys *(post-Mike)*
  163, 164, 168-9, 231
Bishop, Rosemary *(Mike's brother's wife)*
  24, 25
Black Sabbath 43, 118
Bland, Bobby 'Blue' 93
Blue Harlem 169, 174
Blue Rhythm Boys 78, 168
Blue Whale 119, 120
Blues, Elwood 89
Blues Band 97, 232, 248
Blues Brothers 89, 90
Blunt, Micky 53
Blunt, Robbie 170
Bohnsack, Jo 248
Boll, Bert 218
Bonham 131, 169
Bonham, Jason 131, 228
Bonham, John 131, 228
Boone, Pat 23, 267
Bowel, Billy (& The Movements) 170
Boyer, Louise 223
Bradshaw, Tiny 270
Brand, Russell 272
Brawn, Ricky Lee 127, **141**
Brilleaux, Lee 122, 123, 124, 130, 191
Broes, Walter 235
Bronze, Dave 92
Brooker, Franky 94, 120, 172

Brooker, Gary
  91, 92, 94, 95, 98, 100, 101, 102, 103, 104, 107, 111, 120, 123, 124, **137**, 146, 172, 177, 178, 179, 181, 186
Brooks, Elkie 232
Brovoll, Kjell-Inge 179
Brown, Boots (& His Blockbusters) 274
Brown, Charles
  79, 81, 120-1, **139**, 149, 272, 274
Brown, Clarence 'Gatemouth' 103
Brown, James 188, 268, 270, 273
Brown, Joe 101
Brown, Nappy 270, 275
Brown, Roy 84, 269, 270
Brown, Roy 'Chubby' 125-6
Brown, Ruth 270
Brown, Sam 101, 108, 195
Brown, Vicki 108
Bruce, Jack 130, 222
Bryant, Johnny 170
Bublé, Michael 264
Buena Vista Social Club 265
Bugge, Tormod 126, 165, 168, 173
Bull, Tom
  214, **216**, 235, 247, 249, 256, 259
Bunting, Ted 108, 256
Burgess, Sonny 179
Burke, Solomon 229, 265
Burke, Tony 202
Burlison, Paul 49
Burnette, Billy 103, 104
Burnette, Johnny (Rock'n'Roll Trio)
  23, 29, 110, 115, 201, 267, 268, 270, 274
Burnette, Rocky 110
Burton, Trevor 114, 154, 155
Bush, (Vice Pres.) George H.W. 99
Bush, Kate 106, 126, 127
Butler, Geezer 43
Buzzcocks 43
Calloway, Cab 274
Cannon, Freddy 275
Cantaloupe 44
Carlin, George 272
Carlisle, Jim 78
Carr, Budd 185
Carr, Wynona 270
Carroll, Ted 73, 89, 101, 118, 123
Carrott, Jasper 90
Carson, Phil 88
Chaplin, Chas 161
Chapman, Ernest 120
Chapman, Roger 195
Charles, Ray 151, 228, 273

Chas & Dave 98, 195
Checker, Chubby 23, 267
Cheney, Oliver – *See* Darling, Oliver
Chester, Gary 169
Chester, Katrina 169
Chevalier Brothers 78, 85
Chicken Shack 76, 101
Church, Charlotte 185
Clabby, Imelda – *See* May, Imelda
Clapton, Eric
  53, 92, 93, 94, 95, 97, 98, 102, 104-5,
  115, **142**, 146, 147, 154, 155, 163, 195,
  200, 228, 229
Clarke, Dave 82, 182, 202
Clarke, Paul
  72, 96, 99, 100, 113, 114, 115, **133**
Clayton, Steve 190
Cleary, Vic 'Valves' 88
Cochran, Eddie
  23, 29, 49, 60, 115, 155, 157, 268
Cocker, Joe 200
Cole, Nat 'King'
  22, 27, 156, 258, 264, 274, 275
Collins, Bootsy 189
Collins, Phil 98, 123
Collins' Hot-Club, Ray 233-4, 244
Colman, Stuart 31, 60, 87, 117, 118, 128
Coltrane, Robbie 102, 106, 109, 201
Conde, Elizabeth 60
Coni, Tony 57, 117, 121, 131, **142**, 145,
      146-7, 162, 249, 264
Cook, Pete 174, **207**
Cooke, Sam 270
Cool, Ricky
  36-8, 42, 43, 44, 47, 59, **69**, **70**, 76, 77,
  78-9, 80, 81, 82, 83-4, 85, 86, 87, 88, 89,
  90, 91, 112, 129, 158, **210**, 217, 227, 232,
  233, 256
  With the Icebergs: 37, 42, 78
  With the Rialtos: 42, 43, 44, 76, 232
Copeland, Johnny 110
Corea, Chick 169
Corry, Paul 230
Costello, Elvis 74
Cowan, Little John 122
Cramps 55
Cray, Robert 105
Crazy Cavan (& The Rhythm Rockers) 60
Crudup, Arthur 'Big Boy' 195, 268
Curbishley, Bill 107
Curran, Brian 129
Cush, Sandra 111, 201, 257
D'Arby, Terence Trent 109

Darby, Alan 185
Darling, Oliver
  201-2, 203, 224, 230, 234, 235, 236, 243
Davidson, Jim 90
Davies Rhythm Combo, Drew
  234, 244, 257
Davies, Mark 'Beefy'
  35, 36, 39, 42, 47, 48, 49, 50, 52, 54, 55,
  56, 57, **67**, 256
Davis, Maxwell 159
Dawkins, Richard 272
De la Serna, Victor 257
Deamer, Clive
  99-100, 106, 107, 114, 116, 120, **135**,
  138, **139**, 145
Dean, James 60
Dee, Sean 48, 59, 131
Deltas 60
Díaz, Remedios
  (Mike's paternal grandmother) 17, 18, **62**
Dickens, Norman 58, 80
Dickson, Lee 93
Diddley, Bo 37, 109, 268, 271, 275
Dirty Robbers 235
Dixie Hummingbirds 153
Dixon, Floyd 109, 149, 272, 275
Dixon, Wayne 35
Dixon, Willie 271
Dobson, Anita 126
Dolan, Steve 148
Domino, Fats 30, 264, 269, 271, 272, 275
Don & Dewey 132, 145
Donegan, Lonnie 39, 158
Donovan 186, 222
Dowd, Tom 93
Dr Feelgood
  107, 122, 124, 130, 149, 171, 191
Dr John 30
Draper, Ian 57
Draper, Stephen 38, 47, 54-5, 57
Drew, Martin 185
Drifters 249
Dudley, Anne 109
Dunn, Donald 'Duck' 222
Dunn, Phil 130
Dupree, Champion Jack 100
Duran Duran 43, 44
Dury, Ian 272
Dynamite Band 78
Eagle, Roger 100-1, 109, 111
Eastwood, Eva (& The Major Keys) 204
Eddy, Duane 26
Edgar, Donna 52

Edmondson, Adrian 102, 250
Edwards, Nadine 157, 168, 169
Electric Light Orchestra 90
Ellington, Duke 22, 269
ELO 90
Emerson, Billy 'The Kid' 30, 149
English, David 189
Epps, Stuart 129
Ertegun, Ahmet 228-9
Esquerita 30
Everly Brothers 29, 267
Extraordinaires 174, 190, 202, 203, **207**, 223
Fairweather-Low, Andy
   92, 98, 102, 103, 112, **143**, 147-8, 149,
   151, 152, 154, 155, 156, 157, 159, 163,
   183, 195, 202, **205**, 263
Faith, Adam 23, 30, 267
Fame, Georgie (& The Blue Flames)
   85, 172, 178, 181, 186, 188, 189, 193,
   195, 196, 197, 200, 274
Farran, Natalia 222, 223, 224
Fearnal, John 35
Feathers, Charlie 60
Fenech, Paul 77
Ferguson, Craig 185
Ferrone, Steve 98
Fields Orchestra, Ernie 275
Finnigan, Judy 222
Fisher, Sonny 60
Five Blind Boys of Alabama 117, 265, 268
Five Keys 274
Flawless 109
Fleetwood, Mick
   53, 97, 98, 103, 104, 109, 119, **137**,
   159-60, 170-1, 193
Fleetwood Mac 82, 97, 104, 147, 193
Floyd, Eddie 196, 197
Fonz, The 34
Forced Entry 125
Ford, Stuart 130-1
Ford, Sugar Ray (& The Hotshots) 85
Foreigner 228
Forrester, Roger 93, 98
Forshult, Håkan 149
Foster, Melanie 52
Frampton, Peter 195
Franco, (Gen.) Francisco 16, 18
Franklin, Aretha 228
Freed, Alan 173, 190, 271
French, Dawn 102, 106, 250
Frenchy La Femme 228
Fry, Stephen 272
Fulson, Lowell 99, 269

Fury, Billy 30, 267
Gable, Clark 18
Gallup, Cliff 49, 78, 115-16
Gammond, Kevin 110
Garcia, Catherine 228
Gare, Al
   167, 174, 184, 194, 200, **207**, **209**, 225,
   226, 227, 230, 232, 233, 235, 236
Gare, Saffron 167, 227
Garnett, Alf 24
Gatica, Lucho 270
Gavino, Priscilla 244-5, 246
Gayles, Billy 270, 274
Gayten, Paul 30
Gelato, Ray (& The Giants of Jive)
   78, 84, 85, 106
Geldof, Bob 127, 186, 189, 195
Genesis 123
Gervais, Ricky 272
Gibbons (Band), Steve 80, 114, 154, 200
Gil, Josefa *(Mike's maternal grandmother)*
   15, 16, 17, **61**
Gilmour, Dave 101, 108, 127, 186, 195, 200
Glee Club 114
Golding, Peter 129
Goldsmith, Harvey 98
Gonzalez, Dave 145
Good Time Charlie 167, 170, 181
Goodfellas 227, 234, 244
Goodwin, Geoff 161
Goodwin, Tony 39-40, 161, 203
Gorbachev, Mikhail 116
Gordon, Rosco 96
Grand, Otis 130
Graves, Robert 222
Green, Benny 114
Green, Leo 114-15, 120, **139**, 151
Green, Peter (Splinter Group)
   98, 147, 148, 150, 195, 265
Guy, Buddy 92, 103, 105
Hadley, Steve 192
Haley, Bill (& His Comets) 23, 78, 116, 274
Hall, Bob 110
Hall, Jerry 194
Hamblett, Mike 159
Hamilton, Colbert 57
Hammond Jr, John 92
Hampton, Lionel 271
Hamsters 88
Hardy, Tim 181
Harlem Horns 174
Harman, Mark 78
Harris, Bob 148

Harris, Wynonie 182, 268, 269, 270, 275
Harrison, George 90, 98
Hart, Dean 231
Hartley, Ian 260
Harvey, Dave 226
Hatton, Ian 'Tat' 131, 169, 170
Hayriders 256
Hayworth, Rita 18
Hendrix, Jimi 115, 273
Henry, Clarence 'Frogman' 30, 271, 275
Hickey, Ersel 60
Hickman, Jim 114
Higham, Darrel (& The Enforcers)
    154-5, 156, 157, 173-4, 223, 226
Hilfiger, Tommy 160
Hill, Jo 224, 225, 259-60, 261
Hillebrandt, Yvette 250
Hinton, Bruce 44
Hitchens, Christopher 272
Hjønnevåg, Iren
    167-8, 171-2, 173, 174, 177, 181, 182,
    185, 187, 188, 191, 193, 194, 200, 220
Hodges, Chas 98
Holder, Noddy 90
Holland, Jools (& His Rhythm & Blues Orch.)
    59, 106, 108, 110, 130, **143**, 153, 155,
    158, 195
Holly, Buddy 23, 29, 30, 35, 40, 267, 274
Honeydrippers *(Robert Plant group)* 76
Hooker, John Lee 99, 109
Hoola Boola Boys 108, 110, 114, 232, 256
Howlin' Wolf 99, 149, 268, 271
Hughes, Joe 103, **135**
Humperdinck, Engelbert 78
Hunniford, Gloria 129
Hunter, James 117, **140**, 229
Hutchence, Michael 127
Hutchison, Richard 99
Hynde, Chrissie 108
Iron Maiden 148
Isaak, Chris 225
Jacquet, Illinois 271
Jagger, Mick 160, 194
James 105
Janes, Anders
    60, 127, **141**, 168, 170, 171, 173, 199
Jennings, Ian
    34-5, 36, 37-8, 39, 43, 44, 47, 48, 50,
    54-6, 59, **67, 68, 69, 70, 71, 72,** 73, 76,
    77, 78, 79, 80, 81, 86, 87, 99-100, 106,
    112, 114, 115, 117, 119, 120, 121, 122,
    123, 125, 129, 131, **133, 135, 136, 138,**
    139, 140, 142, 143, 146, 147, 150, 151,

152, 154, 156-7, 159, 160, 163, 164, 179,
201, 202, 226, 227, 231, 256, 258, 260,
263
Jennings, Malcolm 34, 43
Jets 60, 117
JoBoxers 85
John, Little Willie 268, 270
Johnny & The Hurricanes 23, 267, 275
Johns, Glyn 103
Johnson, Johnnie 97, 181, 271
Johnson, Lonnie 269
Johnson, Plas 271
Johnson, Sherman 82
Johnson, Willie 180
Jones, Allan 117, 125
Jones, Charlie 110
Jones, Howard 58, 74-5, 80
Jones, Mick 228
Jones, Paul
    91, 97, 126, 130, 145, 145, 149, 153, 159,
    189, 194, 231, 232, 233, 251
    BBC radio show:
        91, 145, 153, 189, 194, 231
    Jazz FM radio show: 126, 149
Jordan, Louis 85, 269, 271
Journeymen 114, 126
Juice On The Loose 85, 94
Kidd, Johnny (& The Pirates) 275
Kilmister, Lemmy 106, 226
King, B.B. 179
King, Ben E. 229
King Jr, Martin Luther 197
King, Stephen 157
King Cole Trio 275
King Pleasure (& The Biscuit Boys)
    132, 167, 183
Knock-Out Greg & Blue Weather
    149, 153, 178, 179-80, 182-3, 184-5, 189,
    190, 191, 219
Knopfler, Mark 101, 151, 195, 200
Kollenbroich, Andreas
    – *See* Collins' Hot-Club, Ray
Korner, Alexis 130, 147, 167
Kravitz, Lenny 231
Lamarr, Mark 201, 231, 260
Langdon, Emma 21, 22
Last, James 27
Le Bon, Yasmin 102
Led Zeppelin 43, 53, 118, 131, 197, 228
Lee, Albert
    92, 172, 177, 178, 183, 189, 194, 196,
    197, 198, 200, **206**, 228, 263
Lee, Alvin 228

Lee, Brenda 23, 26, 267
Lee, Rustie 38
Lee, Stan 21
Leiber & Stoller 89
Lenin, Vladimir Ilyich 220
Lennon & McCartney 39
Lennon, John 120, 170, 273
Lennon, Sean 120
Lennox, Annie 189
Lewen, Anders 149, 179, 182, 233, 243, 263
Lewis, Jerry Lee 27, 30, 34, 97, 106, 109,
              198, 224, 264, 271, 274
Lewis, Linda 248
Lewis, Smiley 275
Liggins, Joe 81
Linna, Ivo (& Rock Hotel) 204
Little Junior's Blue Flames 275
Little Richard
    23, 30, 84, 106, 116, 117, 150, 201, 224,
    264, 265, 267, 268, 270, 271, 273, 274,
    275
Little Walter 81, 84, 268, 274
Littlefield, Little Willie
    30, **70**, 84, 86, 89, 92, 94, 100, 103, 110,
    150, **212**, 222, 230, 272, 275
Long, Pete 114, 115
Long, Trevor 150, 151, 153, 160, 164, 169
Lopez, Rohan – *See* Rohan Thee Man
Lucas, Ronn 105
Lunt, Nick
    59, 115, 123, 127, 132, **141**, **142**, 146, 150,
    158, 163, **213**, **214**, **216**, 230, 231, 264
MacDonald, Robert 91
Mad Tubes 246
Madeley, Richard 222
Madonna 109
Magnum 128
Mancini, Henry 20
Manilow, Barry 75
Mann, Ed 92, 93, 96
Marley, Bob 273
Martin, Barry 88
Martinez, Tayva
    222, 226, 227, 228, 229-30, 230-1, 232,
    233, 235, 243
Mases, Leif 118
Matchbox 60
Matheson, Pete 111
May, Brian 126, 199
May, Imelda
    151, 161, 174, 181-2, 189, 191, 195, 202,
    203, 204, **207**, **209**, 219, 221, 222, 223,
    225, 227, 230, 249, 251

Mayall, Rik 102
Mayfield, Percy 182, 275
Mayhew, Helen 107
Mazelle, Kym 124
McCartney, Paul 201, **210**
McCartney, Stella 107
McCormack, Danny 230
McCracklin, Jimmy 105, 274
McDevitt, Chas 199
McEnroe, John 164
McGuinness, Tom 97
McNeely, Big Jay
    86, 115, 159, 234, 248, 268, 271
McVie, Christine 82, 97, 104
Mead, Frank
    85, 94, 95, 123, 128, 132, **142**, 155, 158,
    159, 177, 197, 199
Medeiros, Britta 153, 218
Merris, Jim 89, 264
Meteors 77
Metti, Christian 44
Metti, Justin 44
Mighty Flyers 92
Milburn, Amos
    30, 79, 81, 82, 84, 97, 120, 149, 168, 198,
    265, 272, 274
Milichip, Robert 35, 36, 57
Mills, Heather 201
Mills, Lisa 202
Milton, Roy 81
Mitzi 146
Mizell, Hank 275
Monroe, Marilyn 218
Montrell, Roy 30, 274
Moody Blues 90
Moone, Ian 54
Moore, Gary 95, 101, 158
Moore, Jenny 118
Moore, Roger 222
Moore, Sam 229
Moore, Scotty 49, 189, 197, 199-200
Moores, Julian 196
Moreno, Sue 201, 218
Morgan, Mark
    96, 121, 123, 125, 126, 127, 128, 131,
    140, **141**, **142**, **143**, 145, 146, 147, 149,
    151, 154, 161, 164, 173, 174, 184, 194,
    199, 201, **207**, **213**, **216**, 225, 230,
    234, 235, 236, 238, 244, 249, 256, 257,
    263
Morrison, Van 151, 152, 179, 229, 230
Motörhead 106, 226
Move 154

Muddy Waters 271
Mundy, Julie 155
Murray, Tracey 119, 125
Neal, Screamin' Joe 270
Nelson, Jimmy 103
Neville, Aaron 131, 265
Neville Brothers 131
Newman, Paul 93
Nicholls, Al
    72, 95, 96, 99, 100, 101, 104, 113, 115,
    127, **133**, **135**, **141**, 159, 169, 174, **207**
Nine Below Zero 126
Nixon, Laura 218
Nottingham, Chris 194
Nutini, Paolo 228
O'Neill, Brendan 121
Ono, Yoko 120
Otis, Johnny 173
Page, Jimmy 94, 115, 179, 228
Paladins 145, 146
Palmer, Earl 99
Panico, Tony 177, 187
Parker, Athene 105
Parker, Howard 22
Parker, Little Junior 275
Parker, Maceo 188
Parry, Lawrence 90
Parsons, Nicholas 222
Pasternak, Johnny 94
Patigny, Renaud 248
Patino, Marco 228
Payn, Nick 130, 158, 197, 199
Peabody, Dave 110
Peel, John 85
Pereira, Kate 114
Pérez de Cuéllar, Javier 17
Perfect, Christine 82
Perkins, Carl 34, 60
Peters, Mike 155
Phillimore, Hugh 151, 160, 172, 249
Phillips, Dave (& The Hot Rod Gang)
    60, 78, 110
Phillips, Don 49
Phillips, Lynne 154, 164, 169, 183, 184
Phillips, Sam 269
Piazza, Rod 92
Pickett, Bobby 'Boris' 23
Pictures In A Dark Room 94
Pink Floyd 123
Pitt, John 58, 74
Planer, Nigel 250
Plant, Carmen 53, 75-6, 110
Plant, Logan 232

Plant, Maureen 75, 232
Plant, Robert
    53, **71**, 74, 75-6, 88, 90, 94, 105, 107,
    108, 110, 112, 120, 127, 150, 169, 179,
    216, 224, 231, 232, 256, 257
Polecats 60
Porter, Tim 160-1, 170, 202, 262
Portishead 106, 120
Powell, Dai **72**, 96, 99, **133**
Powers, Johnny 275
Presley, Elvis
    23, 26, 30, 34, 35, 39, 50, 78, 121, 189,
    195, 200, 226, 264, 267, 268-9, 273, 275
Price, Big Walter 182
Prima, Louis 274
Primo de Rivera, José 16
Priseman, Dave 174, **207**
Procol Harum 26, 91, 172, 178, 179
Professor Longhair 30
Pryce, Martin 108
Pumping Special 153
Q-Tips 158
Queen 123
Rea, Chris 101
Red Lemon Electric Blues Band 90
Redding, Otis 268, 270, 273
Reed, Jimmy 78, 81
Reeves, Jim 27
Reeves, Vic 201
Rent Party **71**, 85, 90
Restless 60, 78
Reyford, Pat 85, 127, 128, **141**
Rhythm Kings
    103, 129, 154, 157, 158, 172, 177-9, 181,
    183, 185, 186-8, 189, 190, 191, 192, 193,
    194-9, 200, 202, 203, 222, 224, 228-9,
    265
Rich, Buddy 222
Rich, Charlie 275
Richard, Cliff (& The Shadows)
    23, 267, 275
Richardson, Alice 250
Richardson, Jim 185
Richardson, Marta 153
Richardson, Peter
    102, 105-6, 108-9, 111, 153, 201, **216**,
    250, 257, 263
Richie, Lionel 187
Ricochets 60
Riley, Billy Lee 179
Rivingtons 180
Robinson, Alan 114
Robinson Band, Tom 107

Rockets 36, 47-60, **67**, **68**, **69**, 73-80, 81, 85, 86, 115, 122, 127, 257
Rockettes 59
Rockin' Renegades 36, 57
Rocos, Cleo 201, 221-2
Rødal, Anette 126, 132, 146, 151-2, 162
Rodgers, Paul 126, 228
Rogers, Jimmy 180
Rogers, Richard – *See* Cool, Ricky
Rogge, Olaf 169
Rohan Thee Man 107, 113, 114
Rolling Stones 22, 58, 197, 222, 228, 268
Rollins, Henry 272
Rookes, Ali 167
Rookes, Rusty 167
Rose, Paul 122
Ross, Doctor 60
Rouen 44, 79
Rush, Otis 271
Rutherford, Mike 98, 186, 218
Sagoe, George 21
Sajak, Pat 103
Sanborn, David 159
Sánchez, Alfonso *(no relation)* 127
Sánchez, Angela *(Mike's father's sister)* 18, 19, 25, **62**, 166
Sánchez, Jesús *(Mike's father)* 17, 18-21, 22, 23-6, 33-4, 50, 51, 56, **62**, **63**, **65**, **66**, 132, **133**, 156-7, 166, 186, 237-42
Sanchez, Louie Ray *(Mike's son)* **215**, 249, 251, 257, 258, 264
Sánchez, Manuel *(Mike's paternal grandfather)* 17, 18, **62**
Sanchez, Sarah *(Mike's wife)* – *See* Wynne, Sarah
Sánchez, Teresa *(Mike's father's sister)* 18
Sánchez, Victoria *(Mike's father's sister)* 18
Sanchez Rhythm & Blues Revue, Mike 173-5, 177, 178, 181, 189-90, 193, 194, 196, 199, 200, 202, 203, **207**, **208**, **209**, 217, 218, 219, 223, 225, 226, 250
Santo & Johnny 275
Saunders, Jennifer 102
Savoy Brown 76
Schok, Martijn 248
Schwanke, Gabi 171
Seatsniffers 233, 234, 235, 244
Seeley, Bob 181
Setzer, Brian 153
Severn Valley Skiffle Kings 39

Sex Pistols 43
Seyssel, Vanetia 202-3
Seyssel, William 202-3
Shakespeare, Jane 223
Shakin' Pyramids 60
Sharif, Omar 20
Showaddywaddy 60
Silvester, Andy **69**, **70**, **71**, **72**, 76, 77, 78-9, 81-2, 83-4, 87, 88, 89, 90, 91, 92, 93, 94, 96, 97, 98, 99, 100, 101, 102, 106, 107, 108, 110, 111, 112, 113, 117, 120, 121, 123, 130, **133**, **135**, **137**, 145, 149, 151, 155, 158, 159, 161, 164, 170, 173, 174, 182, 184, 191, 193, 199, 201, 202, **207**, **209**, **210**, 231, 232, 236, 256, 257, 260, 263
Simms, Hazel – *See* T, Sugar
Simpson, Bart 170
Simpson, Dee 196
Simpson, John 196
Sinatra, Frank 22, 156
Skeete, Beverley 172, 177, 183, 186, 189, 193, 196, 197, 228
Skepper, Catrina 155
Skinny Bop Trio 124
Sledge, Percy 229
Slim Harpo 60, 149, 274
Small Faces 268
Smalley, Anthony 35
Smith, Brian 82, 83, 101, 174, 202
Smith, Pine Top 97
Sonics 275
Sounds of Blue 82
Spandau Ballet 43
Spann, Otis 271
Spinetti, Henry 92
Spinetto, John **69**, **70**, **71**, 78, 81, 93, 232
Squeeze 106
St John, Tim 165
Stainton, Chris 200
Stallone, Sylvester 160
Stargazers 60, 85, 127
Starr, Ringo (All Starr Band) 186
Status Quo 43
Steel, James 132, 165
Steele, Jan 94
Stevens, Shakin' 60, 117
Sting 118
Stone Roses 74
Storyville Big Band 146
Strange Sensation 120
Stray Cats 53, 55, 57, 74, 153
Strummer, Joe 273

Suissa, Maurice 202
Summer, Donna 43
Supremes 160
Swaddle, Paul 112, 113, 114
T, Booker (& The MGs) 269, 275
T, Sugar 217
T. Rex 127
Tarrant, Chris 186
Taylor, Eddie 'Playboy' 79, 81
Taylor, Martin 195, 200
Taylor, Mick 126
Taylor, Roger 186
Taylor, Terry 129, 172
Taylor, Vince (& His Playboys) 35, 274
Temptations 160
Then Jerico 126, 155
Thompson, Ron 119
Tichy, Brian 228
Tonner, Kevin 150
Toussaint, Allen 30
Traffic 82
Trashmen 274
Travolta, John 34
Trio Los Panchos 270
Turner, Ike 81, **206**, 221, 268, 270, 274
Turner, Ruby 75
Turner, Tina 270
Turrell, Nigel 48
Tyler, Rob 121
U2 74
UB40 90
Utley, Adrian 114, 120, **138**, **139**
Van Doren, Mamie 60
Vernon, Paul 82
Vicious, Sid 44
Vincent, Gene (& His Blue Caps)
    29, 78, 115, 122, 201, 262, 268, 275
Vito, Rick 97, 103, 104, 109, 263
Wagstaffe, Doug 233
Wakefield, Will
    50-1, 52, 54, **68**, 75-6, 126, **141**, 164-5,
    234, 262
Walker, T-Bone 84, 149, 180, 182
Wallace, John
    71, 84, 85-6, 88-9, 90, 91, 92, 93-4
Walwyn, Steve
    121, 122-3, 124, 126, 130, 131, **140**, 148,
    149, 157, 161, 171
Warman, Bob 107
Watkins, Geraint 85, 229
Watson, Johnny 'Guitar' 183, 270
Watson, Tony 82, 202
Weapon of Peace 131

Wells, Junior 92, 103
West, Sonny 157, 158
Wheeler, Gilly 110
Whitfield, Nick
    111, 124, 145, **213**, **214**, **216**, 225, 227,
    233, 234, 235, 236, 249, 256, 258
Who 58, 107, 268
Wicked Whiskey 121
Wicket, Alan 'Sticky' 121
Wigfall, Michael 168, 173-4, 223
Williams, Esther 18
Williams, Larry 29, 268, 275
Williams, Roy
    101, 105, 106-7, 114, 122, 128, 131, **141**,
    148, 150, 152, 154, 263
Wilmot, John 90
Wilson, Jackie 270
Winning, Martin
    84, 132, 179, **213**, **214**, **216**, 229, 230,
    244, 262, 264
Winwood, Steve 195
Witherspoon, Tracy 36, 39, 47, 48
Wonder, Stevie 43
Wood, Chris 82
Wood, Natalie 60
Wood, Ronnie 98, 102, 200
Wood, Roy 90
Woodward, Keren 98
Woolley, Stephen 107
Wray, Link 78, 275
Wright, Billy 30
Wright, Neil 35, 36, 38, 42, 57, 256
Wroe, Chris
    111, 115, 117, 118, 131, 151, 161, 162,
    165, 175, 190, 191, 194, 255-6, 264
Wroe, Jenny 165, 184
Wyman, Bill
    53, 95, 102, 124, 129, 154, 157, 158, 172,
    177, 178, 179, 181, 183, 185, 186, 188,
    189, 190, 191, 192, 193, 194, 195, 196,
    197, 198, 202, **205**, **206**, 221, 224, 228
    See also Rhythm Kings
Wynne, Peter 231
Wynne, Sarah *(Mike's wife)*
    161, 168, **215**, **216**, 219, 222, 223-4,
    224-5, 226, 229, 231, 243, 245, 246,
    247-8, 249, 250, 251, 257, 258, 261,
    264, 265
Yates, Paula 127
Yeats, David 'Rowdy'
    82, 87, 97, 161, 165, 168, 181, 262
Young, Kenny 249
Young, Paul 158, 167

Zingg, Silvan 248
Zombies 195
Zuko, Danny 34
Zwingenberger, Axel 248

INDEX OF SONGS & ALBUM, VIDEO & DVD TITLES

■ = Album   ▦ = VHS videotape   ◉ = DVD

■ *6 Pack* 157
20th Century Boy 127-8
68 Guns 74
■ *A Few Short Lines* 248
◉ *A Tribute To The King* 200
A Whiter Shade Of Pale 26
Ain't Got No Home 275
Ain't No Big Deal 131
Ain't That Lovin' You Baby 78
■ *Alexis Korner Memorial Concert (Vol. 3)*
130
All Shook Up 200
Almost Grown 189
■ *Almost Grown* 189-90, 225, 250
Anna 268
■ *Anyway The Wind Blows* 157
■ *Babes And Buicks*
219, 222, 233, 236, 243-4, 259
Baby Please 100, 102, 106, 109
■ *Back For More* 97
■ *Back On Top* 230
Batman Theme 275
Be Careful 130
■ *Be My Guest* 97
Be-Bop-A-Lula 115
Big Town Playboy 79
Black And White Rag 35
Black Magic Woman 195
■ *Blue Boy* 165, 168, 170, 172, 173
■ *Blues According To..., The* 119
■ *Blues On 2* 91
Bony Moronie 275
Booty Ooty 183
Brand New Cadillac 35, 53, 274
Buckeye 275
Can't Get My Ass In Gear 97
Cat Man 275
Chicken Shack Boogie 179, 198, 274
Chicken Walk 78

■ *Chuck Berry's Greatest Hits* 271
Coal Miner 275
Crazy Legs 115-6
■ *Crazy Legs*
31, 108, 112, 115, 117-18, 119, 120,
121, 122, 261
Do It If You Wanna 183
Dock Of The Bay 270
Doopin' 102, 191
Down Down 43
Down The Road Apiece 88, 103, 130, 274
Easy Easy 189
Everybody's Got A Buick
219, 243-4, 259
(Every Time I Hear)
That Mellow Saxophone 274
Fanfare For The Common Man 228
Feelin' Good 275
■ *First Burnley National Blues Festival, The*
100
Flatfoot Sam 203
Flying Home 271
Gamblin' Woman 182
(Get Your Kicks On) Route 66 275
Glory Of Love, The 274
Going Down 119
Good Golly Miss Molly 274
Good Rockin' Tonight 48, 269
Goodnight My Love 274
Gotta Do More For My Baby 88
Great Balls Of Fire 27, 35, 221
Green Onions 275
Half Blind 234
Heartbreak Hotel 23, 26, 275
Heeby-Jeebies 275
Hey Baby 218
Hip Boots 244, 274
■ *Hip Joint*
123, 127, 128, 129, 130, 131, 148

Hold Me, Hug Me, Rock Me 268, 275
Hole In My Pocket 86
Honky Tonk Train Blues 185
Hungry Man 102, 109, 129
I Got A Woman 203
I Like It 88, 89, 154
I Want To Do More 88, 154
I'm Left, You're Right, She's Gone 48
I'm Mad 180
I'm Ready 275
I'm Sorry 26
If I Can't Have You 203
Imagine 170
In The Middle Of the Night 109
It'll Be Me 184, 275
It's My Life, Baby 93
Jitterbug Boogie 154, 179, 203
Johnny B. Goode 23, 48
Jungle Rock 185, 275
■ *Just A Game* 150
Just Because 78
■ *Just Can't Afford It* 161-2, 164, 165, 167
■ *Just For A Thrill* 183, 190, 194, 195
K.C. Loving 89, 275
Kansas City 89
Knock On Wood 196
Knocking On The Backside 246
Lawdy Miss Clawdy 200
■ *Layla* 93
Let The Good Times Roll 189
◉ *Let The Good Times Roll* 195, 197
■ *Live* 203
Lonesome Tears In My Eyes 57
Lonesome Train 119
Long Blond Hair 275
Love Is A Drug 78
Love Me Tender 39
Love That Burns 147
Lovin' Machine 275
Lowdown Dog 91
Lucille 201
Mailman, Bring Me No More Blues 35
Midnight Express 78
Milk And Alcohol 107
Money (That's What I Want) 275
Monster Mash 23
Mumblin' Guitar 275
My Babe 271, 274
My Baby Left Me 200, 268
My Brother Was A Sailor 248
My Girl 106
My Heart Is Mended 274
Nature Boy 274

Night Time Is The Right Time 270
No Coming Back 270, 274
No More 234
Normal Service 97
■ *Now Appearing* 106, 111, 116, 191
■ *Numero Uno!* 246
■ *Off The Clock...Live* 151, 155
Oh Marie 274
■ *On The Road Again* 188
One Night Of Sin 275
Ooh Little Girl 275
Ordinary Life 44
Papa-Oom-Mow-Mow 180
Peggy Sue 40, 274
Peter Gunn 35
Philosopher's Stone 230
Pink Panther Theme, The 271
■ *Playboy Boogie!* 84, 88, 154
Please Release Me 78
Please Send Me Someone To Love 275
Pledging My Love 197, 274
Race With The Devil 203
Ramblin' Boogie 175
Rampart Street Rock 35
■ *Ray Collins' Hot-Club Goes*
    Intercontinental 234
■ *Ready To Rock* 127-8
Real Wild Child 184, 274
Reconsider Baby 130, 269
Red Hot 185, 218
▣ *Red Hot...Live!* 175
◉ *Red Hot...Live!* 190
Red Hot Mama 82, 100, 103, 106
Right Here In My Arms 234
River, Stay Away From My Door 275
Rock Me Again 102
Rocking And Rolling Tonite 234
Roll 'Em Pete 203
Rooming House Boogie 274
Route 66 275
Rudy's Rock 274
Safronia B. 106
Sapphire 184
Sea Cruise 106
■ *Sgt. Pepper's Lonely Hearts Club Band*
    26, 268
Shake Your Hips 86, 262, 274
Shakin' All Over 275
She Loves You 26, 268
She's Not You 23
Sleep Walk 275
Slow Down 29, 268
So Glad You're Mine 268

Somethin' Else 29, 268
Something True Became A Lie 183
■ *Songs The Lord Taught Us* 55
Statesboro Blues 248
Stop Messing Around 98
■ *Stretching The Blues* 129
Struttin' Our Stuff 157
■ *Struttin' Our Stuff* 154
Summertime Blues 29, 268
Surfin' Bird 274
Sway With Me 248
Sweet Louise 124
Tainted Love 78
Tallahassee Lassie 275
■ *Tango In The Night* 97
Tear It Up 48, 53
Teen Flip (Texas Twister) 275
Tell You A Secret 179
■ *Telling It Like It Is* 183
That Mellow Saxophone 274
That's All Right 48, 268
Tie A Yellow Ribbon Round The Ole
    Oak Tree 26
Tomorrow Night 269
Train Kept A-Rollin', The
    48, 53, 119, 270, 274
■ *Travlin' Band* 179
Trouble 185
Twenty Flight Rock 48
Ubangi Stomp 185
Under The Boardwalk 249
■ *Unplugged* 147
Voice Within, The 182, 264
Well Oh Well 154
What'd I Say 151
When I Leave This World Behind 260
When I Lost You 260
Without You 73
Wobble, The 105, 106, 274
■ *Women & Cadillacs*
    182, 183, 184, 189, 190, 191, 219, 243,
    264
Yeh, Yeh 274
Yellow Submarine 26
Yesterday 35
■ *You Better Dig It!* 229-30, 231, 236
You Can't Judge A Book By The Cover
    37
You Fat Bastard 125

INDEX OF FILMS & SHOWS

For Paul Jones's BBC and Jazz FM radio shows see his entry in the *Index of People's Names*.

A Concert By The Lake 98
Alexis Korner Memorial Concert
    130, 147, 167
Americana International Festival 196
Amsterdam Blues Festival 91
Banbury Blues Festival 161
Basildon Blues Festival 89
Bathing Beauty *(film)* 18
Beersel Blues Rock Festival 161
Bergen Blues Festival 167
Bergen Jazz Festival 126
Bewdley Festival 203, 227
Birmingham Jazz Festival 118
Bishopstock Blues Festival 156, 159
Blues & Rhythm 20th Anniversary Party 202
Blues At Broom Hill 161
Blues At The Fort 203
Blues Nights *(Eric Clapton)* 105
Blues On The Farm 130, 156, 196, 218
Bradford Festival 118
Breda Jazz Festival 152
Bremerhaven Festival 118
Burnley International Rock & Blues Festival
    100, 257
Burnley National Blues Festival
    100, 151, 167, 174, 184, 230, 260
Capital Radio Christmas Party 124
Children In Need *(TV show)* 124
Class Of '58 *(TV movie)* 184
Color Of Money, The *(film)* 93
Comic Strip Presents..., The *(TV show)*
    102, 105-6, 153
Coventry Jazz Festival 169
Daffodil Charity Ball 129, 147
Darlington Rhythm & Blues Festival
    161, 188-9
Downton Abbey *(TV show)* 148
Edinburgh International Jazz Festival 103
Elvis Week 226
Escuela de Sirenas *(film)* 18
Falmouth Festival 156
Five Go To Rehab *(TV show)* 250

Gaildorf Festival 178
Glasgow Jazz & Blues Festival 118
Glasgow Rhythm & Blues Festival 159
Glastonbury Festival 103, 107
Gloucester Rhythm & Blues Festival
    161, 202
God's Jukebox *(radio show)* 231
Godfather, The *(film)* 187
Goodwood Vintage Festival 203
Grand World Skiffle Group Contest 39
Grease *(film)* 34
Great British R&B Festival *(Colne)*
    118, 170, 181, 190
Happening *(TV show)* 106
Happy Days *(TV show)* 34
Hayfield Jazz Festival 92, 96
Heart Beat '86 90
Heineken Music Big Top *(tour)* 107
Hell Blues Festival 149
Hell Station Blues Cruise 170
Henley-on-Thames Festival 186
High Rock-A-Billy Festival 219
I'll Be There *(film)* 185, 186
International Rock'n'Roll Festival
    (Brean Sands) 110, 116
Irish World Awards 194
It's Rock'n'Roll *(radio show)* 31
JFK *(film)* 185
Jive After Five *(video)* 91
Jools Hollands's Happening *(TV show)* 106
Langbaurgh Blues Festival 110
Lee Brilleaux Memorial Show 130, 191
Leominster Fringe Festival 153
Leverkusen Festival 150
Live At The Apollo *(films)* 83
Love Thy Neighbour *(TV show)* 24
Maryport Blues Festival 202
Milan Blues Festival 154
Molde International Jazz Festival 131, 169
Montreux Jazz Festival 178-9
National Music Day 126
Natural Born Killers *(film)* 185

Nice Jazz Festival 179
Notodden Blues Festival 153
Ørland Blues Festival 189, 232
Pat Sajak Show *(TV show)* 103
Pebble Mill At One *(TV show)* 129
Peer International Blues Festival 92, 117
Pope Must Die, The *(film)* 107, 109, 110-11
Pori Jazz Festival 153
Pot Black *(TV show)* 35
Ravenna Blues Festival 96, 112
Red Balloon Ball 101, 107-8
Rhythm Riot! 222-3, 246
Rock At Sea 245
Rockabilly Bombardment 248
Rockers' Reunion 233
Rockin' 50s Fest III 226
Rockin' Cruise 251
Rocking Gone Party 223
Ronn Lucas Show *(TV show)* 105
San Sebastián Jazz Festival 187
Screamin' Festival 200
Sheffield Festival 118
Shipston Proms 161
Silk Ball 161
Skanderborg Festival 103
Soho Jazz Festival 107
Sopranos, The *(TV show)* 180
South Blues Festival 154
Southall Festival of
    Music Speech and Dance 22
Southbank Blues Festival 103
Speyer Festival 235, 236
Starlight Foundation Ball 124, 129
Swank *(TV show)* 88
Third Man, The *(film)* 18
This Is Ricky Cool & The Icebergs *(TV show)*
    37
Till Death Us Do Part *(TV show)* 24
Tom & Jerry *(cartoon)* 167
Top Of The Pops *(TV show)* 60
Truman Show, The *(film)* 128
Twister *(film)* 185
Vienna Jazz Festival 195
VIP *(TV show)* 155
Viva Las Vegas 226
Water Rats Ball 199
WOMAD 103
Zeitgeist *(TV show)* 272

PHOTO & ILLUSTRATION CREDITS

Ad on page 71 courtesy Dave Clarke.

Flyer on page 140 courtesy Will Wakefield.

Photos on pages 61, 62, 63, 64, 65, 66, 67, 68 (bottom), 69 (top), 137 (top), 141 (top) 205, 206, 210 (top) and 215 (bottom) courtesy Mike Sanchez collection; photo on page 68 (top) by John Pitt, courtesy Will Wakefield; photo on page 69 (bottom) by Stuart Colman; photo on page 70 by Jill Furmanovsky, courtesy Mike Sanchez collection; photos on pages 71, 72 (bottom), 133, 134, 135, 208, 209 and 214 by Brian Smith; photo on page 72 (top) by Rupert Conant, courtesy Mike Sanchez collection; photos on pages 136 and 212 (top) by Paul Harris; photos on pages 137 (bottom) and 138 by Chris Wroe; photo on page 139 (top) courtesy of Chris Wroe; photos on page 139 (bottom) and 142 (top) by Andy Silvester, courtesy Mike Sanchez collection; photo on page 140 by Steve Addison; photos on pages 141 (bottom), 142 (bottom) and 143 by Will Wakefield; photo on page 144 by Gordon Ayres, courtesy Mike Sanchez collection; photos on page 207 by Chris Nottingham, courtesy Chris Wroe; photo on page 210 (bottom) by Robert Knight, courtesy Jeff Beck; photo on page 211 (top) by Anna Anderson; photo on page 211 (bottom) by Aigars Lapsa; photo on page 212 (bottom) by Tate Taylor; photos on page 213 by Andrew Elias; photos on pages 215 (top) and 216 by Chris Martin, courtesy Mike Sanchez collection.

Posters on pages 70 and 136 courtesy Dave Clarke.

Ticket on page 144 courtesy Will Wakefield.

OTHER TITLES FROM MUSIC MENTOR BOOKS

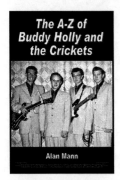

The A-Z of Buddy Holly and the Crickets
Alan Mann
ISBN-13: 978-0-9547068-0-7 *(pbk, 320 pages)*

The A-Z of Buddy Holly and the Crickets draws together a mass of Holly facts and info from a variety of published sources, as well as the author's own original research, and presents them in an easy-to-use encyclopaedic format. Now in its third edition, it has proved to be a popular and valuable reference work on this seminal rock'n'roller. It is a book that every Holly fan will want to keep at their fingertips. It is a book about a musical genius who will never be forgotten.

American Rock'n'Roll: The UK Tours 1956-72
Ian Wallis
ISBN-13: 978-0-9519888-6-2 *(pbk, 424 pages)*

The first-ever detailed overview of every visit to these shores by American (and Canadian!) rock'n'rollers. It's all here: over 400 pages of tour itineraries, support acts, show reports, TV appearances and other items of interest. Illustrated with dozens of original tour programmes, ads, ticket stubs and great live shots, many rare or previously unpublished.

Back On The Road Again
Dave Nicolson
ISBN-13: 978-0-9547068-2-1 *(pbk, 216 pages)*

A third book of interviews by Dave Nicolson in the popular *On The Road* series, this time with more of a Sixties flavour: Solomon Burke, Gene Chandler, Bruce Channel, Lowell Fulson, Jet Harris, Gene McDaniels, Scott McKenzie, Gary S. Paxton, Bobby 'Boris' Pickett, Martha Reeves & The Vandellas, Jimmie Rodgers, Gary Troxel (Fleetwoods), Leroy Van Dyke and Junior Walker.

The Big Beat Scene
Royston Ellis
ISBN-13: 978-0-9562679-1-7 *(pbk, 184 pages)*

Originally published in 1961, *The Big Beat Scene* was the first contemporary account of the teenage music scene in Britain. Written before the emergence of the Beatles, and without the benefit of hindsight, this fascinating document provides a unique, first-hand insight into the popularity and relevance of jazz, skiffle and rock'n'roll at a time when Cliff Richard & The Shadows were at the cutting edge of pop, and the social attitudes prevailing at the time.

British Hit EPs 1955-1989
George R. White
ISBN-13: 978-0-9562679-6-2 *(pbk, 320 pages)*

Fully revised and expanded second edition of the only chart book dedicated to British Hit EPs. Includes a history of the format, an artist-by-artist listing of every 7-inch hit EP from 1955 to 1989 (with full track details for each record), a trivia section, the official UK EP charts week by week, and much more. Profusely illustrated with over 600 sleeve shots.

The Chuck Berry International Directory (Volume 1)
Morten Reff
ISBN-13: 978-0-9547068-6-9 *(pbk, 486 pages)*

For the heavyweight Berry fan. Everything you ever wanted to know about Chuck Berry, in four enormous volumes compiled by the world-renowned Norwegian Berry collector and authority, Morten Reff. This volume contains discographies for over 40 countries, plus over 700 rare label and sleeve illustrations.

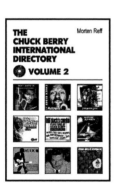

The Chuck Berry International Directory (Volume 2)
Morten Reff
ISBN-13: 978-0-9547068-7-6 *(pbk, 532 pages)*

The second of four volumes in this extensive reference work dedicated to rock'n'roll's most influential guitarist and composer. Contains details of bootlegs; radio albums; movies; TV shows; video and DVD releases; international tour itineraries; hits, achievements and awards; Berry's songs, roots, and influence on other artists; tributes; Chuck Berry in print; fan clubs and websites; plus annotated discographies of pianist Johnnie Johnson (post-Berry) and the ultimate Berry copyist, Eddy Clearwater.

The Chuck Berry International Directory (Volume 3)
Morten Reff
ISBN-13: 978-0-9547068-8-3 *(pbk, 608 pages)*

The third volume in this award-winning reference work dedicated to rock'n'roll's most influential guitarist and composer. Contains details of over 4,500 cover versions of Chuck Berry songs including many rarities from around the world. Alphabetical listing by artist (brief biography, comprehensive details of recordings and relevant releases, illuminating commentary and critiques), plus dozens of label and sleeve illustrations.

The Chuck Berry International Directory (Volume 4)
Morten Reff
ISBN-13: 978-0-9547068-9-0 *(pbk, 546 pages)*

The fourth and final volume of this groundbreaking work contains an A-Z of cover versions of Chuck Berry songs, details of hit cover versions, cover versions in the movies and on TV, over 900 Berry soundalikes, a 'No Chuck' section (non-Berry songs with similar titles), games, and even a brief chapter on Chuck Berry karaoke! Also over 100 pages of additions and updates to *Volumes 1, 2* and *3*, plus useful indices of Berry's releases by title and by label.

Cook's Tours: Tales of a Tour Manager
Malcolm Cook
ISBN-13: 978-0-9562679-4-8 *(pbk, 324 pages)*

Throughout his 44 years in the entertainment industry, Malcolm Cook met and worked with some of the biggest names in show business. In this humorous, fast-paced biographical account, Cook lifts the lid on what it takes to keep a show on the road and artists and audiences happy. It's all here: transport problems, unscrupulous promoters, run-ins with East German police, hassles with the Mafia, tea with the Duke of Norfolk, the wind-ups, the laughter, the heartbreak and the tears. A unique insight into what really goes on behind the scenes.

Elvis & Buddy – Linked Lives
Alan Mann
ISBN-13: 978-0-9519888-5-5 *(pbk, 160 pages)*

The achievements of Elvis Presley and Buddy Holly have been extensively documented, but until now little if anything has been known about the many ways in which their lives were interconnected. The author examines each artist's early years, comparing their backgrounds and influences, chronicling all their meetings and examining the many amazing parallels in their lives, careers and tragic deaths. Over 50 photos, including many rare/previously unpublished.

The First Time We Met The Blues – A journey of discovery with Jimmy Page, Brian Jones, Mick Jagger and Keith Richards
David Williams
ISBN-13: 978-0-9547068-1-4 *(pbk, 130 pages)*

David Williams was a childhood friend of Led Zeppelin guitar legend, Jimmy Page. The author describes how they discovered the blues together, along with future members of the Rolling Stones. The climax of the book is a detailed account of a momentous journey by van from London to Manchester to see the 1962 *American Folk-Blues Festival*, where they got their first chance to see their heroes in action.

Jet Harris – In Spite of Everything
Dave Nicolson
ISBN-13: 978-0-9562679-2-4 *(pbk, 208 pages)*

As a founder member of the Shadows, and a chart-topper in his own right, bassist Jet Harris scaled the heights of superstardom in the 1960s. A helpless alcoholic for most of his adult life, he also sank to unimaginable depths of despair, leaving a string of broken hearts and shattered lives in his wake. In this unauthorised biography author Dave Nicolson examines his eventful life and career, and how he eventually overcame his addiction to the bottle.

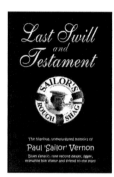

Last Swill and Testament
– The hilarious, unexpurgated memoirs of
Paul 'Sailor' Vernon
ISBN-13: 978-0-9547068-4-5 *(pbk, 228 pages)*

Born in London shortly after the end of World War II, Paul 'Sailor' Vernon came into his own during the 1960s when spotty teenage herberts with bad haircuts began discovering The Blues. For the Sailor it became a lifelong obsession that led him into a whirlwind of activity as a rare record dealer, magazine proprietor/editor, video bootlegger and record company director. It's all here in this one-of-a-kind life history that will leave you reaching for an enamel bucket and a fresh bottle of disinfectant!

Let The Good Times Rock!
– A Fan's Notes On Post-War American Roots Music
Bill Millar
ISBN-13: 978-0-9519888-8-6 *(pbk, 362 pages)*

For almost four decades, the name 'Bill Millar' has been synonymous with the very best in British music writing. This fabulous book collects together 49 of his best pieces – some previously unpublished – in a thematic compilation covering hillbilly, rockabilly, R&B, rock'n'roll, doo-wop, swamp pop and soul. Includes essays on acappella, doo-wop and blue-eyed soul, as well as detailed profiles of some of the most fascinating and influential personalities of each era.

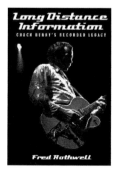

Long Distance Information
– Chuck Berry's Recorded Legacy
Fred Rothwell
ISBN-13: 978-0-9519888-2-4 *(pbk, 352 pages)*

The lowdown on every recording Chuck Berry has ever made. Includes an overview of his life and career, his influences, the stories behind his most famous compositions, full session details, listings of all his key US/UK vinyl and CD releases (including track details), TV and film appearances, and much, much more. Over 100 illustrations including label shots, vintage ads and previously unpublished photos.

More American Rock'n'Roll: The UK Tours 1973-84
Ian Wallis
ISBN-13: 978-0-9562679-3-1 *(pbk, 380 pages)*

The long-awaited follow-up to *American Rock'n'Roll: The UK Tours 1956-72*. Like its predecessor, it's crammed full of information about every American or Canadian rock'n'roller who visited Britain during the period covered. If you love rock'n'roll, you will wish to relive memories of all those nights spent in hot, sweaty clubs amongst the honking saxes, pounding pianos and twanging guitars. It is 'the greatest music in the world', and all those wonderful memories can be found again within these pages.

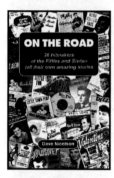

On The Road
Dave Nicolson
ISBN-13: 978-0-9519888-4-8 *(pbk, 256 pages)*

Gary 'US' Bonds, Pat Boone, Freddy Cannon, Crickets Jerry Allison, Sonny Curtis and Joe B. Mauldin, Bo Diddley, Dion, Fats Domino, Duane Eddy, Frankie Ford, Charlie Gracie, Brian Hyland, Marv Johnson, Ben E. King, Brenda Lee, Little Eva, Chris Montez, Johnny Moore (Drifters), Gene Pitney, Johnny Preston, Tommy Roe, Del Shannon, Edwin Starr, Johnny Tillotson and Bobby Vee tell their own fascinating stories. Over 150 illustrations including vintage ads, record sleeves, label shots, sheet music covers, etc.

On The Road Again
Dave Nicolson
ISBN-13: 978-0-9519888-9-3 *(pbk, 206 pages)*

Second volume of interviews with the stars of pop and rock'n'roll including Freddie Bell, Martin Denny, Johnny Farina (Santo & Johnny), the Kalin Twins, Robin Luke, Chas McDevitt, Phil Phillips, Marvin Rainwater, Herb Reed (Platters), Tommy Sands, Joe Terranova (Danny & The Juniors), Mitchell Torok, Marty Wilde and the 'Cool Ghoul' himself, John Zacherle.

Railroadin' Some: Railroads In The Early Blues
Max Haymes
ISBN-13: 978-0-9547068-3-8 *(pbk, 390 pages)*

This groundbreaking book, written by one of the foremost blues historians in the UK, is based on over 30 years research, exploration and absolute passion for early blues music. It is the first ever comprehensive study of the enormous impact of the railroads on 19th and early 20th Century African American society and the many and varied references to this new phenomenon in early blues lyrics. Includes ballin' the jack, smokestack lightning, hot shots, the bottoms, chain gangs, barrelhouses, hobo jungles and more.